To Glenn,

Blessings,

Jon

SAMUEL'S MISSION

A Family's Return to Joy

SAMUEL'S MISSION

A Family's Return to Joy

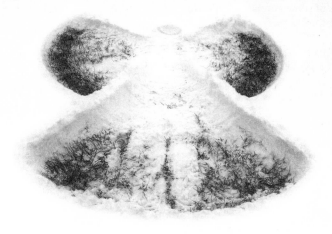

JOHN HENKELS

BEAVER'S
POND
PRESS

ISBN 10: 1-59298-228-X
ISBN 13: 978-1-59298-228-8

Library of Congress Catalog Number: 2011961746

Printed in the United States of America

First Printing: 2012

16 15 14 13 12   5 4 3 2 1

Cover and interior design by James Monroe Design, LLC.

Beaver's Pond Press, Inc.
7104 Ohms Lane, Suite 101
Edina, MN 55439–2129
BEAVER'S   (952) 829-8818
POND
PRESS   www.BeaversPondPress.com

To order, visit www.BeaversPondBooks.com
or call (800) 901-3480. Reseller discounts available.

To Suzanne.
My life started over the night we met.
Her grace, character, and devotion carried us through the storm.
Twenty years now, she still dazzles.
And to our sons and the constant joys and surprises
that fill our days.

CONTENTS

So we're not giving up.
How could we!
Even though on the outside it often looks like
things are falling apart on us, on the inside,
where God is making new life,
not a day goes by without his unfolding grace.

—2 CORINTHIANS 4:16 (MSG)

FOREWORD

When a child dies, it is always out of season. Dreams die and the world is diminished by the loss of the child's human potential. Samuel Henkels was just such a loss to the world.

Yet his story, as told through his father's eyes in *Samuel's Mission: A Family's Return to Joy,* is redemption of that loss. One sweet, brave little boy who endured the ravages of an incurable disease. We all know times of sickness and times of wellness, but Samuel's time was never equalized.

Samuel's Mission does not bring messages for the intellect, but for the soul. This book is not a text to be read or understood, but simply felt. It is about feeling Samuel's arduous experience. It is about understanding courage, commitment, and the experience of love.

Samuel's parents, his grandparents, and his caregivers are remarkable voices of goodness, courage, and selflessness. They were transformed by Samuel's life and, in my view, the greatest validation of Samuel's mission on earth was to allow those who loved him the most to learn that letting one's heart to break is better than denying the heartbreak. A broken heart can be reborn, but a heart filled with anger and denial has no strength to love again.

Samuel's parents, John and Suzanne, have transcended Samuel's death and have continued to love and nurture each other and their children. They find comfort in friends, in family, in their faith and in the firm belief that Samuel's time on earth was purposeful and important.

I read this story one cold, rainy Saturday morning and found myself weeping at page two. I kept reading and was inspired by the faith John describes—it touched my heart in a way I always want to remember. I came away knowing (or relearning) the impact every word, every phrase, every act of kindness has on a family. I hope to impart that message to the leaders and staff at Le Bonheur Children's Hospital in an inspiring way. I came away thanking God that my own son is healthy and happy. I came away wanting to embrace John and Suzanne.

Samuel's mission was to be an angel. He was a mirror for us to see the unlimited beauty and goodness in life . . . and beyond. Settle back—breathe deeply—be still—and you will hear his angel voice talking.

—Meri Armour
CEO/Administrator,
Le Bonheur Children's Hospital,
SVP, Rainbow Babies and Children's Hospital
Cleveland, Ohio

PROLOGUE:
Life on a Thrill Ride

Suzanne and I seemed to live on a roller coaster. Despite commitment and love, the good times during our marriage never seemed to last more than a short while before life's twists, flips, and turns took over. On the day this story begins, we were atop the world and could only envision a future of joy. Our humble dreams had all come true. The bliss was so great that I failed to hear the familiar *click . . . click . . . click* of the roller coaster as it approached the summit of the thrill ride—and the inevitable plummet that would follow.

My best day ever had just ended. Family and friends from all over attended our twins' baptism. Suzanne sported her signature thousand-watt smile as we paraded our babies around the church, as is the custom in our congregation. Later our home was flooded with well-wishers and frivolity as we celebrated this occasion that for many years had eluded us. If only I could have stopped the ride and captured the ecstasy of the day. As we celebrated, I had a powerful feeling that only smooth waters lie ahead.

I was so mistaken.

That magical time on top of the world did not last.

I remember the exact moment and the accompanying rush of adrenaline when I heard our son's diagnosis. How could it be? Our sons Jacob and Samuel were born in perfect health. How could Sammy be so sick in just those few months? More than the words, I remember the emotions when we were told our child could die.

"I must warn you. This disease is life threatening," Dr. Berman, Sammy's physician said. He had identified the illness that afflicted Sam as extremely rare and similar to cancer. The moment is frozen. I can picture the doctors and staff who were present. The hospital conference room reminded me of a cozy den with the earth-tone colors, plush leather chairs, modern artwork on the walls, and a desk of rich walnut. I remember the look of dread on Dr. Berman's face while he awaited our barrage of questions. Mostly I remember the shock, dismay, and the feeling in my stomach that felt like the first plunge of the roller coaster. My top-of-the-world joyfulness dissipated in a *poof!* and was replaced with nausea, goose bumps, and butterflies. When I shut my eyes and go back to that moment, I can still recreate that awful feeling. But I don't do that often.

Many people described our seven-month-old son as "pretty." Samuel was blessed with huge brown eyes, long thick eyelashes, and a beguiling smile that would light up a room. The nurses who cared for him referred to Sam as the "Gerber baby."

At first, I wasn't sure I liked my son being called pretty. But that night, as I watched him sleep peacefully in his hospital crib, I realized Sammy *was* the prettiest thing I had ever seen. That we could lose him was indescribably frightening. Our precious child was in trouble—big trouble.

There was so much we didn't know. Suzanne and I were not trained for this fight. We were unprepared for the suffering that Sammy was to endure and our utter helplessness to stop it. The scary things about the disease we would learn soon enough. In time we were able to gird ourselves for Sam's battle for survival. But other life changes took me by surprise and came without any warning. There was no preparation for how every relationship in my life would change. I could not foresee that marriage and my bond with Suzanne would be so altered. No one warned us that our healthy children were to suffer also, although in more subtle ways. It was almost as if we were suddenly transported to a parallel life in an alien land.

Just those few days earlier, we had been living our dream. I thought then the roller coaster ride of life was over. Suzanne and I had reached the point we had longed for. Happily married, successful in our careers, and ecstatic over raising our three sons, life was perfect. Little did we know how far down the plunge would take us.

"What exactly do you mean by life-threatening? Can he be cured? And what is the name of the disease again?" I asked.

"It's called hemaphagocytic lymphohistiocytosis. We'll use HLH for short," Dr. Berman responded—to the easiest of my questions. "Dr. Nieder will be taking over Sam's care," he continued, nodding to his associate. Dr. Michael Nieder had been introduced at the beginning of the meeting as the hospital's chief oncologist.

"The only cure is through stem cell replacement, which is better known as a bone marrow transplant," Dr. Nieder explained gently. Suzanne and I stared back in shocked silence.

"Have you seen this disease before?" Suzanne asked, finally finding her voice.

"Twice in the ten years that I've been here," he answered. My raised eyebrows and tensed shoulders asked the next question for me.

"They both passed away," Dr. Nieder answered quietly.

"What are his chances?" I asked bluntly.

The consultation ended with few answers. But then, Suzanne and I hardly knew what questions to ask. Tears streamed down Suzanne's face. I sat frozen, stunned by the news, in the now-empty conference room. Dr. Nieder's answer to my last question echoed in my mind.

"Maybe one chance in two," he had said.

"Not one for sugar-coating, is he?" I commented to Suzanne, as we dazedly made our way back to Sam's hospital room.

We were now the parents of a critically ill child. Sam could die. These two thoughts were difficult to comprehend. Life turned upside down with the diagnosis. Our daily conversations now were filled with frightening words such as chemotherapy, transplant, and remission. Sam's doctor was no longer a pediatrician, but an oncologist. Instead of reading how-to books on babies and raising twins, we researched a rare disease and studied survival rates. Suddenly we were enmeshed in a crisis that would devastate our family.

This, then, is our story. It is the story of a child with enormous spirit fighting for his life. It is a story of how our world flipped upside down and turned inside out. It is the story of lessons learned and relationships altered. It is a story of courage few in this world have witnessed. And it is a story of stunning ways our family learned to connect with God.

We had a long, dangerous, and frightening journey ahead. Although the ending was unknown, only one conclusion was acceptable. Sam must survive. At the outset, his mission was only to stay alive. Samuel's mission, however, would grow into something much greater.

Sam had many lessons to teach as he battled his disease. He would touch many lives and change more than a few. In the months ahead, our family would encounter much death—and learn so much about life. Sam's mission, we quickly learned, was not directed by his parents, but by a force far more powerful.

With a battle in front of us, our family prepared for a siege. Sam would be the foot soldier. Suzanne and I could only provide logistical support. With no choice but to fight, we armed ourselves with hope, moved forward with faith in our God, and relied on the support of hundreds of family, friends, doctors, nurses, coworkers, church members, and complete strangers.

CHAPTER 1

The Night of Two Moons

It took Suzanne and me a long time to find top-of-the-world moments in our lives, and Sammy's story can't be told without detailing some of the trips, falls, and recoveries we each made on the road that brought us to those heady days just before Sam's disease dropped the floor from beneath our feet.

Each of us grew up in a loving Midwestern home with hardworking, simple-living parents. The media call it flyover country. You can believe the rich and famous are sound asleep when their aircraft pass over Marshalltown, Iowa, where I was raised. Excitement is rare and the roller-coaster rides are few in this land of flat cornfields and little neon.

The sixth-born of nine siblings, my personality was that of the classic middle child. I never got much attention and never really earned any, negative or positive. I learned to avoid confrontation, go with the flow, and fit in without drawing attention to myself. Dad worked hard traveling the state selling furnaces and air conditioners to a loyal network of small-town dealers. He must have been pretty good at it, as he managed to support a very large family.

Mom was like the classic TV mom of the 1960s—you always saw her in the kitchen, laundry room, or in front of the ironing board. I don't remember that she dressed as well as June Cleaver, though, and she never wore a strand of pearls to dinner. Mom had a seriousness about her (or maybe a lack of joy) that I accepted then as simply who she was. She was never mean or angry; she just didn't smile often. As a child, I assumed she was just too busy to have fun or give hugs. Today as a husband and father in my fifties, I'm really struck by how little I knew about my mother and the forces that shaped her personality. Her life was never a cakewalk, and I knew little of the upbringing she had survived . . . and the tragedy she had endured.

The big family life had plenty of personality clashes and competition, but then I knew nothing else. Looking back, I am grateful for the solid, loving parents who instilled a great work ethic in me and my siblings. We were raised as devout Catholics, attended Catholic schools, and never missed a mass, Holy Day of Obligation, or other available service. In fact, our parents sent us to mass every morning before school. I realize now that the extra hour without eight kids in the house was a precious respite. But somehow, after all that religious training, I grew into adulthood with little connection to my faith and an inability to speak or listen to God.

I kept the middle-child aspect of my personality throughout high school, never overachieving and finding relationships difficult. Like my position in the family, my grades were middle of the road. I was an average athlete, average golfer, and usually got only average girls. My parents recommended trade school after graduation, and I started out in a one-year technical school. Unhappy with the prospect of a life of hard work with low pay, I decided to make a change in the middle of the first semester. With my sister Judith's guidance—and without my parent's knowledge—I enrolled at Iowa State University, in civil engineering, an above-average curriculum. Then a junior at ISU, Judith mentored me through the difficult physics and calculus classes. Looking back, Judith was the first to really believe in me and she instilled in me the confidence to find my way in the world. As a younger brother, I always looked upon her in a bit of awe. Judith's grades were always at the top of her class. She was very active in clubs and activities in school and popular with her classmates. She too was one of the middle children in our family of nine kids but the one most of us in the younger half looked to for guidance.

Iowa State doesn't sound impressive in these pages, but I loved campus life. The independence, classes, friendships, social life, sports—girls, it was all great. I came out of my middle-child shell, developed into a man, and found I could be a leader. Paying tuition wasn't easy. Mom and Dad provided one semester of tuition, room, and board for each child, and the remainder was up to us. I worked as a resident assistant in the dorms, wrote parking tickets for campus security, and drove home twice a month to sack groceries at the supermarket where I had worked throughout high school.

Four years later, armed with my degree, I left the state of Iowa looking for adventure.

I didn't find any.

I was hired as a field engineer with a heavy construction company operating in the Midwest and Southwest.

Although travel sounded romantic, I ended up living like a gypsy, moving from state to state, building roads for a highway contractor. For a time, the travel was so extreme that, like others on the construction team, I lived in an RV. The locations were not glamorous. When not in the RV, I stayed in cheap hotels or temporary apartments in cities like Marshall (Texas), Shreveport, Wichita, Tulsa, Little Rock, and West Memphis (Arkansas). I felt like I was living in that Johnny Cash song about all those little towns he'd been to.

I settled down once for several years near much of my family in Des Moines, where I managed to meet someone and get married.

It didn't last long.

The gypsy side of me took over, and I again headed out to build highways everywhere but home. The marriage fell apart soon after I began coming home every other weekend.

Connected only to my career, I moved from one construction site to another. Nighttime and weekends found me lonely and sad. Some of those Saturday nights with no one to talk to felt too much like the Jimmy Buffet song—in which my only visitor was the pizza man. After a few years, feelings of emptiness overwhelmed me. I found myself yearning for a spiritual side—and not knowing how to get there.

It was years before I realized what I missed the most: I wanted roots. I craved stability—to find a place to call home. I didn't have any idea that would happen when I accepted a job in one more drab city. But Toledo, Ohio, is not as bad as it seems. I quickly found a circle of friends in a similar situation and felt contented for the first time as an adult.

Now in my thirties, I finally realized I didn't have to think of myself as average. In the mirror, I saw a tall and lean grown-up man. I had a solid career and a license to practice engineering, and I was respected in my industry. I enjoyed building airports and superhighways. I liked wearing denim to work and spending the days outside. My job was rewarding in that at the end of every work day there was something tangible to see. I learned to socialize with multimillionaire owners as well as uneducated ditchdiggers, and enjoyed both. I learned that wisdom and intelligence were not always associated with social class. The guy with the shovel taught me as much about life as the guy in the Bentley. It was one of those guys that taught me an important lesson about women as I went through my sixty-three-dollar Oklahoma divorce. (Seriously, a couple could get divorced for sixty-three bucks in Tulsa, Oklahoma, in 1989).

"Mr. Henkels," he drawled, "one thing I learned about women is that they don't think like you think they think." It was a semideep thought that I tried to remember. Of course it took my associate four marriages to gain that wisdom. I hoped I wouldn't need as much practice.

During this period, I determined it was time to shed my middle-child fit-in mentality. I was a leader at work and found that I could be a leader socially. People liked me. And in Toledo, unlikely as it sounds, I found the adventure I had been seeking. Groups of us would go boating on Lake Erie in the summer and skiing in Michigan when the snow came. The guys in the group took to danger-seeking. We rafted the whitewater in West Virginia, jumped out of an airplane in Michigan, and took the dive from a bungee platform in Toledo. We water-skied the Maumee River at night with the boat lights turned off. The group partied together at downtown festivals and created our own celebrations in the winter.

I dated several of the women but never found one for to give my heart. Then a weekend excursion brought the entire gang to Put-in-Bay, Ohio, on Middle Bass Island in Lake Erie. Thousands of partygoers flock to the island every weekend in the spring, summer, and fall. When the sun sets in Put-in-Bay, the families skedaddle and the nightclubs overflow. Like New Orleans, a strand of beads will get you a peak at a drunken girl's boobs. And like Las Vegas, "what happens at the Bay, stays at the Bay."

My first visit to this resort island, I felt like I'd stepped right off Ohio and into Key West when the ferryboat landed. It was like no place I had ever been. Ladies flirted with the men in our group from the moment we boarded the Jet Express ferry. I was halfway, "kinda-sorta" dating one of the women in our crowd at the time and couldn't take advantage of opportunities that were presented to meet someone new. My roommate and I returned the very next weekend—without our girlfriends— determined to meet the women that flirted with us so easily seven days earlier.

The youngest of three sisters, Suzanne was raised in rural Ohio. Known as Suzie during childhood, she played sports and music in her small-town school. Her mother, Marilyn, remembers that Suzie was absolutely driven as a student. After school Suzanne would set her books on the table in perfect alignment and complete her homework without any prompting from Mom. She graduated from Smithville High School at the top of the class. But Suzanne wasn't just into studies. She dated the same boy for several years and was popular with the party crowd as well as the jocks and music geeks.

When driving through Suzanne's hometown, I love to point out to others the gentlemen's club where she took her first job. Suzanne is quick to mention that the building used to be a chain restaurant and she didn't pay her way through college by stripping but rather by schlepping cheeseburgers. At Kent State University, Suzanne didn't wait for graduation to start a career at IBM. She finished her senior year while working nearly full-time using newly earned computer-science skills. As is the Smithville custom and following in the footsteps of her sisters, Suzanne wed right after college. Like my own practice marriage, it lasted less than four years and was followed by a clean break with no children. Also like me, Suzanne devoted herself to her career. She found much success working in Cleveland as a sales rep for IBM. A few relationships followed but she held out for Mr. Right. Suzanne formed deep friendships during this period. She and her girlfriends enjoyed the Cleveland social scene, vacationed in the Caribbean, and made weekend forays to the Lake Erie islands.

I often think of that night at Put-in-Bay as the moment my life started over. Suzanne and I spotted each other across a U-shaped bar at a crowded night spot. A band was playing Caribbean music. Her smile dazzled me. She was one of the most beautiful women I had ever seen—and she was looking at me. After a few swigs of courage, I made a move to approach her. Suzanne still likes to tell how I walked halfway to her before losing my nerve and returning to my side of the bar. When I finally made it to her table, I was quickly under her spell. Her girlfriends gave me the once-over. I was asked to spin around to be checked out.

I did a bad thing that night. I had come to the island that night with my buddy; we had planned to catch the last ferry to the mainland and drive back to our Toledo apartment. But when the ladies were ready to call it a night, I ditched my friend to walk Suzanne to the campground where she and five girl-friends were ensconced in an old motor home. They'd hinted at finding me a place to sleep.

In our family lore, this night became the Night of Two Moons. I was left outside lying on a picnic table while the ladies prepared for sleep. I remember staring up at a beautiful harvest moon when a powerful feeling came over me—a feeling that Suzanne might be the one I had been searching for. The feeling was so powerful that I revisit it now and again when viewing such a moon. Since I had missed the last ferry to the mainland and left my friend without a car or a place to stay, I hoped my feeling was right. When the ladies allowed me inside, I made my move to snuggle up with Suzanne on the big bed at the back of the motor home.

"You sleep on the floor," Suzanne ordered. I accepted her rebuff along with the offered blanket and wiggled down to the narrow floor and planned the story I could tell the guys about my night in a motor home with five hot single women. I soon fell asleep, only to be awakened an hour later by the arrival of a sixth woman tip-toeing over me to her adjacent bed. I instantly learned that Linda likes to sleep in the buff as I was rewarded with the second moon of the night as she climbed into her space.

My roommate made it back to the mainland but, as I had the keys to my car, he was left without a ride or a place to sleep. He seemed fine after I bought him breakfast. I didn't think that breaking into a fish company truck and sleeping through the chilly autumn night with newspapers for a blanket was the smartest decision he ever made . . . but decided to keep my opinion to myself. I must have checked a hundred times that the paper with Suzanne's phone number was still in my pocket.

Suzanne and I began dating one week after the Night of Two Moons. I drove the two hours from my Toledo home to hers in Cleveland. This soon became our weekend habit. I lost interest in hanging out with the gang as we moved slowly into our long-distance dating, each of us in turn taking chances with our hearts, like running into the cold surf and running back out while trying to get used to the water. We talked of our previous hurts and failed marriages. Over time we developed trust in each other and began healing the wounds of our pasts.

We didn't *fall* in love. We didn't float on clouds. We took each other by the hand and trekked through the twisted forests of our previous lives—creepy forests like those on the yellow brick road. We spoke frankly of our hopes and dreams, failed relationships, and the mistakes we had made.

Our talks weren't always fun. Oftentimes we left each other angry and befuddled. Phone conversations were the worst. Suzanne loved to lounge on her sofa under a warm blanket, pick up the phone, and talk for an hour. My theory of telephone conversation was more along the lines of "state your business and get off the phone." I could do that in a few minutes: "Hi honey, how was your day? I miss you. I can't wait to see you this weekend."

During this period of courtship, I found that Suzanne's outward appearance was not her true beauty. Inside I found a woman of courage, character, intelligence, and sweetness, and a sense of humor to go along with her great set of ta-tas.

Dating Suzanne was the new highpoint of my life, at least when she was not making me talk about past relationships. We were compatible and shared a number of interests. We both loved travel, and one of us loved adventure.

Our first trip together was one of trepidation for Suzanne. She readily recalls the tremors of panic in her stomach when the aircraft landed in Denver on our way to ski at Vail. But she put her fears aside, took a few lessons, and conquered the mountain. And what a smoking hot ski bunny she made! Whew—I was falling for this one. I let her know my feelings during an après-ski party at the bottom of the Eagle Bahn Gondola lift. The gondola is an enclosed chairlift that can zoom eight skiers halfway up the mountain in about eight minutes. We had just ridden the gondola together for our final run of the day. Suzanne was elated about completing her first blue (intermediate) run down the mountain after several days of lessons. The room was crowded with skiers enjoying a bite to eat and other libations at the end of the day. The front picture window with a view of the mountain was fogged over, and skiers were writing jokes, notes, and pictures on the glass. Laughter and frivolity filled the room. The time was right. I walked over and wrote my feelings on the window.

Across the room Suzanne broke into a dazzling smile and mimed her response. She pointed to herself, clasped her hands over her heart, pointed at me, and held up two fingers. "I love you too." A smattering of applause broke out from the patrons nearby.

When I added these words, "In the Gondola," the place went nuts.

Another weekend brought us to Las Vegas. By this time, our love had grown and we thoroughly enjoyed being together. It was good that Suzanne already liked me because the hotel room I had purchased on some promotion scam was a bit seedy and wouldn't have made a good impression if this had been our first trip. The blackjack dealer we gravitated toward looked like Elvis, except for the missing teeth. Redneck Elvis, perhaps. Our time together was satisfying like nothing I had experienced before. We saw some shows, enjoyed being the best dressed couple in the rundown resort, and held hands like teenagers all the way up and down the Strip.

And then came the most frightening trips—meeting the parents. We left late in the morning for the twelve-hour drive to Iowa and didn't quite make Des Moines. Grinnell, Iowa, is quite rural and our motel was even less impressive than Bob Stupak's Las Vegas Resort. In the morning, Suzanne opened the blinds to find corn growing right up to our window. She must have felt right at home.

Dad loved her from the first moment and claimed Suzanne was the best woman I had ever dated. Mom liked Suzanne, too, but she was harder to please—after all, I was the favorite among her kids. She had never admitted to it, but my siblings gave me enough crap about it that it must have been true.

Suzanne's parents, Curt and Marilyn, seemed to approve. If you look up the definition of "country folk" in a dictionary, you'd probably find their picture. Curt is a cabinetmaker/remodel carpenter with his own business. He often dresses in bib overalls and covers his flattop haircut with various tractor company hats. Curt is always quick with a laugh, knows everyone in a three-county area, and needs few luxuries in life to be happy. Marilyn is a little conservative and finds most of her pleasures in life are centered on hard work; mowing her five acres with a push mower is a great day for Marilyn. I'm not sure if she has ever seen the clock strike midnight and the hardest drink she's tasted is apple cider. Suzanne's two sisters both had kids, and I quickly learned that Marilyn loved grandchildren even more than mowing and ironing.

In time, Suzanne and I each knew we had found our life partner. We took turns making the Friday night trek but eventually found weekends were simply too many days apart. Thence began a Wednesday night rendezvous at the halfway point. The hundred-twenty mile space between us somehow needed to be closed. Still, with histories of failed relationships, we were both reluctant to disrupt our careers as well as our homes to move across Ohio, even as it became apparent that neither of us wanted to live without the other. To her credit, Suzanne took the initiative and offered to relocate to Toledo. Her transfer would allow us to be with each other every day.

If that's not love, I don't know what is.

Suzanne owned a home and had worked at IBM for more than ten years, yet she was willing to move to Toledo to be with me. Her offer melted my heart—and I gave my two months' notice to my employer the next week and made plans to move to Cleveland. I hunted for a new job and an engagement ring at the same time.

I planned the proposal at the fanciest restaurant in town, and yes: Toledo does have some nice eateries. But the plan took a detour when Suzanne popped in while I was admiring the diamond before dinner. The proposal went off a bit early, and then—well, we became distracted and were late for dinner. Our courtship was over. But our life together was just beginning.

The journey through our pasts and our time together brought us to the point where we were deeply in love and had a foundation of trust and commitment. As it would turn out, the years ahead would not be easy ones, and we would need that solid base in the future.

But at the time, life was carefree and rosy and we looked

forward to a marriage that would last. I moved in a few months before our wedding and began working for the Allega Company.

When I say moved in, I mean my person and my clothes. I brought a whole truckload of furniture along with my car and boat to Cleveland. Most of the furniture was dropped at the curb (must not have had the right *feng shui*) and the boat was sold with the alleged intent of buying a bigger boat (still waiting). The move was a huge culture shock that shouldn't have taken me for such a surprise; I left my home, my city, my friends, my job, and my independence to move in with Suzanne. I was in her house and in her life—as in everything about her life. Our social life was hers, and the furniture, sheets, décor, city, sports teams—everything. It was disorienting to have so many changes at once. I suffered a minor identity crisis when I moved in with Suzanne as I was inserted in the middle of her life while at the same time she wasn't really inserted into mine.

Good thing she was hot.

We immediately began planning our wedding. In Suzanne's conservative country family, our living arrangement created some unease and was perhaps seen as a bit scandalous. Suzanne was the first divorcée in her family and the only daughter to shack up before marriage. Nonetheless, I was welcomed and included in family events—another insertion into Suzanne's life.

One of the ways we meshed was in our wedding plans. We agreed that the wedding was to be by us, about us, and for us. We opted for a ten-day cruise with a stopover on St. Thomas, U.S. Virgin Islands, for the wedding. Family and friends were welcome to meet us on the island but not required for our celebration.

Not content to enjoy the bliss of finding our soul mate and letting life ease on by, we discussed conceiving a child on our ten-day honeymoon—and did everything possible to achieve that goal.

Back into reality after our trip, we slipped into a

comfortable lifestyle that included long work days and lazy evenings lounging on the couch. But the months flew by and the pressure to conceive began to build. One year of marriage slipped by, and Suzanne had not become pregnant.

At the time of our wedding, Suzanne was age thirty; I was thirty-six. We fully expected to produce children in the normal, natural way. When that did not happen, the quest for pregnancy began to control our lives. Sex was no longer for pleasure. Ovulation week became known as "business week," complete with strict rules: no alcohol, no caffeine, no hot tub, and no excuses. Romance was left out of the process.

The highest and lowest points on this emotional roller coaster came after we began fertility treatments. As it was throughout this process, Suzanne had the difficult, painful parts. My role was simple. Nonetheless, the first appointment at the fertility clinic was unsettling. I knew what was expected of me that morning, yet I still felt uneasy. The waiting room was full of women, some with their partners. Suzanne filled out the lengthy paperwork while I looked around the room wondering if all the men were as nervous as I. Moments after Suzanne turned in the completed documents, I heard my name being called to the front desk. Showtime!

The nurse handed me a plastic cup along with a few rules. "Make sure nothing but the sample gets into the cup, please," she warned. "Leave the cup in the room when you are done."

I'd seen this scene played out in several TV sitcoms. On television, though, there was always videotapes, a rack of magazines, and a comfortable couch. I found no such luxuries. The narrow bed was fitted with plastic sheets and the only erotic literature was three tattered *Playboy* magazines. *I wonder if the nurses have a pool on how long it takes us guys in here. Who cares! I've got a job to do, and I'm going to do it.* Being a loving supportive husband, I was able to deliver the goods. I even stayed a bit longer to read one of the articles in the magazine. *I never knew they had articles.*

The sample passed muster.

At first, I thought that was good news. But I still didn't know much about how women think. If only they had found a low sperm count, Suzanne might have felt less pressure. Numerous other tests revealed nothing physiologically wrong with either of us. The doctor prescribed a mild fertility drug called Clomid for Suzanne. Soon after, I came home from my job building a new runway to find Suzanne at the door radiating her thousand-watt smile.

Saying she had something to show me, she led me into the bedroom where she had left the home pregnancy test. That test, along with seven others she took that weekend, was clearly positive. Suzanne was indeed pregnant!

After agreeing to keep the news a secret for two months, we both phoned everyone we knew. It was a joyful time. We talked for hours and made plans for the nursery. We bought books of baby names and had fun negotiating and rejecting choices. We enjoyed one of those top of the roller coaster times in life when everything seems perfect and nothing but excitement lies in front of you.

But the joy did not last. I arrived home one evening two weeks after we'd gone public to find Suzanne crying and in great abdominal pain. We hurried to the nearest emergency room. Suzanne was in severe distress, yet I refused to believe she was having a miscarriage.

Over the next several days, Suzanne endured many tests, as well as laparoscopic surgery. Once again, she did all the physical suffering. The emotional suffering we shared. As was my custom, I played my masculine role—as the strong one— well. Suzanne cried many tears as I held her close. Although miscarriage is a common occurrence, the pain and anguish were new to us.

Our relationship during the years of infertility alternated between intimacy and distance. The weeks following the miscarriage were our most loving. We leaned on each other for emotional support, talked intimately, and spent hours holding each other. I shed a few tears at odd moments—in my truck, or while working out—but always when alone. The saddest times for me were during church services when the minister would summon the children from Sunday school for a short sermon. The kids would flow down the aisles in waves, some with bright and cheery smiles and others bashful and reserved. Parents in the congregation would stretch and lean to catch a glimpse of their child and then grin at each other like they'd just won the lottery. Suzanne and I would share a different kind of look, usually biting our lip at the same time. Suzanne would often need to dab her eyes and always had a tissue out during children's sermon.

Infertility and miscarriage can dominate a relationship, and the hurt is usually carried silently. Unless one has been through it, it is hard to understand the depth of pain couples feel as they desperately try to start a family. Of the trials we would face in the future, infertility ranked near the top as far as stress on our marriage. But somehow in that time our marriage survived as we leaned on each other. Of course I didn't know at the time just how much of the problem was my fault, but was about to find out.

We then moved into what I recall as a black hole of fertility treatments. We tried heavier doses of fertility drugs, intra-uterine insemination, and finally decided on IVF, or in-vitro fertilization. IVF was the last—and most expensive—step on the ladder of fertility treatments. A single cycle of IVF cost $7,500 at the time.

With IVF, the ovaries are induced to release multiple eggs in one cycle. Once mature, the eggs are retrieved through a minor surgical procedure and then fertilized in a petri dish. Three days later, several resulting embryos are placed into the uterus. Additional embryos can be frozen for transfer into the uterus at a later date.

Optimistic once again, we began the procedure. First came the onslaught of fertility drugs: one Suzanne injected daily into her thigh, another I injected into her hip each evening. Suzanne also took a daily dose of estrogen. These drugs advertised some nasty side effects, the worst being mood swings. I found the advertising to be misleading. A mood *swing* would indicate that there are both highs and lows. Suzanne became depressed and angry at the beginning of the process and stayed that way throughout.

As usual, mine was the easy role. I took two doses of patience and understanding daily. Sometimes that wasn't enough. Our good friends, Jeff and Natalie, who later went through the same process, developed an effective theme for surviving the protocol that Jeff shared with me during one of our private manly conversations. These conversations usually would begin with one or the other of us bitching about our wife's mood and how little we understood about women. Jeff explained that he would remind Natalie while giving injections to remember two things: "We want to do this, and I am not the enemy."

The drugs worked as advertised. I paid another visit to the little room with the plastic sheets and old *Playboys* to provide my portion of the procedure. The doctors fertilized sixteen mature eggs, and nine good embryos formed over the three-day incubation period. Suzanne and I were ecstatic with anticipation. We chose to transfer three embryos into Suzanne's uterus and have six frozen for later use. The embryo transfer required a short hospital stay but went smoothly. We were at peace, and Suzanne rested for several days with the knowledge that three potential babies nestled in her uterus.

The process made it easy to believe that pregnancy was

nearly automatic once the embryos were placed. The pregnancy test was scheduled in the clinic for the day after Christmas. Anticipating a wonderful gift, we agreed to try a home pregnancy test on Christmas morning. We arose early, excited to be sharing a special moment. Suzanne took the test strip into the bathroom. A few minutes later, she called me in to watch it change color together. We stared at the strip willing it to turn blue. But it never changed color. When a single tear fell onto the strip, I knew the test was negative. I held her close, but Suzanne was not to be consoled. Christmas was ruined.

I learned some things from Suzanne during our tear-filled talks throughout this period. Since our wedding day, she had felt enormous pressure to conceive—much of it from me she had said, although I remain clueless to this day how she got that impression—and now she felt like she had failed. Instead of defending myself, I listened—a hard concept for a man—as she let out much of her pain and feelings of inadequacy. I was so surprised to learn that my woman—my perfect, powerful, intelligent, sensual, successful life partner—could feel somehow inadequate.

At IBM where she worked as a sales rep, Suzanne's nickname was "Suzanne with the Plan." Her plan for us was to immediately undertake another IVF cycle using our frozen embryos. Our research indicated that success rates for frozen embryos were nearly as high as fresh cycles. Our research proved correct. Through two frozen IVF attempts, we achieved the exact same success as the fresh IVF—none.

Photographs from Chapter 1 can be viewed at:
SamuelsMission.com

CHAPTER 2

A Family Is Born?

We had talked of adoption but as a backup plan that I had not really embraced. It was unclear to me how the process worked, and I worried that we would come to love a child only to lose it to a flawed court system. We were divided on the issue but neither of us had a passionate stance. We both wanted to undergo IVF again. However, Suzanne felt if we started the adoption process, she would feel less pressure to conceive. I was more willing to wait. When we learned of an informational seminar on Russian adoption being held at a local hotel, I agreed to attend, but without enthusiasm.

Suzanne and I arrived to find a large crowd. We were given a stack of papers and found a seat among perhaps sixty other couples. Margaret Cole, the director of European Adoption Consultants (EAC), introduced herself. She described her own experience adopting a daughter from Russia without the benefit of an agency. Margaret then rambled from one subject to another with little direction, while I wondered how she could possibly organize an adoption eight thousand miles away. We then sat through an hour of lawyerspeak on Russian and U.S.

adoption laws, including endless warnings about the things that could go wrong.

My metal folding chair became mighty uncomfortable. Suzanne and I were ready to sneak out when recent adoptive parents began speaking. They had their new babies and toddlers with them. The kids were beautiful. Our attitude began to change. We heard several couples talk of their treks through paperwork. We learned of the costs, then listened raptly as couples described traveling to Russia and bringing their children home. Many of these couples had been through the fertility wars, decided on adoption, and were thrilled with their children. One dad described my exact thoughts.

"You know, we sat right in those seats just six months ago thinking exactly what you're thinking. Margaret doesn't come off as the most organized person in the world. And she's not the most dynamic speaker you have ever heard. Forget about that. EAC's operation in Russia is incredible. We met many other EAC families in Russia, and every one had a happy story to tell. Now I would like you to meet our happy story. This is Alex." When his wife held up their beautiful six-month-old baby, I was sold.

Suddenly, I was eager to move away from IVF. One would think I was making all the sacrifices to get pregnant. But Suzanne was firm. We would pursue the adoption while attempting IVF once again.

We registered with EAC and requested an infant boy from Russia.

Massive amounts of paperwork, documentation, and a home study by a social worker were required to complete an adoption. It became apparent that, while any idiot could become a parent through conception, adopting a child required your life to become an open book for the authorities to peruse. We were required to complete infant- and child-care classes, along with safety and CPR training. A state-certified social worker interviewed us three times to confirm that we would make acceptable parents. Our home had to be child-proofed and then inspected and approved by state authorities. We wrote autobiographies detailing our upbringing, sibling relationships, parental relationships, education, and career paths. We submitted a written plan on how our child would be schooled and disciplined, as well as the religious training he would receive. We provided notarized copies of our birth certificates, divorce decrees, marriage license, and fingerprint cards. Each of these documents then had to be certified by the county clerk of court and then authenticated with an apostille by the secretary of state. (An apostille is a document recognized by most countries certifying the authenticity of a document.) We underwent police background checks and financial scrutiny. We filled out long forms for the INS (Immigration and Naturalization Service, now a part of the Department of Homeland Security), and then waited sixty days for their approval. One other small matter: the cost of the adoption, about $30,000, had to be raised.

We went through IVF again in May 1996. The eggs did not grow as expected. The IVF procedure had to be abandoned. The clinic performed an intrauterine insemination instead. We went home with little hope of achieving pregnancy.

The pregnancy test two weeks later, as expected, was negative. We had reached the end of the fertility battle. Unlike the other failures, there were few tears. Somehow we knew the direction that God was leading us. We moved forward, fully committed to adopting a child. Suzanne with the Plan attacked the paperwork with a vengeance. Many phone calls were exchanged with EAC. Completed documents trickled in. INS approval finally arrived. The social worker gave her blessing. We finished our classes and sold investments to raise the necessary cash. Our packet of documents, known as our foreign dossier, was completed. We were physically, emotionally, and financially ready.

On August 1, 1996, we received a call from EAC. They had a child for us! Suzanne raced the six blocks to the EAC office. She returned with a picture, an eight-second video, and a medical report for a beautiful four-month-old Russian boy named Alexander. The medical report was frightening, but we immediately fell in love with this baby. Suzanne consulted seven pediatricians with the medical report, which was filled with words like perinatal encephelopathy, motion disorder syndrome, and other unpronounceable afflictions. Most of the docs were noncommittal and confused by the terms in the report. The baby looked healthy and happy in the video. We called EAC to say we definitely wanted to adopt Alexander and were told it would take about two months for the paperwork. But we were assured Alexander would be held for us.

There was much to do. The nursery needed to be wall-papered and baby furniture purchased. We applied to the Russian consulate for travel visas, made long checklists of things needed for the trip, and spent our evenings buying baby things. We called EAC three times a week, begging for information on our travel date. We were bursting with anticipation.

Suzanne's thirty-third birthday was to be special. Earlier that week, Patty, our adoption representative at EAC, informed me that we would receive our adoption date and travel itinerary on this day. I kept that information a secret, hoping I could surprise Suzanne with the news on her special day. I phoned the agency from my truck during a quiet moment of my workday.

"Good morning, EAC," the receptionist answered.

"Patty, please, this is John Henkels calling."

"Oh, hi, John, hold on one moment, I'll get her." My heart was pounding as I waited. In a moment, I would know the date I was to become a father.

"John, this is Margaret Cole."

"Hi, Margaret, I was holding for Patty." Margaret Cole is the director of the Adoption Agency who had presented the first adoption seminar.

"I heard your call come in and wanted to talk to you myself."

"Okay, ah . . . sure, go ahead."

"John, I want to make sure you are not driving a car right now." A tremor went through my body. I suddenly felt like I was going to vomit.

"I'm in my truck, but I'm not driving."

"I'm afraid that I have some bad news. A Russian couple has inquired about adopting Alexander. When this happens, the child is taken off the list for foreign adoption. I'm sorry."

We spent Suzanne's birthday grieving for the loss of a child we had never met. She consoled me with the thought that it was just not meant to be.

"We need to let him go," she whispered as she held me tight. So we let him go and prayed for the child meant for us.

During this period of uncertainty and frustration, we relied on prayer for one of the first times in our married life. Our joint attitude that we could achieve our goals through sheer determination, hard work, or perseverance was not working. It was time to let go. We ceded control and admitted we were powerless. We prayed to Jesus for patience and for understanding. We asked God to lead us where he wanted us to go.

He answered us in a most unexpected and stunning way. On a weekend trip to visit family, we stayed at a cheap motel in a small Missouri town. Upon leaving the motel office after checking out, Suzanne suddenly veered away from the exit. *She spotted a coffee pot,* I thought. *Nothing gets her moving like that in the morning except coffee.* When I turned, Suzanne was not getting coffee but standing at a portrait of Jesus hanging on the wall.

"This is a strange picture to be in a motel," she said. *What could be so strange about it,* I thought. *We're in a mom-and-pop motel in the Bible belt.* I finally walked over to have a look.

"Look, I've got goose bumps," Suzanne said with a faraway

gaze. I looked at the goose bumps on her arms, then at the portrait. Goose bumps suddenly appeared on my own arms.

"Something is going to happen," Suzanne said dreamily. "I don't know what, but something good is going to happen." I nodded. My stomach was tingling. As we headed for our car the goose bumps and tingles faded. With heightened awareness, and a cup of McDonald's coffee, we headed down the highway. I never believed in omens before this day. But God's clear message came thirty minutes later. We read the graffiti painted on the bridge in unison:

SUZANNE '96
TRUST JESUS

The message was an awakening. We knew our wait for a child was nearly over. But more importantly, we learned to listen to the special way in which God would speak to us in our forthcoming ordeals, and to trust in His wisdom. Through Samuel, we would reach an awareness that didn't require a four-foot tall sign to hear God's word. Samuel's future lessons would be powerful, but would never have been learned if we hadn't found a way to pay attention to the obvious.

We met our child on videotape two days later.

The director of our adoption agency held a picnic honoring her visiting Russian employees. One moment, we were in the backyard of Margaret Cole's house sipping lemonade. The next, we were sitting in a family room, looking at video of four babies in a Russian orphanage with orders to select one.

Under the gaze of other couples who had gathered around the TV, we studied the children who appeared on the screen.

Suzanne kept quiet until the third child appeared on the screen. "Look at the smile on this one, John. Look how interactive he is." The boy on the screen was dressed in a pink, lace-trimmed girl's sleeper. He grinned broadly at the camera. He giggled when a nurse tickled him. His eyes looked away when a singsong male voice from the side called his name.

"Alexei," the voice called. The conversation was in Russian but the baby talk was universal. Suzanne asked me what I thought. I said he was cute and consulted a data sheet that accompanied the video. He was six months old. The room had silenced. I looked around and saw at least ten people observing. No one said a word. I could hear the hum of the air conditioner and the sounds from the picnic. All eyes were on me.

"Should we go for it?" I asked quietly. Suzanne unleashed her thousand-watt smile and nodded. A smattering of applause from the onlookers followed. Alexei—we had picked a child named Alexei to be our son. Margaret had entered the room. We told her of our decision.

Margaret said she would need us to decide on a name today, gave us a stack of papers, and shut us into her home office to complete them. We had decided on a first name of Zachary long ago. But I wasn't sure what we should do for a middle name.

"Should we keep Alexei in his name?" I asked. Suzanne's wisdom settled the middle name question.

"No matter where he was born or how he came to us, he is our first son. His middle name should be your name."

Two short weeks later, we boarded an airplane. Our flight through eight time zones landed in Moscow at 11:00 a.m. on September 16, 1996. Sheremetyevo International Airport was nearly deserted. After gathering our luggage, some of which didn't make it, we fell into line for customs. We meticulously filled in the customs declarations forms. One line asked how much U.S. currency we brought into the country. I wasn't about to lie to the dour-faced customs agent. I wrote *$10,000* in the appropriate space. I had been nervously carrying this money—most of it the adoption fee—for twenty hours. The agent took my completed form, scowled at me, and turned to talk to a nearby colleague. The second agent grabbed my form and marched over to me. In a very kind voice he asked me, in English, to redo the form.

"Don't write down dollar amount," he said. "We have to report large sums of money. I do not like paperwork."

"Yes, sir," I said smartly. I understood about the paperwork.

Once outside the terminal, as promised by the adoption agency, we found a young woman holding a sign with our last name printed on it. In precise but accented English, Elena introduced herself and explained she would be our escort throughout our time in Russia and would lead us through the adoption process. That afternoon, Elena took us on a tour of Moscow, including dinner at a local pizzeria, and then deposited us at the five-star Metropol Hotel on Red Square.

We were up early the next morning for the four-hour drive to the orphanage in Kovrov, where Alexei had lived all his short life after being abandoned by his mother. The two-story wooden structure looked like an old American schoolhouse.

We were led into an office and introduced to the orphanage administrator and a doctor. Neither spoke English. Elena immediately began a dialogue with the administrator, while Suzanne and I nervously waited. The office was clean, albeit cluttered. A nurse entered and spoke to Elena. Elena directed us to hand over the clothes we had brought for the child. The administrator and Elena were studying handwritten documents. There was no computer in this office, not even a calculator. The administrator used an abacus to calculate figures with Elena. Suddenly, the door opened. The nurse entered holding our brand-new son. I remember my exact thoughts. *He is perfect. He is our prayers answered. He is our son.*

Once again we were riding high. Suzanne cried tears of sheer joy. Her thousand-watt smile shone brighter than ever.

Zachary smiled and cooed as we held him. He seemed to feel the love from us.

Within an hour, we were back in the van with Zachary and off to the city of Vladimir. Next came a blizzard of administrative tasks: passport photos were taken and government documents signed. Thursday's mission was a trip to the U.S. embassy to obtain Zachary's visa. The paperwork was plentiful. We received our adoption certificate, a new birth certificate for Zachary listing us as his parents, and Zachary's visa.

The next day, Zachary John Henkels flew home to America. Suzanne and I flew with him although we could have floated home just as easily.

This time, we were sure that only smooth sailing in calm seas was in front of us. The ups and downs of our past were now just memories—lessons that we could file away and chalk up to experience.

Photographs from Chapter 2 can be viewed at:
SamuelsMission.com

CHAPTER 3

Life and Death

Those who heard our story commented on how lucky Zachary was to be adopted. And perhaps he was. But Suzanne and I felt like we had won the lottery.

Suzanne took four months off work to be with Zachary. She read books and sang him to sleep. She took him on adventures to stimulate his brain and develop his motor skills. I rocked him to sleep at night and held him for long interludes while he slumbered.

We felt it important to teach Zachary about his history and the special way that we became a family. My nightly ritual with Zach included retelling the story of a little baby who lived far, far away in a land called Russia.

For years, when asked where he was born, Zach would respond, "Far away, in a land called Russia." Life was full and rich.

On Valentine's Day, my fortieth birthday, we attended a party and seminar presented by EAC. This time, we were among the happy parents showing off our beautiful son to potential adoptive parents. Four days later, we joyously celebrated Zachary's first birthday. He was healthy, intelligent, and a very happy child. Shortly after his first birthday, Zachary learned to walk. Soon after that, he learned to dance. If music was playing, Zach was dancing. In September, we celebrated Zachary's first Gotcha Day, an annual party commemorating his adoption date.

I nearly broke my face from smiling that day. Not only with the joy of Zachary's big day—but the new life growing in Suzanne's womb made our life even richer. Suzanne was finally pregnant!

We had been planning to adopt a second child when Suzanne decided to try another fertility treatment. She had learned about a doctor in nearby Akron, who had great successes in fertility. Dr. Spirtos put Suzanne through a rigorous battery of tests and then recommended that we try intrauterine insemination, a less-drastic treatment than IVF.

Although the treatment was less invasive, the drug protocol was more aggressive. But calmness surrounded us during this attempt. Zachary had much to do with that. Neither of us felt the need for a home pregnancy test after this cycle. On some deep level, we both knew that Suzanne was pregnant.

She was.

We also felt that the pregnancy would last.

It did.

At six weeks, I joined Suzanne for the first ultrasound at Dr. Spirtos's office. I saw the two sacs on the screen before the doctor announced that we would be having twins. Suzanne lay beaming on the table. We clasped our hands tightly together.

Suzanne had suspected she was carrying two boys. An ultrasound at twenty weeks clearly affirmed her suspicions. I was thrilled. In ten years, I would have my permanent golf foursome all set.

The pregnancy weeks flew by. Suzanne slept very little in the last months and could no longer pick up Zachary, yet never complained.

Zach would lie down by his mommy and sing "Twinkle Twinkle, Little Star" for his brothers. Suzanne would tell the babies to stay in there as long as they wanted. I was telling them to come on out. I couldn't wait to meet them.

Our joyful anticipation was interrupted by a phone call on a sparkling, unseasonably warm March Sunday afternoon. Suzanne called me in from outside, where Zachary and I had been playing.

It was my brother Joe. His tone frightened me. Then he gave me the news. Our father had had a stroke that morning— a bad one. He was in the intensive care unit. Then it was my mother on the line. She told me to not even think of coming to Des Moines. The babies could come any second; I needed to stay where I was.

My other out-of-town siblings were trying to fly in that afternoon. Kathy from California, Tom from Arkansas, Steve from Chicago, Judy from Texas—all were on their way. Suzanne overheard enough of the conversation to understand what was happening.

"This might be an all-night vigil," I told her as she hugged me tightly. One comforting thought came to me as I waited. Quickly, I dialed the phone my mother was carrying.

"Mom, go tell Dad that he is going to see Billy very soon. Tell him to go now if he is suffering. It may bring him comfort." Billy was my firstborn brother. He'd passed away at age five, the summer before I was born.

While Billy was often spoken of during my childhood, I'd never understood the powerful grief my parents carried for him. Not until I was in my thirties did I hear the real story of Billy's death.

A visit home always started with reminiscing around the kitchen table. These were treasured hours, often emotional and always loving. Yet nothing had prepared me for the time I sat with Mom and Dad as they cried their eyes out and described the pain of losing a child forty years earlier.

Billy had fallen ill on a 1956 vacation to our mother's parents' house. Busy earning a living, Dad could not make the six-hour trip from southern Minnesota to Milwaukee, so Mom's parents had driven in to pick up her and the five kids for a summer visit. My mother described how she had repeatedly asked her father to close his window, since the kids were getting a draft in the back seat.

He refused.

Later that night, Billy became sick with respiratory problems. Left without a car, my mother pleaded with her parents to take Billy to the hospital. They refused to be so inconvenienced. Billy rasped and wheezed more and more as the night progressed. By the time he was taken to the hospital, it was too late. Billy died before morning.

The story tore my heart out. Dad described the moment he heard the news. He was in his small-town post office the next morning when his own father located him.

"Jerry, I have something very difficult to tell you," his father had said. Dad could not continue the story. He wiped his eyes to try to dry his tears. I couldn't remember seeing my dad cry before. His voice choked with emotion, Dad reached for my hand, looked me in the eye, and spoke again.

"John, God took Billy from us. Then he gave us you."

While I had known about Billy, I never realized the pain and wounds that lived in my parents. They lived decades with a hole in their hearts. I had no idea they thought of Billy every day of their life. Tension was always high in our house when my maternal grandparents visited. I always wondered about that. And I never knew why my siblings always claimed I was Mom's favorite. It became clearer during that conversation.

Dad was going to see Billy soon. I suspect he was ready and excited.

The phone call came two hours later.

At forty-one years old, I experienced the loss of a loved one for the first time. Later that night, I sat alone and watched old home movies from my childhood. Then I prayed. I prayed that Dad was at peace and with his first son. I prayed for some of the wisdom, patience, kindness, and love this wonderful father had demonstrated while raising eight, I mean nine, children. I prayed in thanksgiving for having him as my dad. He never claimed to be perfect. In fact, his favorite saying was that he knew he was right at least 51 percent of the time when making parenting decisions. He was that and much, much more.

In times of crisis, the kindness of people can be over-flowing. My boss supplied a private airplane for a flight to Iowa. Suzanne made a special visit to her doctor to be certain the birth of our twins was not imminent.

"The babies and I will wait for you," she said.

Through the service, I thought of my two families, my parents and siblings, and my wife and soon-to-be three sons. I prayed for peace and joy to again find a home in my mother's heart. And I prayed to find in myself the character and wisdom of my father. By the time the service ended, I felt a sense of peace. And I felt strong. Boy, would I need that strength in the near future.

Photographs from Chapter 3 can be viewed at:
SamuelsMission.com

CHAPTER 4

Fingers and Toes— Twenty of Each

SPRING 1998

Two weeks after the funeral, the babies still hadn't arrived. I took Suzanne in for an exam on a rainy, chilly April morning. The doctor examined Suzanne and then told her to get dressed and go home. "It could be another week yet," she said.

"I was hoping she would want to induce labor," Suzanne sighed after the doctor left. "I'm ready for these guys to come now." That was the moment her water broke over the floor of the examination room.

The labor and delivery room into which Suzanne was admitted was the same she had been in for IVF egg retrieval. Five years after we started trying to conceive a child, we were finally having not one baby, but two.

Suzanne's labor proceeded very slowly through the night and into the next morning. Contractions began weakly and only after she received drugs to induce labor. Suzanne remained upbeat and excited. I kept eyeing the sleep chair, but hung in there and provided the needed back rubs, foot rubs, and general support that super husbands on TV always seem to provide.

Finally, after fifteen tedious hours of labor, the doctor decided to deliver the twins through C-section. The procedure did not take long. Jacob, born first, came out screaming and kicking. Samuel came to us one minute later, peacefully taking in the trauma of birth like it happened to him every day. And indeed, in the context of his life, birth would come to look like a relatively minor ordeal. Years would pass before I realized that Sammy knew of his mission and accepted it when he came to us.

Our long-awaited babies were finally with us. The date was April 15, 1998. The boys were born healthy. Jacob weighed 6 pounds, 12 ounces; and Samuel was a bit heavier at 7 pounds, 6 ounces. I counted a total of twenty fingers and twenty toes. We immediately noticed obvious physical differences. Jake's head was big and round with thin, light-colored hair. He had a Charlie Brown look as an infant. Sammy's dark hair was thicker. His head was smaller and he had inherited Suzanne's dimples. Like their brother Zachary, they were perfect. Our prayers had been answered in abundance.

We brought the twins home on a Saturday afternoon. By Sunday morning, I was terrified by the amount of work caring for these babies required. We put them together in a crib in our room. Then I lay in bed with every muscle tensed, waiting for one or the other to cry out. It took about a week before I learned to feign sleep when the babies cried out in the night.

From the moment they were born, Sam and Jacob demonstrated uniquely different personalities too. Jacob was boisterous and demanded attention. Sam was sweet and patient. While Jacob was ruggedly handsome (like me), Sam was cute like a TV baby model. Jacob sat in one spot and expected the world to come to him. Sam was always on the move, and became the first to roll over and discover how to explore.

A particularly emotional time came when my mother visited from Iowa. We shared the joy of new life, and we wept together while reminiscing over good times from the past. The kitchen table chats were not the same without Dad. I really missed him and wished he could have lived long enough to meet our twins.

Baptism day fell on Father's Day. Jake and Sammy were two months old. Our minister, Reverend Ron Mowry, proudly carried the twins around the church, showing them off to the congregation. Our families gathered from all over. Jake and Sam reveled in the festivities. This was the first time we had them out in public, and I enjoyed the attention they received. The abundance of our blessings shone brightly on Suzanne's face and on my own. Each child had come to us in a very special way. Our lives were rich. And we were on top of the world—or maybe back on top of the roller coaster—ready to plunge to the bottom.

Photographs from Chapter 4 can be viewed at:
SamuelsMission.com

CHAPTER 5

Hostilities Commence

The first clouds of the impending storm appeared when our three-month-old twins suffered from colds. Jacob recovered quickly, but Sam developed a fever, along with vomiting spells. Suzanne wasted no time taking him to the doctor.

Our pediatrician sensed trouble and ordered up blood tests at a local clinic. That evening he phoned with the results. He wanted Sam admitted to Rainbow Babies & Children's Hospital immediately. He explained Sam's problem, although I didn't understand a word he was saying. He said something about his blood tests and his white blood count. It wasn't long, however, until I learned to carry on an intelligent conversation with the most experienced hematologists.

Suzanne packed a bag to stay at the hospital with Sammy while I called her mother to come and stay with our Jacob and Zachary. We couldn't have guessed that this was to be the first of many nights in the hospital.

As soon as Sam was admitted, frightening events began to unfold. The doctors wanted to do several procedures immediately. Sam was taken to a nearby treatment room. The first procedure was to draw blood for a CBC and Chem 23. I had heard these terms watching the television show *ER*. Now I was to learn what they meant. The CBC is a complete blood count to measure the levels of different types of cells in blood. The Chem 23 measures twenty-three other characteristics of blood. Next the doctors installed an IV. Both measures required several sticks of the needle into this tiny baby.

The third procedure that night was much harder to take. The doctor explained that they needed to do a spinal tap to rule out meningitis. They didn't think the test would come back positive, but if it did, they would need to begin treatment immediately. He was using frightening words. I didn't like that. The doctor slowly explained the process for the spinal tap, also called a lumbar puncture, and then asked us to leave the room because it was a sterile procedure. Suzanne refused and, as the medical staff came to learn, there was no arguing with her.

Gowned and gloved, two nurses, two doctors, and two parents began the procedure. Sammy was laid on his side and curled into a ball. Suzanne, along with one of the nurses, held Sammy tightly to keep him from moving as the doctor jabbed a needle into Sammy's spine. I had hidden my eyes, but the baby's scream told me when the needle was in. Suzanne's presence helped Sammy get through the procedure. He calmed down the moment the needle was removed.

When I look back to that day, I see the beginning of evolution in Suzanne—and my relationship with her. Among the many things I did not expect in Sam's fight for life was the way my relationships changed—and particularly my marriage. Catastrophic illness does that. Virtually every family we encountered throughout our family's ordeal experienced some sort of restructuring of close relationships—some were broken, some made stronger, others just changed in subtle or less-subtle ways.

Suzanne and I were blind to anything but Sam at the time. But the way a mother protects and nurtures her sick child is a powerful instinct men—even a loving, emotionally involved father (like me)—cannot fathom. The most obvious and instant change in Suzanne was physical. It was her thousand-watt smile that brought me to her side on the day we met. It is her most noticeable physical feature and one that turns heads and illuminates rooms. Suzanne's smile radiates warmth, joy, and even frivolity when set on max power. But on this day, the smile was turned down to simmer. Her mouth could still turn up in the shape of a smile but the light in her eyes failed to ignite and her dimples somehow vanished. Her radiant smile didn't just take a vacation either. It packed up and moved out. I would have been aghast if I had known how long it would be until her wonderful light returned.

Being a man of quick intellect, I learned when the twins were born that I was fourth in line for Suzanne's affections. But at least I was in the line and occasionally moved to the front. That changed with Sam's illness. Suzanne still loved me, needed me, and depended on me. But she gave so much of herself—to Sam first and then to Jake and Zach—there was not enough Suzanne left for the rest of us in line. To put it delicately, I learned to take a lot of cold showers.

Over the course of time through Sam's illness I, too, transformed. I couldn't see it in myself as clearly as in Suzanne but from the perspective of ten years later, I am a different person. Catastrophic illness in the family will do that, and when it does, there are several paths one can take. One can rely on faith for strength or bemoan the unfairness of life. My direction remained undetermined.

We had not learned a thing about Sammy's condition as we settled him in for his first night in the hospital. Suzanne stayed with him but found no comfort from the sleep chair provided in Sam's room. It would take some time to learn how to get hospital sleep. There is no such thing as a good night's rest in the hospital, not for the patient or the parent. Slumber comes in random snatches, an hour here, an hour there, interrupted by nurses taking vital signs, equipment beeping, doctors visiting, and so on. We had many other things to learn about hospitals in the coming months. The first and most important skill to learn was waiting. I had some patience, but I was not good at waiting.

I called off work the next day and was told by my boss to take as long as I needed. I arrived back at the hospital, a forty-five-minute drive from our home, to find Sammy crying. The bags under Suzanne's eyes and the lines on her face told me all I needed to know about the night.

That morning we met Dr. Berman, who was supervising Sam's care. Dr. Berman was the chief hematologist at Rainbow. We immediately liked and trusted him and felt fortunate that such a high-level doctor was taking a personal interest in our son's case. Mid-forties, full head of dark hair, glasses, trim— Dr. Berman could easily have worked on the set of *General Hospital*. His manner was warm and his voice soothing. I had no idea what a hematologist did, but he seemed important.

Dr. Berman said he had some good news, though his frown and worried expression made me think the news wasn't all that great. He told us that Sam's spinal fluid was clean, which meant they could rule out meningitis. Suzanne and I exchanged a tight smile and waited for more.

Then he said, "We need to do some more tests this morning. I don't want to worry you but we need to rule out leukemia. We can do that with simple blood work." A tremor went through my body as the word *leukemia* echoed through my head. I hadn't grasped that Sam could be seriously ill until that moment.

As if reading my mind, Dr. Berman said, "He's a very sick boy right now. His spleen and liver are grossly swollen and his fever's spiking at 104 degrees." He pulled up Sam's hospital T-shirt and showed us his swollen belly.

"We'll run a series of tests this morning, and I'll visit with you later today, okay?"

I had paced several miles by the time Dr. Berman visited again. He came with more good news/bad news.

"We've ruled out leukemia," he said with a half smile.

And then, "I would like to move Sam to a different floor, a kind of special care unit where we can watch him a little closer and he can get more one-on-one nursing care than he can get on this floor." I asked if he meant an intensive care unit. "Well, more of a special care unit," he repeated.

Suzanne and I were in a daze as we packed up our belongings and prepared to move along with Sam and his crib. A few moments later, we entered the special unit labeled PICU, which even I knew was an acronym for *Pediatric Intensive Care Unit.*

CHAPTER 6

Lifelines

JULY 1998

Inside the PICU, we followed the transfer team into a special room. A sign on the door warned:

ISOLATION
Hand washing required
Masks required
Door must be kept closed
Laminar air-flow

Suzanne and I donned masks from a container at the door. We entered through an anteroom with a sink where, trembling, we washed our hands. We hurried into the room where PICU staff surrounded Sammy. When Dr. Berman entered the PICU shortly after our arrival, Suzanne stayed with Sam while I hurried outside looking for information.

Dr. Berman explained that they didn't yet know what was wrong with Sammy. They had put him in the isolation room because his white blood count was very low. Thus he was at high risk for infection. The air in the room was constantly vented and replaced with special, filtered air. As for why Sammy's white count was so low, he couldn't say. Some sort of viral infection was his guess.

Sam was hooked up to several monitors, all of which beeped incessantly. He continually received different medications through his IV. The pumps for his meds also beeped intermittently. Four wires were glued to his abdomen and hooked to the monitors. A cable was taped to his big toe that measured the oxygen level in his blood, and twin IV lines were installed in his thigh. The doctors gave us permission to hold Sammy but failed to explain how to move him safely. As carefully as if moving a ticking bomb, and with Suzanne's assistance, I slowly and gently lifted Sam from his crib, wary not to let a wire or line get caught on the crib or tangled up in medical equipment. With the precision of a ballet dancer, I slowly sank into the rocking chair until Sam was safely in my lap. Any time we tried to move him, the lines became twisted or caught.

The rules in PICU were that only one parent was allowed to stay overnight in the room; a sleep chair was provided. As Sam was now critically ill, the nursing staff ignored the one-parent rule and both Suzanne and I stayed with Sammy for several nights. I offered to let Suzanne try the sleep chair (chivalry is not dead). This was a diabolical multifunctional contraption designed to maximize space in a hospital room. During the day, it was a reasonably comfortable place to sit. At night it could be extended to allow some adults (short ones) to lie down and rest. I found a blanket and lay down on the cold, hard linoleum floor.

Already we missed our other sons, whom we had left at home in the care of Suzanne's mother, Marilyn. Zachary would talk to us on the phone, but only for the few seconds a two-year-old's patience allowed. We had almost no connection to Jacob those first days and felt the pain of not seeing him as well as Zachary. But we had left them in the best hands we knew. Marilyn was the iconic, perfect grandma to her seven grandchildren and adored our three sons. Marilyn often left Grandpa Curt to fend for himself in their home an hour away to be with our babies. She had her own bedroom in our house and would now become a rock of stability for our boys.

The long night not sleeping on the floor gave me a chance to study our surroundings. PICU was a locked unit. Admission was granted only when you convinced the voice on the intercom at the door that you belonged. The unit had only about ten rooms. However, there were at least that many more patients in beds in a central room. Monitors, IV poles, and high-tech medical equipment crowded most of the space. Nurses, doctors, technicians, and staff were everywhere. Peace, quiet, and comfort were not found in this place.

When Dr. Berman visited the next morning, Suzanne again asked what was wrong with our son. He explained that Sam's immune system was having an unusually overexuberant—maybe tenfold—response to a viral infection. They were chasing down several possible causes but, frankly, were still in the dark as to what had caused the reaction.

"Sammy's liver and spleen are very prominent, maybe double their normal size," Dr. Berman explained as he pressed on Sammy's belly. Sammy let us all know what he thought of that with a low moan of pain. For treatment, they were using what Dr. Berman called shotgun medicine. Sam was being given many different meds in the hope something would work. Dr. Berman again reassured us that while Sam was critically ill, he was stable and in no immediate danger.

Perhaps more comforting was encouragement from another source. Reverend Ron—his parishioners call him "Rev" Ron—appeared from nowhere into Sam's room in the locked-down PICU.

"Suzanne, John." Just the way he spoke our names brought comfort. Ron's voice and manner resonated warmth and caring. A little rotund, and more than a bit balding, Ron was unlikely to be confused with a leading man in the movies. Yet when he smiled, heads would turn simply from its radiance. After giving us each a bear hug, he looked us steadily in the eye as he asked how we were holding up. Suzanne gave him her honest answer.

"Not too good right now," she cried. "I'm really scared."

Wrapping his arms around her again, he implored her softly to let it out.

"That goes for you, too, John," he said. "I know you are trying to be strong, but don't hold it in too long."

It was too hard to believe that Sammy could be this sick, I told him. Nobody in here could tell us what was wrong with him.

Ron reminded us that we were not alone. Prayers were being said for Sammy from our congregation. He left with a pledge to visit often, a promise that he fulfilled. Suzanne and I were not pillars of our church. We had never volunteered for leadership or committee positions. We did not sing in the choir nor did we show up every Sunday. But Rev Ron was there to remind us that not only were our fellow congregants with us in spirit, but peace could be found in prayer. We quickly found how the church members responded. Meals began showing up at our house regularly as word spread of our plight.

CHAPTER 7

Angels in Ohio

By the third day in PICU, Sam had stabilized enough that I felt able to go home and sleep. I arrived too late in the evening to put Jacob to bed, but Zachary met me at the door with a whoop of joy.

"I miss you, Daddy," Zachary repeated over and over as he hugged me tightly. I sensed a unique, but not unknown, aura around Zach as I rocked him to sleep. Since the moment we'd selected him from the video, Suzanne and I had felt that Zach was protected by angels. It is an unexplainable feeling; but even today we sense the presence of angels around him. I could feel them this night. Drifting to sleep on my shoulder, I asked him about them.

"Zachary, do you have angels with you?"

"Yeah," he sweetly responded. I don't know why, but I then asked him their names.

"Chrissy and Kelly," he answered without a moment's hesitation.

After recovering from my surprise, I asked: "Do you think you could send your angels to see Sammy in the hospital? He is really sick."

"Sure," he murmured as he fell into a deep sleep in my arms. I snuggled Zachary close for a long time while contemplating our conversation.

Before succumbing to exhaustion, I sent the first of what would be many e-mails to our siblings describing Sam's condition. I ended with *Please keep Sam in your prayers.*

I phoned Suzanne the moment I arose, expecting to hear of a rough night. The cheerfulness in her voice took me aback. She sounded rested and calm.

"Sam is a lot better this morning. His fever broke during the night. He is smiling and happy. He's eating. In fact he's on his second bottle already," she said.

"You should see him. He's in his crib right now grabbing his feet and trying to suck his toes, which is kind of difficult with all the wires and lines stuck in his body." Suzanne said the night nurse was wonderful. She came in at ten o'clock and made the room dark and quiet. She fed Sam, gave him his meds, and then rocked him to sleep. Suzanne described a night of blissful sleep for both herself and Sammy.

The next night was my turn to solo with Sammy. The nurse came in around ten o'clock and introduced herself. She took my hand in hers.

"I'm going to take good care of Sammy tonight. I want you to lie down and get some sleep." Just as Suzanne described, the nurse made the room dark and quiet. The pumps never beeped. The constant commotion of PICU never entered the room. The harsh lighting of the unit didn't penetrate the thin curtains. I never heard the door open. The sleep chair for this one night felt soft as a cloud. Sammy and I both slept soundly. When he awoke, Sam responded to his nurse's loving care with smiles and charm. I had forgotten her name, so I checked her ID badge before speaking.

"Christine, what a wonderful night, Sammy and I both slept great. Thank you for taking care of both of us. Are you on duty tonight?"

She said I didn't have to thank her and answered that she would be off the next three days.

On the way out the door she paused and looked at me with a warm smile

"And please, call me Chrissy."

She was gone before it dawned on me. Chrissy was Zachary's angel! Goose bumps filled my arms, tingles went up my spine, and butterflies fluttered in my stomach. Moments later I told Suzanne the story. When we put the time frame together, we realized Chrissy had shown up within minutes of Zach's promise to send his angels to protect Sammy.

An angel among us! It wasn't that hard to believe. God no longer had to put a sign on a bridge to get my attention. I was learning not only to listen but also to trust in God. I began to understand that through Sammy I was going to learn important insights. I didn't know what they were, nor did I know that others would learn valuable lessons from this special child too. I didn't know then that such a little child would deliver powerful messages of faith, courage, love, and joy. I didn't know the way Sammy's life would change me completely from the inside out.

While the presence of an angel brought a sense of spiritual peace, medical science failed to bring similar comfort. Several days after entering the PICU, there was still no diagnosis, only guesses from a group of baffled doctors. Although his fever had broken, Sam's liver and spleen were now swollen to three times their normal size. In addition, an unknown enemy was destroying his blood cells. Sam had received several whole blood transfusions, along with two transfusions of platelets, the component of blood that provides clotting.

I sometimes look back and wonder which was worse—the fear of the unknown that I felt during this period or the fear that came when Sam's disease was finally diagnosed. At the time of course, we had only experienced the unknown. The fears of the what-ifs were so new and so raw that I often found myself shivering as if I were coatless in a wind-driven sleet storm. But back then I could always retreat into that warm cloak of denial when I became too scared to face the frightening unknown.

Although the PICU doctors were now in charge of Sam's treatment, Dr. Berman continued to visit each morning and evening and brought some encouraging news. Sam was responding to some of the treatments. For some reason they didn't understand, he was getting better. And if he continued to improve, he could be moved back to "the floor," hospitalspeak for one of the regular care units. After a week in PICU, moving to the floor sounded like a stay at the Hilton.

The next day Sammy was transferred to the sixth floor, more popularly called Rainbow 6. Sam continued to improve, and his spirits lifted. He became a smiling, sweet little charmer again. Suzanne and I relaxed a little, and I was able to return to work. We continued to alternate nights in the hospital and developed a skill for getting at least some hospital sleep.

Sam's blood counts finally returned to the normal range. His liver and spleen, although still enlarged, were much less prominent. So we sat down with Dr. Berman and began negotiations on a release from the hospital. He said he would feel better if he knew what had caused the violent overreaction of Sam's immune system, but admitted we might never know. "Hopefully this was a one-time event and in five years we can sit down over a cocktail and wonder what happened," he continued. We agreed to monthly visits to Dr. Berman for checkups and blood tests, and he signed Sam's discharge papers. Sam was free to go.

Once at home, it became easy for me to believe that Sam

was cured. In my mind, his immune system simply was under-developed when he had contracted this mysterious viral infection. Now that he had beaten it once, he surely had the antibodies in his system to prevent a recurrence.

To prove it, Sam once again thrived. He and Jacob reached developmental milestones as expected except for the one I wanted the most. When would they ever start sleeping through the night?

Against my mild objections, Suzanne kept Sam isolated. We never took the babies to church, the mall, or any place with crowds. I considered him cured and wanted to enjoy the attention twins bring in public. But Dr. Berman had put Sam's immunizations on hold and Suzanne feared a relapse of his mysterious disease. Until Dr. Berman was satisfied that Sam was well, she was not risking an infection. Motherhood tipped the scales of power in our home.

The children each caught a late summer cold, complete with ear infection. Sam, like the others, recovered after a course of amoxicillin. This was the proof I was looking for that Sam was cured. Four months passed with no sign of Sam's illness returning. Our lives had settled into a chaotic routine of what I now realized was our normal, everyday life. We had finally found the near-perfect nanny, and Suzanne made plans to return to work after an eight-month leave.

The boys grew like corn in an Iowa field. Every day brought a new skill from one or the other children. With each advance seemed to come a new toy. The twins' favorite was a contraption called a bungee chair. This device, designed to develop a child's legs, would attach to the top of any doorframe. The child, suspended from four stretchy cords in a wrap-around safety seat, then bounced up and down like a yo-yo. Jake and Sam took turns in the bungee chair. Jake's shrieks filled the house as he tried to make the thing fly. Not as adventurous, Sammy would turn on his devastating smile and giggle with merriment, satisfied with a steady safe up-and-down rhythm.

Meanwhile Zachary loved cruising the sidewalks outside on his new tricycle.

Then in early November, Zachary, Jacob, and Sam each caught another cold along with the obligatory ear infection. Sam developed a low-grade fever soon after starting a course of antibiotics. Just to be safe, we took Sam to Dr. Berman for a checkup. Upon examining Sam, Dr. Berman seemed unconcerned, yet ordered a blood draw. The blood counts were soon back, and again Dr. Berman was unconcerned. But since it was Friday, he said, he would feel better hospitalizing Sam to keep a watch on him. So Sam was readmitted to Rainbow Babies & Children's Hospital immediately. Suzanne, typically organized, had an overnight bag prepacked and was prepared to stay at the hospital. I drove home, troubled by my remembrance of the tendency for Dr. Berman to soft sell.

Sam's condition steadily declined over the next several days. Once again his blood counts dropped, fever increased, and his liver and spleen became enlarged. He was treated with numerous meds again. The most fearful moment came when the doctors ordered Sammy transferred to the hematology/oncology unit. The Rainbow staff performed countless tests, including another painful spinal tap and bone marrow biopsy as they narrowed in on a diagnosis of Sam's baffling symptoms.

Two weeks after Sam entered the hospital, we heard the diagnosis—and that Sam was in a fight for his life. I could no longer control the shivers of dread in the false security of denial. And I knew for certain that the horror of Sam's disease was far worse than the fear of the what-ifs. My worst nightmare had been that Sam would be diagnosed with leukemia. And now I actually wished he had been.

Our family entered a tunnel. The world outside Sammy's fight for life ceased to exist. Newspaper headlines meant nothing, and I often skipped work. It was like I suddenly lost peripheral vision. I felt out of my body at times, like I was watching a movie about someone else's child. Other times, I felt like my body was encased in concrete, barely able to expand my chest to breathe.

HLH, or hemaphagocytic lymphohistiocytosis, was now a firm diagnosis. The doctors told us what they knew about the disease—which was little—and their experience in curing it—which was none. The disease was so frightening Suzanne cried most of that night. I was too stunned for tears. I yearned for the days when I was afraid of the unknown and had never heard of HLH.

By midnight, I had settled on a macho way to deal with Sammy's disease. I bottled up my emotions and fears in a tight package and buried them. My family needed a strong and fearless husband and father to take care of them. I wanted to educate myself about this disease and try to solve the problem without thinking of the possible consequences. That Sammy might die was a concept I would not grasp.

Upon hearing the news of Sam's disease, our families wanted to help. My sister Kathy, also a mother of twins, dove into the research of HLH. She wrote one of the first Sam updates sent to other siblings. As time went on, her research on HLH provided a complete description of the disease to my family.

Date: November 16, 1998
Subject: Info on Sammy's Disease

After spending about 6 hours last night searching and several hours this morning perusing what I found, I have come to the conclusion that there is not much info available on the net about HLH other than it is an extremely rare and lethal disease. Here is a quick synopsis of what I have found.

HLH is a genetic disease which affects the immune system. It can be set off by viruses, as it appears to be in Sammy's case, or just on its own. It usually appears before age 2, but sometimes not until age 6.

In HLH, the histiocytes (one type of white blood cell, which is an immune cell and should attack invaders to the body) become too populous and start invading other tissues and destroying normal cells, especially in the bone marrow, lymph nodes, liver, spleen, skin, spinal cord, and more rarely, the brain itself. This is generally described as a fatal disease. There is record of attaining remission with some chemotherapy drugs. All patients have relapsed when treatment was discontinued. The only evidence of cure or at least long-term remission is with bone marrow transplant.

There is a 20–30% chance that Jake would be a bone marrow match for Sammy, and less chance that other relatives, but all should be tested, as this is a better chance than finding a match in the general public. Doctors use the terms stem cells and bone marrow interchangeably. Stem cells are the blood cells that continuously produce all the other blood cells in the human body.

Kathy

The Internet quickly became an ally in our quest for information, as well as a communication source for our family and friends. Today numerous free websites are available to support families and patient with critical illnesses. Information on some of these sites can be found in the appendix of this book. As the months went by, a huge network of family, friends, coworkers, and church members became connected to Sammy's fight for survival. Sam updates were e-mailed several times each week either by Suzanne or me, or by Kathy, who became our designated communicator.

One of the uplifting results of Sammy's illness was the way my siblings became closer. Judith responded to our news with some quick research, the most important being the presence of histiocystosis website, www.histio.org. I had always held Judith as one of my favorites. I don't think she ever knew how important a mentor she had been to me through high school and college. That she was available to assist as we needed her brought great comfort. Unlike with Judith, my relationship with Kathy had always been tepid. She is four years older than me, and we shared almost no common ground during childhood. We were nearly always in different schools. We were not close as adults and had no mutual interests. Kathy chose to live far away from the rest of the family. She went away to a small nursing college in Minnesota and never really returned. From college, Kathy moved to Dallas and excelled in her nursing career. She specialized in trauma and eventually supervised the nursing staff in a head injury unit. At some point, Kathy moved on to Southern California, where she continued her career and met David. I was in my senior year at Iowa State when Kathy and David were married; I took my first-ever commercial flight to attend the wedding with my family. In a few years, Kathy gave birth to twins, Matthew and Nicole. From a Midwestern upbringing, she became a Southern California mom, and the lifestyle suited her perfectly. Kathy was the daughter who was expected to do big things in the world. She was a hard-working, driven student with big goals in mind when she left Iowa. But she found her true happiness in being a mother. Kathy and her family rarely visited Iowa. And I would often go an entire year without speaking to her. There was never animosity, only distance that neither of us found a reason to close up. I later learned that Kathy had become moderately disabled with fibromyalgia after her children were born and travel was difficult for her. Sammy's crisis somehow brought Kathy back into the family, for which I will be always be grateful.

CHAPTER 8

Faith, Hope, and Disillusionment

We had quite an office set up in suite 408, Rainbow Hematology/ Oncology. The space was a large laminar-air room with a comfortable couch, plenty of tables, desk, and telephone with Internet connection. We also had a TV/VCR, a nice bathroom with a shower, and a closet with a dresser. Many upscale hotels were not this well equipped. The family-friendly atmosphere of Rainbow Babies & Children's Hospital made it possible to be with Sam 24/7 while conducting our research and achieving reasonable rest.

Sam remained out of sorts with his fever still spiking at 104 degrees. He didn't cry often but he fussed and sucked his fingers for comfort. I wondered if a baby could feel emotions such as fear or know that something is wrong.

Suzanne, refusing to let Sam see her crying, often went off alone to find a quiet spot. It bothered her that I hadn't shed tears yet.

"Don't worry, they'll come," I told her. *I just have everything bottled up now.*

Macho, macho man.

Either Suzanne or I stayed with the baby twenty-four hours a day. The other spent the days on the phone or talking to doctors. We learned, for example, that a bone marrow transplant, or BMT, is an extremely difficult process for the patient.

And thus the days passed. Daylight kept us busy caring for Sammy with an occasional visit home to give Marilyn a break. It was during the quiet times at night that I reflected on the battle looming for this helpless child.

The first priority was to locate a bone marrow donor. Our understanding was that the donor could be either related or unrelated, with the best chance for a match coming from a sibling. Jacob was a fraternal twin, so his chance of matching Sam's marrow was like that of any sibling—only 25 percent. Our prayers were now focused on Jacob being a perfect match.

Our ongoing research led us to Dr. Alexandra Filipovich, a worldwide leader in the care of HLH patients. Fortunately she practiced just four hours away at Cincinnati Children's Hospital and, further, was hosting a seminar the week after Sammy was diagnosed on treating HLH. I remembered my boss had offered to help in any way so I took a chance and phoned him with a big request. Even though I had not returned to work he had phoned daily letting me know to take all the time I needed. That my paychecks continued to arrive in the mail was a true godsend.

While trying to explain my need to travel quickly to Cincinnati, he quieted me.

"John, just tell me when you need to be there and I'll handle the rest." He phoned fifteen minutes later with information on where to meet the private plane and the pilot's cell phone number.

That twin-engine Cessna whisked me to Cincinnati in fifty-five minutes, saving me a four-hour drive. The timing of the HLH seminar was fortuitous, to say the least. It was the only meeting held in 1998 and occurred at the time that we needed it most. There were six other families with HLH children on hand. The meeting started with an introduction from the director of the association, followed by a statement from a representative of each family detailing their experiences with HLH. One by one a parent arose and described his or her experience with HLH. Each speaker needed a tissue to wipe tears; the descriptions were often in halting, choked-up voices. One mom talked of losing her first two children to the disease and the current success of the third in surviving three years post transplant.

Masculine man witnesses real strength.

But all the parents in turn praised Dr. Filipovich as the best specialist in the country. I was last to speak. Fortunately my story was short, because as I described Sam's recent diagnosis, my tears finally unstuck.

Mr. Man has a soft side after all.

It took words spoken aloud to a group of strangers to make them flow.

The seminar concluded with lunch and a presentation by Dr. Filipovich on treating HLH. By the end of the day, I had learned much—most importantly that Dr. Filipovich was the specialist for Sam. The logistics of getting treatment far from home would be difficult, but somehow we would manage.

Back in Cleveland, we met with the hematology/oncology team the next week in a formal conference to review Sam's diagnosis and define the treatment protocol. The reality of the situation finally hit me. There was no escaping the cold fact that Sam was critically ill. He could die.

Dr. Nieder opened the meeting by saying that they were done doing things *to* Sam. Now they were going to start doing things *for* him. The treatment, the same as presented by Dr. Filipovich, consisted of an initial eight-week program of multiple chemotherapy and other medications. Sam would begin with IV chemotherapy. He would also receive a series of painful spinal taps in which he would receive chemotherapy into his spinal fluid. In addition to the chemo, Sam would receive daily doses of IV steroids. Other maintenance drugs would come later in the program. The goal, Dr. Nieder stated, was to achieve remission at the end of eight weeks. He would start the chemotherapy at eight o'clock the next morning. We expressed our desire to go to Dr. Filipovich at Cincinnati Children's hospital for the transplant. Dr. Nieder agreed.

As I drove home that evening for a respite, my thoughts were stuck on all the suffering in front of Sammy and the stress our family faced. How, I wondered, would we ever get through it? It was time to start praying for strength, patience, and courage—to go along with my prayers for Sammy.

The next day we all had appointments to get our blood drawn for bone marrow—compatibility testing. Jacob was our only real hope. The odds of Suzanne and I matching were considerably small. We also had Zachary tested. Mathematically he had less than a one-in-a-million chance to be a compatible donor, but then, we knew that miracles don't follow math rules.

Sam underwent his first chemotherapy treatment, which he tolerated remarkably well. It was the high-dose steroids that would soon intensely affect him. Dr. Berman explained that steroids have different effects on different kids.

"Some get mean and violent while on the steroids, and some kids get on kind of a high and are very loving. All the kids gain a lot of weight. Sam's cheeks will puff up and his belly will get rounded. I've got to warn you, he will get heavy." We took many pictures of Sam that day, now known as the "before" pictures. Sam smiled broadly for the camera. We were grateful that we took them because Sam's appearance would soon change dramatically.

Suzanne contacted both of our medical insurance companies. Making certain of coverage for Sam's treatments was now a priority. Rainbow Hospital had estimated the cost of Sam's transplant at $500,000. With dual medical insurance, we felt comfortable that we were financially protected, but would feel better once the insurers committed to covering the transplant. Suzanne also contacted Dr. Filipovich's office and made an appointment for Sam. We were to meet with her in two weeks' time, on December 1, 1998.

Bone marrow compatibility reports from our family were back the next day. Sam's nurse delivered the news early in the afternoon.

"I'm sorry," she said handing over the papers showing the data. "No bone marrow matches were found." Suzanne left the room in a hurry—looking for a place to cry. I wanted to wrap her in my arms and tell her everything was going to be okay. I wanted to be the protector, the anchor who could and would take care of my family in any circumstance. But I knew it wasn't okay. I had little to give Suzanne and nothing to help poor innocent little Sam. We would have to go outside our family for a bone marrow donor. That meant Sammy's chances for survival had taken another plunge. It also meant that monumental suffering awaited our precious child. Research had shown that a bone marrow transplant from an unrelated donor had significantly less chance of succeeding and came with multiple complications. (Years later I discovered my helpless feeling aptly described by lyrics in the song "I Dreamed a Dream" from the musical *Les Miserables*. I had never seen the show, but the Susan Boyle version from *Britain's Got Talent* really struck me. Maybe there were "dreams that cannot be" and "storms we cannot weather." These were fears I could not verbalize and felt guilty having them. I guess the women of the world don't have a corner on guilt.)

So much of life had seemed like a series of ups and downs.

I had never spent more than a short time on top. Every single time in my life I felt like things were going my way, the roller coaster plummeted to the bottom. This was a drop from an already low level, but nonetheless, it hurt.

The approaches Suzanne and I took to dealing with Sam's illness were on widely diverging paths. Although we both relied on prayer and were committed to our faith, Suzanne turned to a number of her holistic and spiritual friends and mentors. In addition to a psychologist/counselor that Suzanne had visited in the past, she also placed a call to a goofy psychic, a transcendental, spirit-whispering, meditative, guru type. Suzanne and a circle of her girlfriends had visited this woman in groups and individually to learn about their personal spirit guides. Suzanne had convinced me to come along to one of her sessions in the past. I remember a bizarre experience. The woman would be talking to us in a normal conversation when suddenly she would look away and begin a conversation with a spirit that had suddenly appeared to her. It was like listening to a Bob Newhart comedy bit.

"Okay, I understand," she would say to the air.

"Sure, I'll tell her that," she said another time.

Several times she would even argue with the spirit. "Don't you think I know that already?"

This is a bunch of crap, I thought at the time, my mind firmly closed to the experience.

I continued to think the same thoughts as Suzanne searched for emotional support to deal with Sammy's critical illness. As she reached out to others for support, Mr. Tough Guy felt abandoned and alone. She no longer looked to me for comfort. Looking back, I see why: I had nothing for her. We stopped discussing our fears about Sam and his forthcoming ordeal.

I was so afraid that it finally became too much to hold in. With Sam in my arms in the rocking chair, I suddenly began sobbing for no apparent reason. Suzanne jumped up from her chair at the desk where she had been working. At this moment, my emotional rift with her widened to a chasm. She grabbed Sam from my arms and scolded.

"He shouldn't see either of us crying. We have to be positive around him."

But hadn't she told me only a few days ago that she would feel better if I would let my emotions out? When I most needed her support, I felt cold abandonment. I realized that while I had nothing to give her, she also had nothing left for me. I would have to find other outlets for my fears and anguish.

We put our feelings aside the next morning as Sam had two procedures scheduled, both requiring general anesthesia. First was an MRI of his brain, followed by surgery to install a permanent IV tube in his chest. The tube is commonly called a Central line or C-line. The C-line is used to give IV medications, draw blood, and give transfusions. Once the C-line was installed and in use, no more needles were required to draw blood or give meds. During the surgery, Suzanne and I met with a nurse for a training session on Sam's home care. Sam was being discharged soon, but would require substantial medical care along with an abundance of meds. Our duties would include daily flushing of the C-lines with a heparin injection and weekly dressing changes of the C-line site.

Dr. Berman visited after the surgery and described the procedure. "The older kids tell me that they feel like they had been punched in the chest after the C-line surgery. So expect

Sam to be in some pain for a few days. He looks pretty comfortable right now, though."

Sam awoke from his nap feeling happier than he had in weeks and ready to play. Suzanne spread a blanket on the floor and turned him loose. Sam's brown eyes were wide and his smile broad as he plunked his xylophone, reached for Suzanne's hair, and let loose his demure giggle. Suzanne knelt down and played peek-a-boo while I took video. Sam responded by rolling to her, pulling himself to his knees, and reaching for her hands. When Suzanne opened her palms and hooted "Peek-a-boo!" Sam would giggle with delight. Suzanne took the camera and we played another game.

"Sammy, where is Daddy? Where is Daddy?" Suzanne asked. Sammy looked toward where I had been. I peeked out from a hiding place just enough for him to find me and then disappeared again. Sam roared with delight, even the tenth time we did it. His smile simply mesmerized me on this day. His eyes were so deep I got dazed looking into them. He had an aura about him, a quality or depth, something I couldn't fathom. His eyes were those of someone who had seen much, someone involved in a deep mystery. They had a sparkle that was not what one normally found in a baby.

The video and pictures we took on this day—he was seven months old—would become precious, because Sam's features were about to change dramatically. The aura would dissipate as his suffering increased. Sam's eyes would not be as big and bright. Steroids were about to grossly disfigure his face.

All this frivolity happened on the same day Sam was withheld food, anesthetized, put through an MRI, had an operation, and woke up in a hospital room. I was again struck by his indomitable spirit. And again wondered at the life lessons Sam had to teach. I remembered the powerful message from Sam's angel and reminded myself to find a peaceful moment and listen. Sam had something about him—something special. I reminded myself to be aware and let God speak to me, let me hear His word through the innocence and trust of this child.

"Chemotherapy"—the word did not yet feel right coming from my mouth and frightened me each time I heard it. Sam was hooked up to his second dose of chemo early the next morning. Except for the four hours of toxic chemicals dripping through the tube buried in his chest and the multiple leashes of monitor wires and IVs, Sam looked and acted like a typical joyful seven-month-old. He played in his crib and playpen, took a short nap, and giggled to music videos. Sammy smiled at the nurse as she took his hourly vital signs and tried to eat the stethoscope. We read books to him with noisemakers on the pages, which simply delighted him. I found myself grinning from ear to ear during a game of "how big are you," as Sam stretched his arms out wide to show us he was "so big." His sugary smile during these games left my heart pumping with joy and aching with fear. Sam showed no signs that he was critically ill and was unaffected by the chemo.

Dr. Nieder checked Sam out thoroughly late in the afternoon then reviewed his treatment plan with Suzanne and me.

The nurse loaded us with home-care literature and gave us the rules for when to bring Sam immediately to the hospital. Dr. Nieder warned us to prepare for unexpected hospital visits, as most chemo patients are in and out of the hospital frequently. The consultation ended with Dr. Nieder's declaration that Sam was free to leave. After three fear-filled weeks in the hospital, Sam was going home. The fear came with us.

Date: November 20, 1998
Subject: Sam is home

I spoke with John this afternoon and have good news to report. Sam is home. The road is long in front of him but John & Suzanne are joyful to have him home. Over the next eight weeks, the doctors will try to get Sam's disease into remission. He will be receiving chemotherapy twice a week in the Ireland Cancer Center adjacent to the hospital. This is given by IV. In addition he will be taking another chemo drug called Methotrexate one time per week. This drug is injected into Sam's spinal fluid and specifically targets the HLH in his brain. Unfortunately, these spinal taps are very painful and there is no way for Sammy to receive anesthesia. These lumbar punctures will also be used to check Sammy's spinal fluid to gauge the level of the HLH involvement. Appearance of white cells or protein will mean that the disease is busy destroying his brain cells. The next step will be to locate a suitable donor. I'll be researching the process and get back to everyone soon. Please keep Sammy in your prayers.

Kathy

Photographs from Chapter 8 can be viewed at:
Samuelsmission.com

CHAPTER 9

The New Normal

Sammy was safely home. Life returned to what I suppose would be called *normal*. Yet nothing *felt* normal. With a critically ill child amongst our three children, nothing ever seemed under control. Days became a whirlwind of reacting to the most pressing need of whichever child demanded attention. I felt disoriented and out of control. I realized the feeling is not unusual and had a name. It's called parenthood. My parents survived raising eight children, so it had to be possible. But I was sure tired.

Suzanne and I had to literally become Sam's nurses. In addition to administering his medications at a specific time and without fail, we were responsible for daily flushing of his C-line and keeping his dressing clean and sterile.

Once the nursing was completed, the evening brought the joyful chaos of bathing and playing with three little boys. At the end of each day would come a time when every child would be asleep. Suzanne usually had the laundry under control, so my job was to mix formula and fill baby bottles to last the next twenty-four hours.

When the cleanup was done, it was time for the best moment of the day: Suzanne and I would walk upstairs together and look in on our three slumbering angels. These interludes are among my most treasured and precious memories. As parents, we have babies in our life for such a brief span. At the time, it seems like the days never end but in retrospect it is so fleeting. If I had one chance to advise new parents, I would tell them to use all their senses to absorb this scene and save it into their memory banks. When I revisit these moments, I remember everything; the smell of the baby powder, the room so quiet I can hear my sons' breathing (followed by the gentle tinkle of crib chimes bumped while craning for a closer view), the luxurious softness of my child's cheek as I sneak a bonus goodnight peck, and the glow of wonder and utter contentment on Suzanne's face as we drag ourselves away from this tranquil scene. Nothing in life will ever match the peaceful joy of watching your child sleep, and these are the moments to file away under the heading of Total Joy.

Sam and Jacob continued to develop markedly different personalities. Jacob became a little boisterous and developed into an exuberant happy child. There was no feminine side to Jake. He was a thrill-seeking, laughter-producing, type A– personality boy. Sam was getting special attention from Mom, so Jake and I became quite attached. He loved to be tossed in the air gently or fly around like an airplane.

Jake and Sam were different physically also. While Jacob always had minor rashes on his chin and torso, Sam had a perfect peaches-and-cream complexion like his mom. Sam had an abundance of curly hair and those long eyelashes. Jacob had wispy straight hair, short thin lashes, and a mouth that was always open and usually dripping with drool. Although Sam had a sweet smile that captured your heart, Jacob's joy exploded from his whole body. His laugh would get the attention of the entire house, as delightful squeals would erupt amidst flapping arms, kicking legs, and eyes bright enough to light the night.

The most joyful person in our home was Zachary. I have heard parents complaining of the terrible twos. Not me. Of all the phases and stages of growth, I cherished the toddler years the most. Zach expressed love in a way I had never felt before— pure and unconditional. When I think back to all the pitfalls of infertility and adoption, it is clear that I was meant to be his dad. The trials of the past were well worth the reward of loving and being loved by this child.

Although Sam's care kept us busy, I did find time to read the Sunday paper. A story that surfaced about that time left me angry and very upset: a crack mom left her infant son and three-year-old daughter alone for four days while she partied. The baby died of starvation in a filthy apartment. Evidence showed that the three-year-old had attempted to change the baby's diaper and feed him. Her heroic effort at saving her brother failed, yet somehow she survived.

My total helplessness to make Sam better gnawed at me and left me empty. I have always felt that action or change could solve my problems, attacking them head on. But I was powerless to help my own child. That someone *could* help her child and did not drove me crazy with anger.

Then I remembered that I was not powerless, and I could do something for Sam: I could pray. I really had not tapped into the power of prayer often during my life. In fact, I had probably prayed more meaningfully in the past year than my first forty. Quietly, in my Sunday paper—reading recliner, I bowed my head. I prayed for the dead baby's soul and the heroic three-year-old whose life was sure to be a mess. I even tried to pray for the crack mom. I found that praying for Sam then came easy—and provided the comfort I sought.

If I had known then what know now about prayer, I wouldn't have been so reluctant to speak to God. I didn't realize then that God's line was never busy. I did not grasp that God didn't care that I hadn't prayed often. I had no clue that God loved me completely without any conditions, like a toddler loves a parent. I spoke to Him and He listened. I had much to learn about how God hears us and answers our prayers. It is so simple yet the hardest concept to embrace. All those years of going to Catholic school, daily and Sunday Masses, first communion, confession, confirmation, and altar-boy training yet I was clueless and uncomfortable as to how to pray. I was slowly learning to use this powerful support system.

Sammy's outpatient chemotherapy treatments were moved to the Ireland Cancer Center attached to Rainbow Babies & Children's Hospital. An appointment here was not like visiting the pediatrician. There were no kids here with the flu, an ear infection, or broken bones. Most kids were bald from radiation or weak and thin from chemotherapy. Suzanne brought Sam in early and expected to be home by noon, but found that things don't work that way in the cancer clinic. The exacting procedures required to dispense chemotherapy drugs create long delays and boring hours in a tiny treatment room.

The side effects of the steroids didn't take long to appear, and they profoundly affected Sam. His sweet personality was unchanged, but constant ravenous hunger and sleepless nights became the bane of our struggle with Sam's disease.

The only sense of normalcy came during working hours. Supervising construction projects seemed so much easier than before Sammy became sick. Work hours were almost relaxing compared to the stress of our busy life at home. Suzanne kept me informed throughout each day of Sam's progress as well as Zach and Jake's events. Reality hit hard every night when I returned to our home. Outside every entrance to our house we had posted the following notice:

ISOLATION RULES
CRITICALLY ILL CHILD
All visitors must be free of
cough, cold, flu, infection.
Hand washing required when entering.

Support rolled in from church members in the form of nightly meals. But our close friends did not fathom what we were going through. The guys would call to see if I could watch *Monday Night Football* at the local sports bar. Wives would call to see if we wanted to get a sitter and go out to dinner. No one seemed to understand that Sam could die and nothing else mattered to us. It's true that people really don't know what to say to you. Some assumed that since Sam was home, he was fine. I explained the disease HLH over and over and learned how to pronounce hemaphagocytic lymphohistiocytosis. The big elephant in the room was the fact that Sam could die. The odds were not in his favor.

"You should thank God it's HLH or whatever and not cancer," one friend said.

Others told me how bone-marrow transplants are like changing oil in a car. "Routine procedure," someone said confidently. "Two weeks, in and out."

"My cousin's neighbor had leukemia; you're lucky it's not that," another said.

Most of our friends had their own day-to-day problems and couldn't comprehend the thought of losing a child. It's not their fault. No one wants to face this challenge. And we didn't get to vote on it. This is what God put in front of us. Every morning, I would wake up and try to figure out how to get through the day. And every night, I would be frustrated by my inability to help my precious son.

The holidays were upon us, yet Suzanne and I were not in a celebratory mood. Sam spent Thanksgiving Day fussing and crying. He was miserable from the disease, medication, or maybe even normal baby colic.

The next morning he was scheduled in the clinic for chemotherapy and was unlikely to feel better. I was braced for a difficult evening. But arriving home from work that night, I was surprised to find a deliciously happy family. Sam and Jacob were in their ExerSaucers giggling as Zachary attempted to do summersaults in the living room. The babies would erupt in laughter as Zach rolled halfway over before tipping sideways. Between attempts, Zach would crawl to each brother in turn and tickle his feet. Jake and Sam would bounce up and down, slap their hands on the tray, and light up the room with their delight. Jacob howled with robust guffaws. Sammy laughed with sweet little titters.

"How can this boy be so happy?" I asked Suzanne. "Yesterday he was miserable. Today he gets four hours of chemo and look at him. He's living large and enjoying life."

"It's the blood. He got transfused today and that totally changed him," she said.

The idea that Sam was an extraordinary child was becoming apparent. Each of our sons had put meaning into my life. But Sam's lessons were special. The way he seized pleasure from the simple joys of family and laughter began to affect the way I looked at my own life. Even with his bloodstream flowing with toxic chemicals, Sam refused to miss the fun of clowning with his brothers. I could see that the roadblocks life threw at him were not going to deter him from loving—and living large.

Photographs from Chapter 9 can be viewed at:
SamuelsMission.com

CHAPTER 10

Back Aboard the Roller Coaster

We'd decided weeks earlier to take Sam to Dr. Filipovich and Cincinnati Children's Hospital Medical Center for his bone marrow transplant. The decision was based solely on Dr. Filipovich's reputation as a world-renowned expert in the care of HLH patients. We looked forward to getting started. Now Sam's first appointment with Dr. Filipovich was upon us. Once again, my boss, Jim Allega, supplied an airplane for us to travel quickly to Cincinnati and back home again. Sam, Suzanne, and I were in high spirits as we made our first visit to what would be our home for many months.

We were immediately struck by the efficiency and friendliness of the hospital. A car had been dispatched to the airport to meet us. Julia Griffin, Dr. Filipovich's nurse practitioner, met us at the door of the hospital to begin our busy day. We settled into a conference room in the Outpatient Services Building, also known simply as the clinic. This building, connected to the hospital, was the office where Sam would receive treatments both before and after his hospital stay. Dr. Filipovich greeted us warmly with a promise of an extended visit later in the day. She then introduced us to several hospital staff members who would be closely involved with our family throughout our time in Cincinnati.

First was Peggy Kaiser, RN, the hospital's bone marrow search coordinator. Finding a donor for Sammy had been a huge worry, and we were grateful to receive the information that Peggy presented. In fact, we had been under the impression that the search was already underway through Rainbow Hospital, but Peggy explained the Children's Hospital would conduct the search and it would begin at this point.

The search would be funneled through the National Marrow Donor Program and the International Marrow Registry. Peggy explained that both agencies have a computerized data bank with over six million potential donors. She also expressed optimism in finding a perfect match for Sam.

"We have great success in finding matches for people of Anglo-European descent."

After several other meetings, including a visit to Ronald McDonald House, we were introduced to the hospital financial coordinator, Carol Page. Carol's job, she explained, was to make sure billing was handled efficiently with our insurance carrier and to minimize our involvement in the process. Carol explained that all departments of the hospital would send bills through her office and they would then be forwarded to the insurance company directly.

"Hopefully you will never see a bill in your mail," she told us. Carol warned that my insurance company had yet to approve the transplant, but said not to worry, as most insurance companies wait until the last minute to okay such procedures.

Although this was surely unique among most families suffering through such trauma, Suzanne and I spent little time worrying about the money. Although not rich by any means, we had the comfort of two insurers and income flowing. But one can't tell the story of calamitous illness without wondering how others survive financially. I'm reminded of the scene in *Forrest Gump* when Forrest learns he doesn't have to worry about money any longer because his partner, Lieutenant Dan, had invested in Apple computers. "That's good, one less thing," Forrest surmised. That particular "one less thing" was, indeed, a blessing.

Dr. Filipovich returned for a frank discussion on Sam's chances for survival—which she put at fifty-fifty—and a description of the suffering in front of him. We flew home after the meeting heartened by our feeling that she was the right doctor for Sam and that Children's Hospital was the right place. The hospital seemed family-friendly and supportive of our needs to be with Sammy 24/7. I didn't get an institutional feel of the place. The environment was warm, and the staff, while world-renowned, were personable and caring. We were also scared out of our wits once again with the viciousness of HLH and were terrified of losing our precious son. Sam didn't seem worried. He enjoyed the airplane ride and snuggled deep into his mommy's lap.

The weeks that followed while we awaited a donor were far from peaceful. Aboard the roller coaster, we had some major plunges, including a two-week hospital stay for a life-threatening virus and days in the intensive care unit. The search continued for the perfect bone-marrow donor. But the chemotherapy did its job and the disease went into remission. If this were a war, remission would be called a temporary ceasefire. We knew it would not last, but at least for a time, the deadly histiocytes in Sam's bloodstream halted their relentless destruction of his brain and organs. Sam's beautiful features slowly became hidden by the continual swelling from the steroids. The doctors warned us that remission is usually short-lived, but it was a relief nonetheless.

CHAPTER 11

Preparing for War

I was at work on January thirteenth when the news came that a donor had been located. I don't remember a word of the conversation, only the butterflies of relief and a tremor of fear after Suzanne phoned.

Staring into space in the absolute silence of a construction field office trailer, I soaked in the emotions running through me. I felt again the same powerful joy as the day Suzanne shared the news that she was pregnant. But I also felt the adrenaline of fear coursing through my veins, adrenaline I would need to get through the trials ahead. Not only did we have a bone-marrow donor but a date for the transplant. *How many prayers have just been answered?* I wondered. The donor, a perfect match, was a forty-four-year-old Englishman. I prayed to God in thanksgiving for the news, and for the wonderful gift of this stranger from another country. We were not allowed to know more about the donor due to anonymity laws. The transplant was scheduled for February nineteenth in Cincinnati Children's Hospital. The news was a great relief as we scratched one item off our list of worries. Suzanne and I joyfully phoned our families and close friends with the news.

From my office at work, and with Suzanne at home, we set up a telephone conference call later that afternoon with Dr. Filipovich to learn more details.

"First, I must warn you that the donor must pass a physical exam. He must be free from infection or communicable disease. The good news is that he has agreed to go through with the procedure," Dr. Filipovich cautioned. She then reviewed the process. Dr. Filipovich explained that if everything went according to plan, the donor would be admitted to the hospital in England on February eighteenth. After the procedure, the donor's stem cells would be packaged and transported to the nearest international airport to be flown to Cincinnati.

Suzanne and I planned to be together with Sam during the pre-phase of the transplant when he would receive very heavy doses of chemotherapy, as well as the first few weeks after. We expected these times to be the most difficult and the times that Sammy would need both his parents for support. Marilyn would be in charge of Jacob and Zachary's care during our time away, although we made preliminary plans for them to visit us in Cincinnati. Three and a half weeks remained to get us logistically and emotionally prepared for the battle ahead. Everything was coming together for our precious Sammy to get new bone marrow and lose this fearful disease. He was in good shape for the transplant, the donor was perfect, and we were going to the best doctor in the country. The road ahead was fraught with peril, but we were excited to be getting this behind us. Our confidence was high and our faith strong. Sammy was going to beat this! I was certain.

At home one evening during the wait, Zachary talked of not feeling well. "Daddy, you better take me to the hospital."

I hugged him tightly. "Oh Zachary, I hope you feel better soon. I wanted to take you swimming at the rec center tonight."

Seconds later he was back.

"I'm feeling much better, Daddy. Can we go swimming now to the rec center?" Zach continually and pleasantly surprised me. Carrying on a normal conversation with a two-year-old has to be one of the highlights of parenting. We knew the one-in-a-million chance of Sammy getting HLH was some bad luck, but adopting this precious child from the millions of Russian orphans was incredibly lucky.

And I was certain Zachary was to have a role in healing Sam. I had three reasons for this confidence. Zachary had already brought healing powers to our family when he arrived, by releasing us from the pain and stranglehold of infertility. Secondly, Zachary had first-name connections to angels; and thirdly, the blue shirts. For some reason, once Sam was diagnosed, Zachary would insist on wearing only blue shirts. Not just insist, but throw an all-out tantrum until we gave him a blue shirt to put on. Suzanne soon figured it out.

"You know, blue is a very healing color. I think the blue shirts are part of Zachary's healing therapy for Sam," she told me one morning.

"Hey, I'll buy it," I told her. "I know two-year-olds have funny ways of getting their way, but it makes sense to me."

The truth was, I wasn't buying any of it. It wasn't until years later when I did an Internet search on the healing power of the color blue that I finally realized Suzanne had been right. Zach was doing his part to help Sam heal. No doubt his angels Chrissy and Kelly were behind it somehow. Zachary and I had great fun swimming. Later at home, I rocked Jacob to sleep. I even found some intimate cuddling time with Suzanne that night. For the moment, all was well with my world. Such bliss was rare, living in our tunnel—which made it all the more special.

Suzanne was determined to have a family portrait taken before Sam went into the hospital. This meant our entire family went out in public together for one of the few times ever. Sitting in a studio at our local shopping mall, we successfully found a way to get our three young children to cooperate for the picture. We celebrated the accomplishment by going to dinner together as a family at a nearby restaurant. Although taking Sam out in public was not really acceptable to our doctors, we carefully kept him isolated in his stroller behind our table. All of us thoroughly enjoyed the evening. Our boys caught the attention of many patrons, and Suzanne and I reveled in the attention they received.

Pretransplant testing required a short visit to Dr. Filipovich's clinic in Cincinnati. Suzanne packed enough gear in our van to last a month, and we headed to Cincinnati for three days and two nights. Zachary cried a flood of tears as we left the house. He knew this was the start of hard times. Zach was cognizant of the crisis in the family. Fear of abandonment showed in his face as I held him tight.

"I love you, Daddy. I miss you, Daddy," he said between his sobs. My heart ached from the impending separation and swelled with love at the same time as I hugged him good-bye. Seeing his pain brought tears to my eyes. I felt grateful that his birthday party was coming soon; being the center of attention would be good tonic for him. Abandonment at birth must have wounded him so badly, and I fretted about those feelings returning.

Jacob joined in the wailing as we headed out the door. Suzanne and I came in and out of the house several times for one last hug. Jacob gave up crying long enough to reward us with a huge smile, and we finally made our escape. Jacob did not understand the way Zachary did. I worried about him. His feelings would surely come out in some form, and I hoped we would recognize them and give him the special attention he would need.

"I feel like I'm on vacation," Suzanne said as we checked into our hotel. "I haven't been out of the house except for the hospital and clinic in two months." The hotel, a converted hospital floor in a building next door to Children's Hospital, was not quite like the Hilton. The hallways were deserted and dimly lit. The rooms looked and felt like hospital rooms. The all-you-can-eat buffet dinner served on paper plates in the erstwhile waiting room was cooked in a hospital kitchen at the neighboring University of Cincinnati Medical Center. The food looked and tasted like hospital food. Nevertheless, with only one child to care for, Suzanne seemed relaxed. For entertainment we drove around the area orienting ourselves to our temporary home and really talked to each other for the first time in many weeks. Sam was also feeling good. He had been giggly and playful all day and kept our spirits high.

While the evening was relaxing, the nighttime was fitful. The full-size bed was much too small, and the cement pillows blocked any chance for comfort. While tossing and turning, I was imagining the next four months and the trials they would bring for Sam and our family. My brain churned through the hopes and fears one by one. *I'm so relieved that Sam's transplant is coming up, but the poor guy has no idea what's facing him. I don't have much idea what's facing him. How is it possible that he has only a fifty-fifty chance to survive? He's such a fighter. He looks strong. He can do it. Dr. Filipovich is just being conservative. He has a better chance than 50 percent. He'll probably be sterile from the chemo, but no reason to worry about that yet. Now, how am I going to keep everyone happy in the coming months? Suzanne expects me to cover half the hospital time, and I want to be here with Sammy, but Zachary and Jacob need us too. How do we give them the love and parenting they need? Thank God for Marilyn. She is such a rock. I hope my boss understands how long this is going to take. I hope he keeps paying me while I'm gone. What are we going to do if the insurance doesn't come through? They have to, or we've got big problems. I hope, hope, hope the donor is healthy. Does forty-four-year-old bone marrow affect Sam's life span? I wonder why I never thought of that before. I'll have to remember to ask Dr. Filipovich.*

My head was spinning from the worries circling through.

The night passed and I had failed to solve any of the problems. I needed to find a way to keep my sanity and finally remembered a tried and true mantra. I promised myself to get through "one day at a time." The whole process was too hard to comprehend, but I knew I could get through one day.

From the perspective of years later, I realize that one day at a time is the *only* way to get through such a crisis. There is no roadmap or training for this kind of existence. No college classes cover this lifestyle. Every parent or caregiver must figure out how to get up every day and face the calamity in front of them.

But even a one-day-at-a-time strategy by itself leaves one empty of fortitude. And maybe—as in our case—you can't confide in your spouse because he or she is in such a different place than you.

Neither husband nor wife is at fault here. Dads deal with their child's critical illness completely and inexplicably different than moms. It's easy to be angry with our partner but the fact is we simply face crises in different ways. Moms focus like lasers on sick children and then face the guilt of not sharing love equally with siblings. Men don't comprehend the concept of guilt that afflicts women. I'm not talking about guilt from, say, cheating on a spouse; everyday life creates guilt in women. Whether it's working-mom syndrome or some other form unfathomable to men, guilt is a real issue that wives and moms struggle with. And they do it to each other. That's why you don't see women on the golf course for five hours on weekends.

Caregiving women often have nothing left for husbands, partners, or friends. Many dads I spoke with reacted much like me. We needed distractions to take us away from the constant strain. Men are blessed with the ability to take mental breaks from the stress and let it go for short periods of time. Moms can't fathom that we still read the newspapers and care whether our team wins or loses. They can't imagine how we could possibly have a sex drive while our child is ill.

"That is the single farthest thing from my mind," Suzanne would tell me when I was begging . . . I mean, romancing her.

Sometimes I would get lost in a book and be free from Sam's disease for hours. Most moms cannot do that. And they may get angry because men can. But men don't break away for selfish reasons. We have to check out now and again both mentally and physically. Men cannot focus like laser beams on catastrophe 24/7. We are different. Men don't have the emotional stamina of women. Face it realistically: we're Mars and Venus in the hospital.

So where do you go for help to get through that one day at a time? Your spouse doesn't understand you right now. Who do you talk to? Your friends are busy with their lives, and while they care about you, they don't understand your emotions and the intensity of your helplessness to take care of your family. That left me with just the Big Guy. I found that He will listen—anytime, anywhere, any situation. God does not care if you've never prayed before. He doesn't care if you're angry, lost, confused. He doesn't care if you have failed Him or dismissed Him. God will take your prayers while you're walking, reading, eating, kneeling, crying, or watching the play-offs. You may pray with a litany of memorized incantations on your knees, or you can be sitting on the can and simply say, "Help." There are no rules for prayer. It is simply a conversation that you can have at your convenience, and God will be there. I have no training to preach. This is just what I have learned during and after Sam's ordeal. Simply talking with God really does help.

The next morning started peacefully in the clinic. Dr. Fili-povich elected to give Sam an extra dose of chemotherapy to keep him in remission. It's difficult to look back and remember a day your child receives chemotherapy as being peaceful but in our world, it was so.

While Sammy slumbered through the infusion, Suzanne and I relaxed in the spacious treatment room. Sunshine streamed through the window, a reflection of our upbeat atti-tudes. Suzanne worked on her notes and studied the reams of information on bone-marrow transplant, focused as usual. I read a book, mentally leaving the room and toxic chemicals.

We took turns going to the hospital cafeteria for lunch. This was a place Suzanne and I would eat many times in the coming months, so I looked forward to checking it out. At Rainbow Hospital, the eatery was bright, cheerful, and abun-dantly filled with delicious hot foods, sandwiches, soups, salads, and desserts. Remodeled from an open courtyard, the cafeteria was covered with a giant skylight that allowed sunshine to stream through trees, flowers, and bubbling fountains. Tables were scattered to allow privacy if so desired. I had found it to be soothing and uplifting, a place to recharge my spirit. Not so here at Children's Hospital. What a dismal disap-pointing place I found. The lights were so low I could barely read my newspaper. The line for hot food was long, with few choices served by surly attendants.

"The cafeteria sucks," I told Suzanne on my return.

"Good. Maybe I won't feel like eating so much." *How does she put a positive spin on something as important as roast beef and mashed potatoes?*

Sam continued to sleep as the day rolled by and medicine

dripped slowly into his veins. At peace with each other for the time, Suzanne and I talked softly of our optimism that Sam would be cured.

"I can picture the day when my three sons and I are playing golf on Sunday afternoons," I said. "In fact, I expect someday you'll be begging me to take the boys golfing so you can have go shopping or get your hair done or whatever you girls do for fun."

"They might want me to play with them and leave you home," Suzanne teased. Silence filled the air for a moment. I looked at Suzanne serenely staring into space. She spoke softly, almost dreamily. "I picture them walking to the school bus together. Won't that be something to see?"

I could only nod my head; afraid my voice would pop the blissful vision in Suzanne's head. A sweet smile washed slowly over her face. Her eyes twinkled with rarely seen joy. Through the window, the sun was directly behind her head, casting a halo of brightness around her. Suzanne had never looked more radiant. The moment was so peaceful that I could hear a faint chorus of cherubim in the background. Almost afraid to breathe, my head slowly swiveled to peek at Sammy blissfully dreaming the afternoon away. This was one of those moments in life to take a mental snapshot. Just in time I absorbed this scene of tranquility, and stored it in my brain's precious memory file.

Dr. Filipovich briskly entered the room and dissipated the serenity.

"He looks so peaceful," she said, caressing Sam's cheek. "But I'm afraid I have some bad news." Her voice was soft and soothing. The words were not. "We received the results from Sam's spinal tap taken Monday in Cleveland. The disease has reengaged in Sam's central nervous system. He's lost his remission."

She broke our peaceful reverie so suddenly that we didn't know what to say. Once again we had let ourselves be caught off guard with the aggressiveness of HLH. Dr. Filipovich paused to allow us to absorb the news. Both Suzanne and I arose from our chairs and walked over to Sammy asleep in his stroller. As we gazed down upon him, neither of us spoke, waiting for Dr. Filipovich to continue.

"I would like Sammy admitted to the hospital today to begin more aggressive chemotherapy."

"Um . . . okay," I stammered. "I'll call Rainbow and let them know we're coming."

"I'm sorry. Sam needs to be here at Children's Hospital from this point on. Sam is at high risk for a seizure due to infection in the spinal fluid," she said.

Complete understanding came to us slowly.

"Do you mean that Sam will be here the whole time until his transplant?" Suzanne asked. Dr. Filipovich nodded.

"We need to get the disease under control soon. We don't want the HLH active at transplant time."

CHAPTER 12

Into the Fray

Suzanne and I had been preparing for Sam's long hospitalization, yet were stunned by the suddenness of it. We were counting on the remaining days to get organized for a long absence. With little discussion other than to decide that Suzanne would stay with Sam the first few days, we put our emotions on hold. Suzanne took Sam to his cardiology appointment while I went shopping.

It wasn't until I entered the TJ Maxx store that I wished I had stayed with Sam. While I was driving, Suzanne had made a list of things she needed for her unexpected stay. Walking through the aisles speaking with her on my cell phone, I jotted down the items. Jeans, shirts, shoes, I could handle. It was the bras and panties that made me regret skipping the echocardiogram. Suzanne gave me the sizes and I picked out what I thought she liked. This was not fun shopping like Victoria's Secret. *Think practical,* I told myself. I felt silly at the register but the clerk didn't seem to find my purchases unusual. On my way to the drugstore, I phoned Suzanne for her next list, hoping that I didn't need to visit the feminine hygiene aisle.

Suzanne's tears came later that evening after Sam had been admitted. Depression and fear hit hard. Her sobs were audible as she hid in the bathroom of Sam's isolation room. But I made no move to comfort her. The connection we'd made earlier that day had evaporated. I longed for her affection, but knew I was fourth in line and little was there for me.

The nurses settled Sam in and began administering meds. His C-line was hooked up to an IV pump that dispensed the drug cyclosporine to shut down his murderous immune system. He also received an IV dose of steroids.

Sam's room was in a twenty-seven–bed unit named the Manuel and Rhoda Mayerson Bone Marrow Transplantation and Hematology/Oncology Center. The unit, on the fifth floor of the hospital's Tower Building, was commonly known as the Hem/Onc unit. The floor was called T5A, short for Tower Building, fifth floor, section A. The unit was divided into three identical nine-room U-shaped pods. Sam was in a HEPA-filtered laminar-air room with an anteroom for hand washing and gowning. The front of the room was all glass, allowing easy monitoring from the nurse's station. In addition to Sam's crib, the furnishings included one sleep chair, a rocking chair, a built-in bench at the window, one office-type chair with a small swing-out desk, and a telephone. The room also had a TV/VCR mounted above Sam's crib and a private bathroom with shower. This small space was to be our second home for much of 1999.

Sam was not happy. Sedated during his cardiology appointment, he now seemed confused by his surroundings. My heart ached for him and all he would suffer in the coming months. Cuddling my beautiful son helped for a moment. Sam, however, cried for his mommy, and I quickly handed him over.

I stayed with Suzanne and Sammy that night until both were calm and ready to face the first of many hospital nights.

Early the next morning, I headed home to spend the day with Zachary and Jacob. These were hours to be treasured, because soon they would be rare.

When we'd brought Zachary home from Russia, either Suzanne or I was with him every second. We missed nothing. His first crawl, his first steps, his cries in the night—we were there to comfort him. Zach had faced the trauma of being abandoned at birth and then institutionalized; at seven months he was uprooted and moved halfway around the world. That last part was the first good thing that ever happened to him. Now he was a trusting, happy, and well-adjusted toddler who was about to face abandonment again. Suzanne and I were going to be leaving him for long stretches. Like everything in our life, it was so unfair.

Jacob, too, was getting a raw deal, and I was sad for him. Jacob received much of his primary care from Marilyn. Although she was wonderful with him, I rued the time we missed with him. But despite my regrets, Jake was thriving. His disposition was sweet. He was happy, playful, and growing like crazy. Jake's bond with Grandma was strong, but if Suzanne or I were nearby, Jake demanded our attention. And one dare not play with Zachary without letting Jacob in on the fun because his screams would shatter glass.

Less than twenty-four hours after arriving home, I was on the road back to Cincinnati. I had spent most of the morning playing with two happy boys. Jacob enjoyed flying above me like an airplane. His delightful shrieks came with a shower of drool, but I didn't mind. Zachary preferred riding on my back like a rootin' tootin' cowboy. Their jubilation was pure. I marveled at the ability of a child to live for the moment. I wanted to relearn that emotion. I wanted to be able to embrace the total joy of life as it happened without looking ahead. But my heart was conflicted even as it swelled with the love of these special guys. Like a wicked witch's hourglass, the grandfather clock in our great room flowed toward our looming separation. Zach refused to take his nap before I left and insisted on watching me drive away from the window. I bit my lip to keep my emotions in check as I pulled onto the street. I stopped for a final wave. But Zach's face was drawn. Only gloominess showed through the glass. He didn't return my wave. Marilyn's voice cracked when I phoned an hour later to check up on him.

"He's pretty upset," she explained. "He sat at the window calling for you. 'Daddy, come back. Daddy, please come back.'" I had to bite my lip again to keep from crying.

Sammy was in the middle of a rough day when I arrived at Children's Hospital. He had been sedated twice, once for a spinal tap, and again for an MRI of his brain. Halfway through the MRI, he awoke and the test was not completed. Sam's list of medications reached an all-time high with twenty-four different doses on this day.

The little guy had every right to be upset, yet still managed some smiles and laughs that evening. Suzanne accepted his jocularity as a good time to call it a night and headed over to our fabulous hospital/hotel room. We were on the waiting list for a room at Ronald McDonald House. I was alone with Sammy for my first night at Children's Hospital. Exhausted, I waited for Sammy to fall asleep then laid myself down on the sleep chair and waited for my nighttime worry demons to keep me company. Knowing that Sammy had immeasurably worse days in front of him kept me tossing and turning for hours.

Earlier in the day, and to her delight, Suzanne had discovered a holistic health department within the hospital. Before she left, Suzanne asked me to read the brochure and agree to let her schedule an appointment with a healing touch therapist. *This garbage ought to put me right to sleep,* I thought as I picked up the brochure during my restlessness. "Holistic health therapies are used to bridge the gap with traditional medicine to achieve harmony and balance among body, mind and spirit," I read. *Yeah right, whatever. Okay, I read it.*

The next morning before she left for Cleveland, Suzanne set up an appointment with a healing touch therapist. Picking up the brochure, I read more about what to expect. "Healing touch is an energy-based therapy that supports the body's natural healing process." *I have no clue what that means. But I'm going to try to be supportive. I probably won't even be here when this happens. Surely Suzanne scheduled this for when she gets back from home.*

As it turned out, Suzanne was away when the therapist visited. Determined not to show disdain, I greeted Kristine warmly and welcomed her to Sam's room. Surprisingly, I found our conversation pleasant and informative. I watched with interest as she moved her hands above Sam while he slept peacefully, missing the whole session.

"Can you explain what you are doing?" I asked hoping not to disturb the process.

"Sure. This is a method we use called healing touch, although sometimes I don't actually touch the patient. I work on balancing and smoothing out the energy field around him. The therapy will help Samuel heal."

Something about Kristine and her ways caught my attention. Her voice was soft and melodic as she talked. She kept a smile on her face while she worked. She moved her hands around and over Sammy like she was smoothing a sheet that was blowing in a breeze.

"Do you feel something there," I asked after a time. She

seemed to be concentrating on an area above his head.

"The energy around his brain is very unsettled. But I'm getting it smoothed out." *Maybe she does feel something. I mean the HLH in Sam's brain has me so worried.* Sam continued to slumber as Kristine did her work. After thirty minutes, she finished up.

"Would you like me to come back again? I think we made a lot of progress today," Kristine said, the smile still on her face.

"How often do you usually work on a patient?"

"Usually once a week. Sammy seemed to really accept the therapy. His energy field feels much smoother." Kristine beamed at Sammy and gently caressed his cheek.

"That'd be great. Hopefully Suzanne will be here next time. She'll enjoy watching you."

"I'll look forward to it," Kristine said. "And it was nice to meet you." Kristine grasped my hand in both of hers while saying good-bye.

"Kristine, do mind if I ask you a question?"

"Sure, ask me anything."

"Do you ever see angels?"

"Wow . . . I've never had any parents ask me that before," she answered cautiously. Kristine looked at me suspiciously for a moment, then seemed to decide to go for it.

"I sometimes see angels around the kids. Other times I sense them in the room." She went on to describe a case of a terminally ill child, only weeks to live according to the doctors, whom she provided comfort from pain with her touch therapy.

"When I came in his room to work on him, I would see little blue angels surrounding him. They were so pretty, just floating around him, little blue angels about six inches tall." She spoke softly and smiled broadly while describing the angels. I got tingles listening to her. *Zach's blue shirts,* I suddenly remembered. *Maybe Zach's insistence on wearing only blue shirts have something to do with angels.* I believed the old story that if one gets tingles while hearing an angel story, then the story is true.

"People around here still talk about that boy," she continued with an almost dreamy look in her eyes. He walked out of this hospital one day. He walked out on his own, disease free."

"Really?" I said, "Kristine, may I ask you a question? Does anyone ever call you Krissy?"

"Oh, sure, all my friends call me Krissy—why do you ask?"

"I thought maybe they did." I told Krissy about Zachary's angel Chrissy, and our encounter with her in the PICU so many months before. I quickly determined that this Krissy, too, had some connection with angels. I had one more question as she packed up her music at the end of the session.

"Will you let me know if you ever see angels around Sammy?"

"Sure," she said with a nod. "I really never expected to have this conversation with a new parent on the floor, but yes, if I see angels, I'll tell you."

Sammy, Suzanne, and I were the new family on the block those first few days on T5A. We had much to learn about our surroundings and the routines of our new home away from home. We soon figured out that parents had the run of the place. We found sheets and blankets to which we helped ourselves. We discovered a cache of little snacks and drinks provided by the hospital at the nurses' station. We were shown how to check out *Barney* videos from the playroom. We learned the hard way that Sam was not allowed in the playroom when we were kindly evicted by the volunteer.

"Just bring a permission slip from Sam's doctor and we will be delighted to have him with us," the volunteer told us.

"Absolutely not," Dr. Filipovich told us later when we asked about the playroom. "Sammy's immune system is compromised from all the medications. He really shouldn't leave his room except for procedures," she lectured.

A Ronald McDonald House room became available during this time, and we settled into our new space.

One concept we had difficulty learning was the hierarchy of doctors treating Sammy. Hospitals don't explain this very well to inexperienced sick people or families of sick kids. It was confusing to figure out who was Sam's physician at any given moment. We came to CCHMC to be under the care of Dr. Filipovich, but that did not mean that she would always be Sammy's main physician. In fact, we learned she would only occasionally be involved in his day-to-day care. Dr. Filipovich, along with three other physicians—Dr. Morris, Dr. Harris, and Dr. Gross—headed the bone-marrow transplantation service at CCHMC. These doctors were known as attending physicians and would rotate monthly on the floor. The "attending" would be responsible for the care of all BMT patients during his or her month on service and would also supervise the fellows and residents. Fellows, in this case, were physicians who had completed their residencies and had chosen to specialize in hematology/oncology or bone-marrow transplantation.

During the time of Sammy's sickness, we encountered scores of doctors who had responsibility for his care at some level. The four attending physicians at Cincinnati Children's Hospital would most influence Sammy's survival. We had come to respect and depend on Dr. Filipovich, but we didn't know her personally. She reminded me of my seventh-grade English teacher in the way she dressed and carried herself. She didn't spend much time styling her long straight hair, but I expect there's little time for vanity when you're a world-class doctor. Her ankle-length skirts and dresses didn't come from Saks Fifth Avenue, but she wasn't paid to be a fashion leader. But Dr. Filipovich's voice was soft and melodic when she uttered carefully chosen words and her smile could warm a frightened child and calm a frantic parent.

Dr. Harris directed the BMT service. A bone marrow–transplant specialist, he seemed less an HLH authority than Dr. Filipovich. By the time Dr. Harris was scheduled to take over Sam's care, the HLH was expected to be destroyed and no longer an issue. Sam's post-transplant care and recovery would perfectly fit Dr. Harris's considerable talents. Just under six feet tall, with straight, thin brown hair, Dr. Harris was generally unflappable. He didn't bubble over with enthusiasm, nor did he panic during difficult times. Dr. Harris always seemed solid, dependable, and in control. His face was not unpleasant, just never smiling or particularly warm.

Dr. Morris moved, talked, and practiced medicine at a high level. Taller than my six-foot-three, his shiny dome protected a powerful brain. He reminded me a bit of Dr. Nieder at Rainbow in that one had to think quickly to keep up with his discussion. Dr. Morris seemed always a step ahead of his fellows and residents and wasn't afraid to get creative with medicine. There would come a time when Dr. Morris prescribed a medication for Sammy that he had seen work "maybe once." A rock in times of crisis, Dr. Morris would earn our respect in the future.

The day-to-day caring of patients was left to the residents (known as interns on most TV medical shows). These were the least trained of all the doctors, yet provided the most care. Suzanne and I found the residents who treated Sammy to be outstanding physicians. Each month, one resident would be assigned to care for Sammy, along with several other BMT patients. The residents would make rounds with the attending physician each morning in order to be up to speed with the issues of all the children in the unit. Since even a resident cannot be expected to work seven days a week, twenty-four hours a day, the "Who is your resident?" issue became clouded during nighttime and weekends. The residents would often work thirty-six-hour shifts and alternate the nighttimes. Other times, a moonlighting resident or fellow would cover the night-time shifts.

Once we learned the routine of the rotating residents, we came to dread the first week of the month—when a new doctor would be assigned to Sammy. As the weeks passed and we came to trust the resident, our level of comfort increased. The residents worked very hard to quickly learn about Sammy and his issues. The life of a resident physician couldn't be much fun. These doctors worked an enormous number of hours on the floor in addition to participating in continuous seminars and training. None of the residents who cared for Sammy went through the motions. They each developed a devotion to him and were normally available when we needed them.

But when the door to Sammy's room opened on the first day of the month and a new resident walked in, he or she quickly learned there were three personalities to win over. Sammy was the most suspicious and hardest to please. Suzanne, with her copious notes and need for detail, tested the resident immediately on Sammy's issues and treatment protocol. My only expectations were that Sammy be comfortable, residents be available when we needed them, and that they never, ever wake Sammy up at night.

My first weekend with Sam in CCHMC was quiet. Few people were around, and there was little activity on the floor. Suzanne and I had already developed a routine of alternating hospital time. In that routine, the caregiver was left without a car in Cincinnati. Looking back, it seems very odd to be left without transportation for days at a time, but it worked out well because our only place to go outside the hospital was Ronald McDonald House next door. It never occurred to either of us that we would leave Sammy alone long enough to drive anywhere.

Sam and I missed the frivolity of Zachary's birthday back home that weekend. The party had been scheduled weeks early to avoid conflicting with Sam's hospitalization, but Sam's disease ruined that plan. Now I felt low during the weekend. Still, Sammy's sparkling smile brought me back up; he had many life lessons to teach, and I learned to enjoy the time with him.

I had brought Sam's playpen, bungee chair, and a pile of toys from home. When Sammy felt good, he enjoyed his playthings that made noise or music. When he watched his videos, little smiles periodically crossed his face. He also loved to observe the goings-on outside his room. Sam was also a people watcher from the day he moved into Children's Hospital. He liked that his front wall was all window. As people moved past Sam's room, he would lean over and stretch as far as he could to keep them in his vision until they had passed. It wasn't long until staff, parents, and the older kids on the floor began smiling and waving at Sammy. At first bashful, he would lower his eyes or turn slightly sideways and sheepishly grin back at his visitor. Although it was almost unnoticeable at first, Sam learned to wave back. With his arms at his side, he would open his palm and shyly flick his wrist once or twice. The move became Sam's signature wave and regular passersby watched closely for his greeting.

During the weekend, I began meeting other parents and kids on T5A. Sharing stories with other parents of sick children helped me learn how to handle myself during Sam's ordeal. I first met Marcia and her two-year-old son Nathan. Nathan had recently been diagnosed with leukemia—the worst kind, AML. Marcia and I shared fears for our children and discussed how we each expected to survive the coming months and years. I soon made a habit of greeting the other parents and quickly became acquainted with many of the kids in T5A.

Sam and I planned a big Super Bowl party on Sunday. I warned the nurses we were going to order pizza, drink beer, and maybe have a few dancing girls in at halftime. Our plan did not quite come together. Sam enjoyed a nice blood transfusion before some delicious baby formula. I did get my pizza, but settled for Diet Coke. The dancing girls never showed, and the game was a blowout. Looking back, however, it was one of the best Super Bowl parties ever. Sam and I enjoyed the one-on-one time. He suffered through vomiting and diarrhea spells, yet maintained his indomitable spirit.

When the weekend finally ended and Monday arrived, I was able to leave the hospital and go home. Sam was not. Three nights in the hospital was plenty for me, and I was grateful to leave. Suzanne had arrived at noon bearing gifts. She brought video of Zachary's birthday party, which I quickly inserted into the VCR; she also brought toys, balloons, and music videos for Sam. All too soon, it was time for good-byes.

Suzanne and I were adjusting to living apart, although not enjoying the experience. And leaving our children—on either side of the state—was an even more difficult adjustment. The good-byes that came with the departures brought much heartache, and never became tolerable.

Three short days later, I was back. Before I left home, Zachary made it clear how much the separation was affecting him. He climbed into my bed in the middle of the night.

"Dad? Are you awake?" he whispered. I rolled over and mumbled something unintelligible.

"DAD, ARE YOU AWAKE?" he repeated, not with a whisper.

"Zach, what's the matter? Are you okay?" I asked, very awake now.

"Are you leaving me again, Daddy?"

"Well, Zach, I have to go back to Sammy's hospital in the morning, but Mommy will be coming home to be with you."

"Can't you stay with me, Daddy?" Zach begged. He snuggled against me. I could feel the wetness from his tears on my face. He pleaded with me several more times.

I delayed my departure until noon—a few extra hours that were not nearly enough. Throughout the morning, Zachary refused to smile. His face drooped, and the light in his eyes was missing. He persistently held my hand or kept his body in contact with mine. Jacob, not yet understanding the comings and goings of Mommy and Daddy, giggled and wiggled the precious hours away, oblivious to our impending separation.

A major conference to sign a consent form was scheduled with Dr. Filipovich the next morning, so Suzanne and I planned to spend an entire day together. Medically, Sam was doing okay. High blood pressure continued to be an issue, along with continued vomiting and diarrhea.

While Sam napped, Suzanne and I walked the floor and met a few more families on Hem/Onc. The nurse's grapevine revealed that another child had been admitted with the same rare disease as Sammy. We searched out, and then introduced ourselves to Steve and Tammy Carter. Their one-year-old son, Zachary, had recently been diagnosed with HLH. We bonded instantly with the Carters. We had much in common and much to share. Steve and Tammy asked a hundred questions about the disease and Sammy's treatment to that point. We expressed our deep sorrow that they had to go through such a crisis. They expressed similar feelings to us, and we moved along with a promise to visit every day. Next door to Sammy we found a room occupied by Jason, a teenager from Cincinnati. We met Jason's mother, Debbie, later that afternoon. Debbie described the thirteen-year battle with leukemia that Jason had so valiantly fought. Jason was nearing the end of his battle, Debbie said softly. He was living out his last few days in a coma. Debbie's story was only the beginning of the horrors we would encounter in Hem/Onc. The Grim Reaper was always nearby on T5A, and Jason's impending death was not to be the only one that would affect us in the coming months.

Over the years, I have thought often and long about Debbie and Jason and other families afflicted with leukemia. The trauma of Sammy's illness did not last thirteen years. I only experienced our own version of catastrophe and have no way of understanding the devastation left behind in Debbie's life following Jason's death. During our visits, I learned she had divorced during Jason's illness . . . but little else. While it is pointless to compare family traumas, I can only speculate that Debbie's heart, hopes, dreams, career, finances, and relationships were left in shambles in the wake of Jason's long illness and death. Debbie likely doesn't remember me, but I still keep her in my prayers now and again and I hope she has since found happiness and fulfillment.

Dr. Filipovich, at the consent conference the next day, detailed the complete process for Sam's bone-marrow transplant. We met in a consultation room on T5A. She described the symptoms Sam would experience; the side effects of chemotherapy he would endure; the time it would take for the new marrow to graft; the potential complications, many of which could be fatal; and, finally, his statistical chances of surviving the ordeal, which she again put at 50 percent. Fifty percent—one chance in two—were the odds of Samuel surviving. Dr. Filipovich further stated that Sammy would absolutely not be able to go home until one hundred days after transplant.

"He may be able to leave the hospital before the one hundred days, but only to go as far as Ronald McDonald House. They have several isolation suites set aside for transplant patients."

The conference ended with a bit of good news. The donor had passed his physical; everything was "go" for transplant on February nineteenth.

The battle against the HLH inside Samuel would commence

for real ten days before the transplant on February 9, 1999. At that point, the docs would begin the conditioning phase of the transplant by administering chemotherapy to destroy every single bone-marrow cell in Sam's body.

The calendar with months and weeks no longer meant anything to us. Our system of keeping track was now based on the number of days before or after Sam's bone-marrow transplant. For example, transplant day was known as Day Zero. February ninth, the day chemo was started to destroy Sam's bone marrow, was known as Day Minus Ten. We did refer to the traditional calendar to calculate Day Plus One Hundred: May 31 was the day we could expect to take Sammy home.

Although Sam's room was our home during the long months to come in the hospital, Ronald McDonald House became our haven. Ronald McDonald House Charities sponsors the Ronald McDonald Houses near many children's hospitals throughout the country. A plaque on the wall of Ronald McDonald House describes the mission of facility.

This is the house
Where families meet
To continue their lives,
To eat and sleep,
To find their strengths
And dry their tears,
To look forward with hope
To better years.
This is the house
That becomes their home.

This is the home
That love built.

I'm not sure how we could have survived Sam's ordeal without Ronald McDonald House. The comfort and security this home brought to our family was immeasurable. Suzanne generally used Ronald McDonald House only for sleep; I found the other families and the fellowship key to my emotional survival. The Cincinnati house, which has been replaced with a fabulous new structure since our visit, was designed with approximately twenty private rooms set up with a bathroom for every two rooms. Our room, like most, was tiny. We had one full-size bed, a small dresser, nightstand, and a small closet. Many public areas were available for use by all residents. The house included living areas with TVs, a library full of books, a kitchen stocked with plenty of food, a game room for older kids, and a toy room for babies and toddlers. The large private outdoor patio came complete with grills, lawn furniture, basketball hoop, and a fleet of tricycles. Several nights each week a private group or service organization prepared a hot meal. Love abounded in Ronald McDonald House. Families quickly bonded, brought together by similar crises. Friendships were made in minutes at Ronald McDonald House; some probably last a lifetime. The management was warm and helpful, and always found time to listen when a parent needed to talk. A friendly smile, an open ear, a shoulder to cry on, and a hugs were always available from the generous volunteers that cleaned, cooked, and provided childcare. There are now 300 Ronald McDonald Houses in 54 countries around the world. Since our stay, I've been unable to pass by a Ronald McDonald House collection tray without throwing in a few bucks or at least my loose change. I also think they should change the name to Ronald McDonald Home, for it is so much more than a house.

Photographs from Chapter 12 can be viewed at:
SamuelsMission.com

CHAPTER 13
Search and Destroy

FEBRUARY 1999

Suzanne was alone with Sammy when the Bone-Marrow Transplant War commenced. Day Minus Ten marked the beginning of the destruction of Sammy's bone marrow, or stem cells. The stem cells produce all the white blood cells, red blood, and platelets in the human body. Sammy's stem cells were genetically flawed lethal killers that needed to be replaced. The healthy stem cells would come from a generous man who lived thousands of miles away. Before the donor marrow could be introduced, however, every one of Sammy's stem cells would be destroyed through a rigorous ten-day course of toxic chemotherapy. This period was known as the conditioning phase.

To deliver the Busulfan, the chemo used for the first four days, the docs ordered a feeding tube inserted into Sam's stomach. The feeding tube, called a nasal-gastric or NG tube, was a very thin flexible tube inserted into Sam's nostril and pushed through his esophagus into his stomach. Sam would live with the NG tube for many months and did not seem bothered by it once it was inserted. The NG tube would also be used in the coming days to pump baby formula into Sam's stomach when his mouth was too sore to eat or drink.

After missing the opening days of the war on Sam's bone marrow, I returned on the morning of BMT Day Minus Seven. Six years earlier on this date, Suzanne and I had joyfully been married on sun-drenched St. Thomas Island. There was little joy on this anniversary. Suzanne looked haggard, like a battle commander on the front lines.

"I'm glad to see you," Suzanne greeted me with a half-hearted hug as I walked into the room. *At least she's happy to see me. That's a good sign.*

"I'm really exhausted," she said before I could respond with an anniversary greeting. "We didn't sleep much at all last night."

I went to Sammy's side. He was snoring softly in his crib.

"I'm going to head right home as soon as I give you the update. It's been a hard few days." *She looks tired. I hope she's okay to drive home.*

"Wow! Sammy looks different. I can't believe how much he is swollen. He looks miserable," I said.

The change in his appearance, after I'd been away for three days, was startling. Sam's face, grossly disfigured from steroids and chemo, no longer would be confused with the Gerber baby. To visitors, his appearance was unnerving. Few called him cute. Those who did were only being nice.

"He's been in a pretty good mood considering what he's going through." Suzanne handed me the charts that we kept for tracking Sam's meds, feeds, and outputs. Since our twins were born, we had been charting when they each ate, slept, and had diaper changes. We had continued that practice with Sam in the hospital, as well as keeping an additional chart with his meds. Each week I would print up a new chart listing all the meds and with scheduled times.

"I'm ready to go. Where is the car parked?" Suzanne asked.
"I'll walk you down. Here are the keys." That it was our
anniversary never came up. Neither of us felt like celebrating.

"Are you sure you don't want to take a nap before you go?
You look so tired," I offered.

"I'll grab a cup of coffee for the road." After a peck on the
cheek and a quick hug, Suzanne was gone. We had spent
twenty minutes together. There were no cards, no flowers, and
no romance.

It had now been about three months since Sam had been
diagnosed. My relationship with Suzanne had changed drasti-
cally in that time. We were most definitely a team in the arena
of Sam's illness and raising our boys, but beyond that our
marriage and interpersonal relationship was on the shelf. I
craved the closeness we once shared but knew not how to get
back to it. I could not explain to her how frightened and powerless I felt. The role reversal was another unexpected side effect
of Sam's illness. We all know it's supposed to be the male who
doesn't share feelings—and frankly I was okay with not sharing
mine—but I felt unneeded when Suzanne kept me at a distance.

Again, looking back from the perspective of ten years later,
I understand why. While not claiming any particular wisdom
on how women tick, I learned much by being married to one of
the strange creatures while living through our ordeal. As
described earlier, her total commitment and focus on our children simply left her tank empty of outward affection. As we
have talked over the years, it's become clear how desperately
grateful Suzanne was to have me at her side throughout
Sammy's fight. She's talked, too, of missing the intimacy of
our marriage during that time and thanked me for my patience

with her.

The lesson for husbands is the same one we learned the moment we discovered girls don't have cooties. Females are definitely from a strange planet. But they really like when you're patient with them.

Sammy and I were alone again. He'd been sound asleep when I crept into the room. Suzanne's chart from the day before (actually we started a new twenty-four-hour chart every midnight) was lying on Sam's bed. It gave the details of her hard night. She had made a notation every hour—a doctor visit, diaper change, or Sam awoke hungry.

But now the room was quiet. I dozed in the rocking chair next to Sam's crib, enjoying the tranquility. He awoke two hours later with a giggle. I looked at him through the crib bars, lying on his side. He had one eye cracked open and two fingers in his mouth. I smiled and he giggled again.

"Hi, Sammy, how's my boy? I missed you so much." Neither of us moved. I talked to him softly, my own eyes barely opened. Sammy cooed.

Daddy, you're with me. I'm so happy to see you. His face radiated the words that he couldn't yet speak. When the drowsiness vaporized, Sam was ready to frolic. We played all his favorite games. Peek-a-boo, how big are you? Where's Daddy? Sammy tittered with delight, not allowing deadly chemotherapy to affect his mood. His smile was so different from his presteroid days. His puffy cheeks pushed his mouth inward so it was almost round. His eyes were just slits compared to the deep round chocolate saucers of three months earlier. That Sammy could feel so joyful while under assault from chemotherapy left me pondering my own dark moods. Sam's ability to lift me up gave me an insight into his powerful spirit—again. And he left me to marvel at his courage.

Heavy artillery was brought into the battle against Sam's bone marrow on BMT Day Minus Five. His happy mood dissipated as the hostilities inside his body escalated. To the rest of the country, this Valentine's Day was about flowers, candy, and romance. To Sammy it was about combat. Cytoxan became the primary chemo weapon in the destruction of his stem cells. Sam's nurse Sarah started hooking up medicine to Sam's C-line early in the day. He first received side-effect medicines to prevent nausea and to protect his bladder from bleeding. Sam was feeling okay until late morning when the chemo started. The Cytoxan took an hour to drip into the artery near his heart. Once the medicine arrived in his blood-stream it found its way to the battleground deep within Sam's bones. It took just minutes for him to start feeling the misery. Once his cries started, they didn't stop. I tried holding him on my lap, over my shoulder, and cuddled in my arms. I carried him around the room as far as his IV leash would allow. I played music, turned on *Teletubbies* and *Barney*. Nothing helped to stem his wails. When the Cytoxan was completed, Sarah hung a bag of VP-16 on Sam's IV pole and hooked it to his C-line so he could endure another four hours of chemo.

Sam was trapped in the middle of the war. He had no escape. Yet there were times in the day when I left the room, leaving him moaning in pain, while I took a walk. My thoughts punished me. *Sam doesn't get to take breaks from chemo. Why don't you stay with him? He's the one suffering, not you.* Sam worked hard to avoid vomiting during these hours. He finally took a two-hour nap late in the afternoon. I knew this was only a tiny sample of the misery in front of Sam, but I was worn out from trying to comfort him.

Sam felt better after his snooze, but faced numerous doses of IV meds throughout the evening and night. Sam's IV pole was getting crowded. It now supported four pumps and five bags of chemo and other drugs.

The nighttime hours ticked excruciatingly slow. I could only wonder how Sammy endured the discomfort. He awoke every hour either hungry or in pain. The nurse seemed to be in Sam's room all night, either drawing blood for labs or monitoring his vital signs. She was only missing when the pumps beeped—which always happened about the time that I started to doze. Yet no matter how long or how miserable the night, morning's arrival was always welcomed. Daylight seemed like the finish line of a marathon. The prize was coffee—lots of coffee. I often joked to the nurses about starting an IV line in my arm for coffee, but they told me it was strictly a P-O (oral) drug.

CHAPTER 14

The Heroes of T5A

That was a special place, the hematology/oncology/BMT unit. Our time there was like no other in our lives.

Living in a cancer unit was like being in another dimension. When you left for a time, you missed it. And when you returned from the outside world, it took time to get in tune with the heartbeat of the unit. Every fiber of every person there was focused on the children.

In many ways, Hem/Onc was hell on earth. Yet in other ways, it was a miraculous place that brought out the best in the people who resided and worked there. It was a place that can't truly be described—you had to feel it—but Dan Mahoney, a nurse on the unit comes close:

HEM/ONC/BMT

How do you express your feelings about Hem/ Onc/Bmt?
Do you have a rope long enough to circle so many emotions?

Hem/Onc/Bmt is a ride—with direction and
destination unknown.
It encompasses all—sheer joy and sheer
sorrow—
Sometimes at the same time.
The ride is like the roller coaster at the park.
You share it with many, but you also must ride
alone.
It is up, down, around. And over and under.
You must hurry on and feel each section.
Hem/Onc/Bmt is also an island.
But—more importantly—it is an island of
families.
All that matters are the families and the
children.
When I arrive on the island—nothing else
matters—as much.
What needs to be accomplished is known.
Sometimes it is to help live—sometimes it is to
help die—
Sometimes at the same time.
Sometimes my feelings are overwhelmed.
Crying and laughing at the same time is
difficult.
Sometimes you want to burst.
Sometimes you do.
Other people on the island are always there to
pick you up.
The sorrow and pain of a dying child
can only be overturned by the joy of a "going
home party."
And these can be happening at the same time
also.
Time, measured in moments, each one to be
felt,

is what matters.
Hem/Onc/Bmt is to be lived in the present.
To me, life is lived and felt to the fullest,
on the island
And, *I can't imagine not being there.*

Suzanne and I were tuned into the rhythm and pace of life on Hem/Onc by the time transplant day approached. We were a part of the landscape now, not simply visitors. We recognized all the nurses, doctors, volunteers, and cleaning staff, and they us. Sam was a star in Hem/Onc. The nurses loved taking care of him. When his primary nurses were off, others fought to take him. We soon picked our favorites. Friendships were made quickly in Hem/Onc. Faces in the elevator told a story with only a glance. There was pain here. There was joy. Mostly, there was weariness. The eyes of the parents at the coffee machine each morning told the story of the night. Most overheard conversations were about the day's "counts." Blood counts were everything. Rising counts were good, falling counts were bad. ANC, a measure of immune cells, was king in Hem/Onc. Sam's ANC would soon be zero, a necessity to receive new stem cells. Our neighbor, four-year-old Colby, was fourteen days post-transplant on this day. His ANC went from zero to 36. Thirty-six is a microscopic ANC number, yet his parents were thrilled. An ANC above zero is the first sign that the transplanted marrow is grafting.

We learned of another baby receiving a bone marrow transplant. Zachary Bowlin was three months old and an orphan, a ward of the county, with no one to hold him except nurses and volunteers. Zachary was born to a crack-addicted mother who abandoned him at birth. If that wasn't enough trauma for a tiny baby, it was soon determined that he was born without an immune system. Suzanne and I had now met two boys named Zachary on the unit. They both had already carved a little niche into our hearts. This Zach's story often caused me to reflect on the joy brought by our own precious Zachary, also abandoned at birth. Suzanne and I both vowed to find time to hold and comfort little Zachary.

The kids in this place were awesome. The strength you sometimes saw in their eyes was breathtaking. The pain you more often saw was heartbreaking. We had gotten to know many of the long-termers. A lot of the kids were regulars— cancer patients in for a short visit, often for chemo, sometimes low blood counts, fever, or whatever. The leukemia kids would come and go for years . . . if they were lucky. Other kids were in for a long term, like Sam. Most of the regulars were once long-termers.

Sam had many admirers here. One was Allison, an adorable four-year-old from Tennessee with thick, bouncy, curly blonde hair and a sweet smile. She was pretty enough to be on stage in one of those goofy child beauty pageants. Allison's outgoing personality matched her lovely appearance; she visited Sam twice a day and made crafts for him, which she taped on his window. Allison seemed to have a lot going for her, until you looked closer. Hers was a sad story: her mom could visit only once a week and her dad even less. The grapevine said they were very poor. Awaiting a bone-marrow transplant, Allison was so weak when she was admitted that her BMT was delayed until she became stronger. Her story got sadder yet: Allison's liver was diseased. If she survived her BMT, she would then wait for a liver transplant. The grapevine indicated that Allison had little chance of surviving.

Then there was Alexandra, age eight, in the final stages of leukemia. I befriended her dad. Scott stayed with Alex most of the week. He had to quit his job because he gave his white cells three times a week for his daughter. Alex had been through much, yet I never saw her without a smile. She recently had a tumor removed from behind her eye. Her face was swollen, and the eye was blind. But every day Scott wheeled her multiple IV poles out to the nurse's station where Alex would sit at her laptop computer and illuminate the unit with her joy. Around the corner from our room was baby Elijah. A Native-American from New Mexico, Elijah had had his bone marrow transplant sixteen days before Sam. Elijah's family was said to be very poor also. In the world of Hem/Onc, however, Elijah was rich. He had his mom, dad, and grandparents to care for him. They had rooms at the Ronald McDonald House, but like Suzanne and me, spent all their time in the hospital. Elijah, also afflicted with a rare immune disease, seemed to be making a splendid recovery. There were many other children here, each with a story. The children sitting alone waiting for someone to love them were the saddest. And there were so many of them.

The nurses more so than the doctors were on the Hem/Onc battlefield line. They would spend hours each day with the patients while the doctors spent minutes. It was the nurses who detected when a child's condition was deteriorating, or becoming critical. The doctors reacted to what the nurses told them or wrote in their reports. The doctors were great, but they were not at the front. The docs were the generals. The nurses were the infantry. And the infantry was sensational.

We had our favorites, of course, and some not-so-favorites. Incompetence, however, was something we rarely witnessed. There were many easier places for nurses to work, always with the same pay, usually with better hours; simply choosing to work in this unit made them special people.

Sarah, Melinda, Niki, and Mark were Sam's primary nurses. The care, dedication, professionalism and love they each provided to Sam won our deep respect. Many other nurses cared for Sam periodically, but if either of these four were on duty, we knew Sam was in great hands. Melinda and

Niki would sometimes work the same shift, and would fight to care for Sam. These nurses not only took great care of our baby, but also protected sleep opportunities for us, and scheduled their procedures in efficient order to minimize distractions to Sam.

Sarah Smiley, late twenties, cute and personable was Sam's day-shift nurse. Sarah was as fun to be with as she was efficient. Other nurses changed shifts, took vacations, or worked in different areas periodically. Sarah, like a rock, was there every weekday and every second weekend. Her routine was like clockwork. She took vitals and gave oral meds each morning at eight-fifteen, and then she weighed Sam. Each of Sam's meds was dosed by his weight, and Sarah was obstinate about weighing him accurately and at the same time each day. Many times I watched Sarah work long after her shift had ended in order to provide extra attention to her primary patients. Sarah liked to take care of chores that could easily have been accomplished on the next shift. She stayed late to deliver blood transfusions, for dressing changes, or even to change the sheets on Sam's crib. If the second shift nurse had not previously cared for Sam, Sarah would spend an extra hour going over his routine and med schedule. Sarah also took care of Allison and kept us informed on her condition during the long weeks of isolation after her bone-marrow transplant.

Niki worked either evenings or nights with an occasional day shift mixed in. No nurse adored Sam more than Niki. Her day was made if she could coax a smile out of him. Holding him thrilled her. Niki was not only fiercely protective of Sam, but her care also included looking after Suzanne and me. She answered any questions about doctors, other nurses, medications, or procedures with candid honesty and a bit of editorial. She shared her experiences caring for other HLH and transplant kids, along with before and after pictures of her favorites. Niki never lacked for an opinion, and her frankness was refreshing.

"Who is this doctor covering the floor tonight, Niki? I've never seen him before," I asked one weekend evening. Niki shook her head and rolled her eyes as she spoke.

"He's a resident picking up a few bucks. He was on this floor a few months ago and impressed no one. I'm not supposed to talk about doctors like this but whatever," Niki continued.

"Go ahead, Niki. I'm sure not going to say anything. I want to know if I need to watch this guy."

"I mean he's all right, but he just doesn't have any interest in Hem/Onc. His residency is almost done, and he is going into practice as a pediatrician in a big group. He just didn't impress me when he was on the floor."

When times were rough and Sam's condition bleak, Niki's care included hugs. I watched Suzanne break down and cry in a Niki hug. Niki was skilled and efficient with her nursing duties, but when her tasks were completed, she liked to hang around and visit with both Suzanne and me. Those visits were appreciated. Adult conversations, especially with someone interesting to talk to, are rare when one is stuck in an isolation room. Niki understood that and used her precious time letting us vent our emotions or idly chatter away. We shared much of our life experiences with her and, in turn, learned much of hers. Niki also developed a special relationship with Jacob over the months of Sam's hospitalization. She cuddled Jake on each of his visits and always found a Popsicle or special treat for him. Since we men love women that feed us, Jake became attached to Niki. One of the first phrases Jake learned to speak was "zip it," which is a common Niki-ism. Like Sarah, Niki was single and enjoying the lifestyle. Also like Sarah, Niki struggled to live on a nurse's salary. Paying off college loans, car payments, and rent stretched a nurse's salary to the limit. I was first astonished, then disgusted at the meager pay scale of these dedicated professionals.

The nights were made far more bearable if Mark was on duty caring for Sam. Unfortunately for us, he split his time between T5A and the clinic. His schedule worked out such that he was on night shift only one week in six. Tall and thin with a receding hairline, Mark closely resembled Dr. Mark Green on the TV show *ER*. Naturally his nickname was Dr. Green—a confusing nickname for a nurse. He was legendary for being able to take vitals, draw labs, give meds, and monitor pumps without waking the child or parent. Mark and I had a tacit agreement that he would let Sam sleep without interruption as long as I paged him whenever Sam awoke. Mark would then complete his tasks while I changed and fed Sam. I timed Mark one night while I fed Sam at two a.m., hoping to get back to sleep quickly. In eighteen minutes, Mark took Sam's vitals, gave him his meds, drew his labs, and changed the sheets. Most of the night nurses would take a minimum of forty-five minutes to accomplish the same tasks while leaving Sam crying and uncomfortable.

Mark had quickly earned my respect, and that of Suzanne's, during the period when Sam was experiencing cardiac arrhythmia in the days prior to transplant. One particular night, Sam was hooked to his heart monitor, which consisted of four wires pasted to his chest. In addition, he was wearing a separate device with six additional wires to record his heart rates over a twenty-four-hour period. Mark, in the room to draw labs from Sam's C-line in the middle of the night, whistled softly to himself as he lifted Sam's T-shirt. Suzanne, awake with insomnia, chuckled softly as she listened to Mark talking more to himself than Sam.

"I feel like I'm defusing a bomb here, Sam. I don't know if I can even find your C-line in amongst all these wires." But he did. And Sam woke up only briefly while Mark completed his tasks.

Mark and I enjoyed sharing fatherhood stories for he also had young children at home. "I'm going to write a book called, *What I Can Do With One Arm*," Mark told me one day while relating his weekend activities of carrying his young child throughout the house. Mark is an awesome nurse. I would bet my house he is an outstanding father as well.

Melinda was a tough-as-nails nurse with a heart of gold. Actually, she liked to put on the Nurse Ratched facade, but down, not too deep, was a soft, sweet woman who loved and protected Sam as if he were her own. Melinda and I barked at each other periodically, but we both knew it was more frustration than irritation.

I met Melinda, a fiftyish bundle of energy, on my first overnight shift at Children's Hospital. She wore her brunette hair short and frosted. She moved around the room and unit rapidly, always on the move to her next task.

"Do you go by Melinda, or do people call you Mindy?" I asked.

"No one dares call me Mindy. I hate that name," she responded with a shudder.

"Great, I'll just call you Min then," I said teasingly. Melinda gritted her teeth and looked at me. She didn't slow down her work changing the meds on Sam's IV tree.

"Grrrrr," she said, trying to intimidate me. It didn't work. I called her Min from that moment on. Secretly, she liked having a pet name. Min opened up only a little bit about her personal life. Over time I learned that she was married and her husband was disabled. They had one daughter. Min was the primary breadwinner for the family.

When we needed information or an opinion, Min was always a good source. Her views were frank and based on years of experience caring for very sick children. She was especially good to talk to about the multitude of different doctors who cared for Sam. Not many nurses care to comment about skills and methods of the docs, but when coaxed, Melinda would let loose with a barrage of uncensored editorials about this or that doctor and her experiences that formed those opinions. Melinda loved Sam and always called him her lovebug in high-pitched baby talk.

More than any other nurse, Melinda was a "by the book" practitioner. She never took shortcuts, gave medicines precisely on schedule, and never was late taking vitals. I was always irritated at night nurses when they awakened Sammy just to take his vital signs. Only once I made the mistake of complaining to Melinda.

"Min, he's sound asleep. Can't you do that later when he wakes up?" I whispered from the awesome comfort of my sleep chair as Min's presence woke me from a light snooze.

"John, you never know when one of these kids is going to go down," she replied. "It's my butt on the line if Sammy crashes and I haven't taken his vitals on schedule, so chill out."

"Chill out! I was chilled out . . . until you came in and woke me up."

We both enjoyed the banter, and Melinda was the first to admit that she was the world's most anal person. But she was an awesome caregiver to Sam. She loved to act as the tough nurse, but the role didn't really fit her. Both Suzanne and I felt great comfort when Min was on duty.

The chaplaincy staff was also an integral care component of Hem/Onc. Reverend Sue began her work at Children's Hospital on the same day Sammy was admitted. He was one of the first patients she was assigned. Sam, always on guard when staff walked in the room, soon figured out that Sue was on his side. She was never going to squeeze his belly or take his blood pressure. Her warmth and sincerity quickly brought us close. As much as she was our minister, she also became our friend. While Sam rested one day, Sue and I got to know each other better.

"Are you married, Sue?" I asked.

"I have a long-term, committed partner," she answered.

That's kind of odd, a minister shacking up with some guy. I thought. *Wait just a second. That's not what she meant, committed partner. That means her partner is a woman. Why am I so naïve? Sue is gay. Do you use the word gay to describe a woman? Who cares? I really like her. Why could it possibly matter if Sue is gay?*

Sue, tall and angular, kept her hair short with a two-inch braid in the back. She always wore a colorful vest and slacks. Sue never pushed her religion on us, yet had a perfect sense when a prayer was needed or when a hug was more appropriate.

Sue's sense of humor, always used with deftness, often brought lightness to a dim day. I always felt uplifted whenever Sue visited. The times we prayed together often left me with a tear trickling down my cheek. Sue didn't simply recite prayers; she delivered them from her heart. We always held hands and touched Sammy while she prayed. God was close; we could feel His presence while she prayed. Nothing is easier to spot than an insincere minister, but there was no doubt about the depth of Sue's passion and compassion.

There were no ministers or priests like Sue in my past. My strict Catholic upbringing never brought me in contact with a woman minister, much less a gay woman minister. The image in my mind when the word *minister* is used would never in the past have been a picture of Sue. One of the lessons I learned from Sam, though, was to open my mind and lose my stereotypes. This lesson encompassed more than my encounters with Sue. The hospital environment placed us among people of all races, religions, and many nationalities. The kids were all treated the same. The parents came together and supported each other. Love transcended attitudes of the outside world. Yes, I came with attitudes of bias and prejudice. My experiences in this awful place wiped many away. Quietly, Samuel's mission was developing. Sammy's students were learning.

Simply wonderful people populated Hem/Onc/BMT. What nobler profession than nursing exists, I wondered? And having catastrophic illness doesn't make a kid a hero, but my memories of the children on the floor will never leave me. In our time on T5A, we witnessed such great courage from the kids and overwhelming commitment from the staff. Should the world ever embrace the love, acceptance, diversity, valor, and generosity found on a cancer unit, human potential would be unlimited. Rich, poor, black, white, Asian, Arab, Native American—Hem/Onc was a micro-melting pot; a place without a hint of hate, racism, or discrimination. Every citizen of T5A, from the patients, families, doctors, nurses, therapists, right down to the guy who took out the trash brought love into this small world. A cancer unit is the worst place in the world. At the same time I found it to be the best of places.

Photographs from Chapter 14 can be viewed at:
SamuelsMission.com

CHAPTER 15

D-Day

Sam's special day was at hand. His new bone marrow arrived at nine o'clock sharp from Hoxworth Blood Center down the street. The life-saving stem cells, in a small plastic bag, looked like typical blood products that Sam had received in the past. The atmosphere in his room was different this day. Suzanne and I were excited and optimistic. I had the video camera loaded and charged, ready to record the momentous occasion.

The transplant was ready to begin, although one wouldn't know that anything eventful was about to happen. There was not a doctor involved. Two nurses and the blood technician were the only staff in the room. Suzanne and I took our places. I was at the foot of the bed taking video, and Suzanne was at Sam's side. Sarah scrubbed Sam's C-line then sterilized the port on the stem cell bag. All was ready. The mood was light.

"Lights, camera, action, go ahead, Sarah. Let's do it," I said as if I were in charge instead of acting as the videographer.

"Uh-oh," Sarah mumbled as she struggled with the bag.

"What happened?" I asked, still looking through the viewfinder.

"The port broke off inside the bag when I tried to hook it up," Sarah said. The video later showed my alarm as the picture wavered all over the place. Sarah was calm. She worked intently on the bag for what seemed like an eternity. The room was silent. Suddenly Sarah finished up and hung the bag on Sam's pole. The marrow began dripping into Sammy's line.

Sarah looked up and giggled nervously. "What's everyone staring at? It's under control."

Thirteen minutes later, the bag was empty. Sam's bone marrow transplant was done. It was, as expected, an anticlimactic event. Sarah, a deft performer, handled the crisis of the broken plug calmly and skillfully. The mood in the room became lighthearted. After it was over and the nurses were gone, Suzanne and I said a prayer together. We thanked God for getting us to this moment of transplant, and then we asked Him for the marrow to join with Sam's body and be one.

Following the transplant, Suzanne and I sat down and wrote thank-you notes to the donor. We weren't allowed to know anything about him, or contact him directly, but the Marrow Donor Program would deliver letters between patient and donor as long as anonymity was kept. The Donor Program would actually censor the letters: any lines providing clues to our identity or our location would be blacked out. Our thankfulness could never be expressed properly to this anonymous angel, and the words to equal our gratitude were difficult to find. Suzanne and I hoped that someday we could return the favor to another person in need.

Reverend Sue came around later. Although the day was medically busy, Sue locked the door for a moment and closed the curtains. Suzanne, Sue, and I gathered in a semicircle around Sammy. We held hands with each other and touched Sammy. Sue prayed.

"Dear God, we gather here in Your name and ask You to be with Sammy, to look after him and protect him. Lord, we ask that You bless this union of bone marrow and child, that

You help Sammy's body accept this gift from a stranger and to heal and recover. Lord, we ask You to provide the wisdom for Sammy's doctors, that they can make the right choices and decisions in the next critical weeks. Father, we pray that Sammy may suffer little and be cured from this terrible disease. Oh Lord, although we don't begin to understand Your mysterious ways, we place ourselves under Your care. We ask this of You who knows what it is like to walk in our shoes and to lie in our beds."

Sam's counts, back later that morning, were indeed plummeting. His ANC measured 300 on its way to zero. The ANC—Absolute Neutrophyl Count—was the data we would watch over the next months. In simpler terms the ANC is a measure of his immune system blood cells. His red cell count was also low. Soon he would need a whole blood transfusion. In the six months prior to transplant Sam had received six transfusions of red cells and four platelet transfusions. We were expecting many more in the coming months. I remember how frightened I was when Sam needed his first transfusion. Now they seemed routine.

Morphine was added to Sam's ever-expanding IV pole. The docs explained that the morphine was delivered manually whenever we felt Sam was getting uncomfortable with pain. The push-button delivery system, however, would only work on fifteen-minute intervals, thus limiting the amount of narcotic to a safe level.

Sam was expected to be getting painful mouth sores soon from the chemo, a side effect that was seen in almost every transplant patient. The mouth sores, known as mucositis, were caused by a breakdown in the mucous membranes lining the mouth. The morphine would ease that pain somewhat, and we hoped it would allow Sam to eat normally.

He appeared to be sicker now than any time previous to the transplant. Throughout the day, Sammy looked more and more out of it, eating less, sleeping more, and filling his diapers often with very wet diarrhea. This was expected. The docs had warned us that the next few weeks would be the worst. Sam still managed some cheerful moments and enjoyed being held with his head resting on Mom's or Dad's shoulder. As some kids have a blanket or Teddy bear for comfort, Sam sucked on his fingers when he felt bad. He used his middle and index finger in his mouth to keep from crying. From this day forward, Sam sucked on his fingers more and more. No matter his condition, Sam still required a view of the nurse's station outside his room. His visitors still waved and smiled. Sam returned the gestures only occasionally but refused to miss the action in the hallway.

A quick visit home was next on my agenda. It would only last one night but even the eight hours of driving with music playing full blast provided a break from T5A. The time at home was purely joyful. Hours seemed like moments. When Zachary and Jacob were asleep, I spent long minutes just watching them and luxuriating in the feeling of being Dad. Sammy's ordeal brought into focus that time with my sons was not to be taken lightly. I vowed as I watched their peaceful slumber to remember this feeling and to let joy be our companion as we raised these children. I vowed to not allow parenthood be just a process, destination, or a survival test, but a precious gift to be nurtured and treasured. And I wondered if I would have found these insights without Sammy's catastrophic illness. And then I wondered how to share this feeling with other parents.

This book is one of the ways I found to spread that message. Through the years of raising our sons, I've found that I indeed enjoyed every stage of their growth. So many times I heard other parents wish for a phase like "terrible twos" or puberty to pass quickly. Suzanne is particularly joyful and patient with the boys' changing personalities, appearance, interests, and attitudes. I'm not always thrilled being with a mouthy teen with selective hearing, but wouldn't change the experience for anything. It is the moments you least expect when you find the most pride in raising your children. A note from the teacher, a comment from a parent, or when you find out your child befriended someone who didn't have one—a single instance that tells you that you're doing something right can make up for many hours of teenager-itis. I've kept that vow to myself. I never wished a difficult phase would pass.

I felt out of sync when I arrived back in Hem/Onc the next day. I was only away for twenty-seven hours, yet it took time for me to get back in tune with the rhythm of the place. Pod 2 was different. Some patients had moved out while I was gone. Sam's neighbor had been released, at transplant Day +21. Incredible! Something else had happened, but I couldn't put my finger on it. There was sadness in the air. The floor was too quiet. What was it? I didn't have time to find out. Sam was whimpering in his crib. I had him in my lap in seconds, but his soft moans continued. Suzanne kissed us both good-bye and left for a nap.

Sam looked different. Most of his eyelashes were gone. I stroked his face gently and ran my fingers through his hair. I came away with a handful of his soft locks. We'd known this day was coming. The docs had told us for months that his hair would fall out—and that was okay; Sam wasn't vain about it. His condition kept the nurses busy. His blood pressure was up and his platelets were down. He received a transfusion then spiked a fever. The nurses drew blood and sent cultures to the lab to check for bacterial infections. The mucositis was in full bloom, and his mouth sores were multiplying. Sam was hurting greatly. He cried almost constantly. The pain team changed his medication to methadone. The narcotic worked slowly. Sam fussed several more hours then finally fell asleep late in the evening, nearly midnight. It was my first chance to walk the floor and get back in touch with Hem/Onc. Strolling by Alexandra's room, I was startled and saddened to find it empty. I returned to Sam's room to find Melinda checking his vitals.

"Where did Alexandra go, Min?" I whispered.

"Alexandra went home," she replied without looking up.

"Oh, good," I said naively.

"It's not good," she said softly. "She went home to die. It's where she wanted to be."

I picked up Sam and put him on my shoulder, then sat silently for quite a spell before I felt able to speak again. "You must be very strong to work on this floor. I don't know how you do it."

"It is really hard sometimes," she choked. I knew Melinda's tears were close so I stopped the questions. Soon Sam and I were alone again. I held him a long time before laying him back in his crib. Neither of us slept much that night. Sam was up every hour or so, crying in pain. Only in my arms did he find comfort that night. His strong breathing soothed me, and I came to realize how truly lucky we were. Sam had reasonable odds to leave this place and live a normal life. Too few of the others in Hem/Onc had the same chance.

I was not alone in my optimism. I found during an emotional interlude the next morning that Suzanne was feeling upbeat.

She told me of her feeling that Sam would be the kid the docs talked about for years. I basked in her cheerfulness. My girl was starting to come back to me. I loved the feeling of closeness. Suzanne described the sensation. In her mind the conversation would start like this: "Remember that baby we transplanted back in '99? What did we do different to get him healed so quickly? He was amazing."

The mood was contagious. Dr. Filipovich fed our hope during her daily examination.

"All in all, how is Sam doing?" Suzanne asked.

"I am just delighted in his progress," she responded with a warm smile. "I think he is doing great. Other than the mucositis, which every child gets, he is having few side effects." Those were exactly the words we had hoped to hear.

Allison visited Sam through his window again on this morning. Suzanne failed to contain her tears when she saw this beautiful lonely girl wandering around dragging her IV pole.

"I'm going to get her a little present from the gift shop this morning," Suzanne said, wiping her eyes. "She's alone so often." Suzanne brought her a stuffed animal that morning and became her good friend. Later that evening, while Sammy slept, Suzanne took me to visit her. Allison looked miserable as she sat by herself watching TV. She was just four years old and in a hospital with no family around. Suzanne brought along a coloring book and some new crayons that she had set aside for Zachary's next visit. Allison's face lit up like Times Square when we came in with this simple gift. We spent an hour coloring and talking with her. Suzanne had to leave the room once to avoid crying in front of this little girl. Our visit ended with hugs and a promise to visit tomorrow.

The optimism lasted through the next two peaceful weeks. Sam's condition improved slowly but steadily. We passed the point where his new marrow started to graft. This meant that the disease was gone, destroyed along with his lethal stem cells. Sam's new stem cells began producing healthy white cells and red blood cells. We learned that platelets were the last cells to be produced and that would occur after a few more weeks. The docs assured us several times that the disease was gone and wouldn't come back. I could finally rest a bit easier knowing that the deadly histiocytes were no longer destroying Sam's brain.

Of course many worries remained. The docs warned of numerous complications like liver disease; they said we should expect Sam to suffer some level of graft versus host disease or GVHD. In GVHD, the donor's bone marrow would launch an attack on Sam's organs and tissues with special cells that normally attack viruses, bacteria, and other foreign matter in the body. When the donor's stem cells fail to recognize Sam's tissues as "self," it considers them foreign matter, and the battle is on. GVHD symptoms can range from mild to fatal, with most cases treatable without long-term disabling side effects.

Indeed, the GVHD appeared in the next week. The initial symptoms came in the form of deep sunburn type rashes beneath Sam's chin, and under his arms. Suzanne and I talked at length about this complication. Sam's new marrow was growing rapidly. With faith and optimism, we accepted the possibility of GVHD as another step in Sam's story and his recovery. We prayed that the disease would be mild and put our faith in God to protect Sam.

The weapon of choice to engage the marrow in this new war was massive injections of steroids. These doses were twenty times higher than what Sam had taken to control the HLH prior to transplant.

Sam's IV tree was getting impossibly overcrowded. I counted seven bags of fluids and meds, along with innumerable syringes of different meds and electrolytes that were all injected through his C-line throughout the day and night. Even Sam's formula was pumped through his feeding tube into his stomach to bypass the mouth sores. We attempted to feed him by mouth numerous times each day, but he would take little of what was offered. The hospital provided disposable single-use formula bottles for Sam, and many of the full bottles went into the trash can. When Sam did take formula, he would often vomit it back up, along with a load of mucous. The good news about his meds was that none of them were chemotherapy. Many were antibiotics; even with the growth of white cells, Sam's immune system remained severely compromised.

AUTHOR'S NOTE:

Graft versus Host Disease or GVHD can be understood as almost the opposite of a transplanted organ being rejected by the body. In GVHD the transplanted bone marrow or the "graft" is rejecting the body or "host." And since the bone marrow manufactures all the weapons as well as the immune system, the body is defenseless without the armor and heavy artillery provided by medicine.

Photographs from Chapter 15 can be viewed at:
SamuelsMission.com

CHAPTER 16

Sam for President?

Sam had a whole new set of doctors in March, due to rotation. Dr. Jennifer Voelker had been Sam's resident physician for two days as she examined Sam in the early morning hours. She had already won the trust of Suzanne, Sammy, and me as she dealt with a new issue of low electrolytes in Sam's blood.

It was really Dr. Filipovich that we most missed, as the attending physicians had rotated as well. Dr. Filipovich would not be on service again for several months. Her replacement, Dr. Harris, an outstanding physician and the director of the BMT department, had just one flaw in our eyes: he was not Dr. Alexandra Filipovich, Sam's protector and healer.

Sam's ANC continued to soar and in my mind was no longer an issue. There were several other issues to be concerned with, primarily the GVHD and side effects of massive steroids. The long-term steroid effects were discussed in rounds on this morning. Dr. Harris warned us that prolonged high doses would probably thin Sammy's bones considerably from loss of calcium. In the short term, weight gain and high blood pressure would accompany the medication.

Sam's GVHD burns were peeling while other rashes spread slowly across his trunk. His legs were speckled with dime-size bruises caused by consistently low platelets, and he was now getting transfusions daily. His hair was nearly gone from the chemotherapy, although he kept a few thin eyelashes. Sam had no interest in taking a bottle. His nutrition was pumped steadily through his feeding tube.

I missed his beguiling smile so much. We saw tiny glimpses of it only occasionally between long periods of moaning or sleeping. Seeing him in constant pain and discomfort was dreadful to bear and starting to wear on my optimism. Sammy was still beautiful to Suzanne and me, but no one called him pretty anymore. I knew somewhere under his disease and steroid-ravaged face was the stunningly cute, happy, sweet baby who had come into our lives eleven months earlier. And I knew we would see him home sometime soon. Sammy would learn to crawl and explore the world as his twin brother was doing.

A new neighbor arrived on the floor, another HLH patient: Maria, a three-and-a-half-year-old, was recently transferred to Children's Hospital from Chicago. I looked forward to visiting with another HLH family. Sharing stories and information with other families is a principal method of emotional survival in Hem/Onc, and I kept watch for the right opportunity to introduce myself. My chance would not come for a time, but I learned through the grapevine that Maria was in bad shape. She had gone undiagnosed for a very long time, and the HLH had deeply infected her brain. As Sammy seemed reasonably stable, Suzanne finally allowed herself a trip home. Our boys had been to see us for a few nights along with Grandma, but Suzanne had not been home in about three weeks.

I spent four consecutive nights in the hospital with Sam. But I was not alone: my brother Steve flew in from Chicago to spend a weekend helping care for Sam.

Steve is two years younger than me. We were once inseparable, but had drifted apart as teenagers and young adults. As kids, Steve and I did everything together. We had a two-man baseball team in the summer; when you're a kid, you find a way to have a team with only two members. In the fall, we played one-on-one football every day in the backyard. The teenage years found us rapidly drifting apart. Although we both loved sports, Steve went into wrestling, and I went into basketball. I hate to admit it, but Steve and all my brothers were better at their sports than I was in mine. The only sport I could ever beat my brothers at was golf—and back then, golf hardly counted as a sport in our family. Now it is the only sport we play, which is good for me.

As a wrestler, Steve was not blessed with an overabundance of talent. He made up for it with grit and determination. Not until he was a senior in high school did Steve win a spot on the varsity team. Although I was in college at the time, I occasionally found myself at his wrestling meets. I remember Steve had a nemesis, a wrestler from a nearby city who was an outstanding state champion. Through different meets and tournaments, it turned out that Steve had to wrestle this guy four times in that season. As the year passed, I secretly planned to attend the meets when Steve faced this guy. His name was Tony something. I remember the cheerleaders had a special cheer about "Tony the Tiger." Steve and I were far from close at this time, so even I was surprised to be supporting him when I could be doing cool college stuff. As it turned out, Tony the Tiger pinned Steve easily the first time they met. The second time, Steve stayed off his back, yet still lost by a large margin. The determination in Steve's face the third time he faced Tony was unforgettable. He hung in there and made Tony work for three periods, and lost by a respectable score, like 9 to 3. The fourth time they faced each other, Steve gave Tony the Tiger the "eye of the tiger" and wrestled like never before. By the third period, Tony was out of gas. Tony probably never called Steve his nemesis. He would have if they had wrestled a fifth time that year. Tony held on for a one-point win and moved on to become state champion.

Although Steve's wrestling career was soon forgotten by most, I never forgot the fight and determination Steve demonstrated in his battles with Tony the Tiger. I also never told him I was watching, until the weekend he visited Sam. In fact, I could see a bit of Steve's courage and determination in Sam.

As the years passed and children came, I developed a deep respect and admiration for Steve. He and his wife, Elise, have two children. Drew was thirteen and Kelly ten at the time of Sam's illness. Suzanne and I were the last in each of our families to have children, so we had many siblings to emulate as parental role models. Steve and Elise became the parents we most admired, probably without their knowing it.

Sam had his medical issues each of the next few days, but they seemed like minor glitches in the big picture. High blood pressure was the principal concern for the week. The nurses continually had a difficult time even getting a blood pressure taken due to the puffiness of Sam's arms. When they did get a pressure, it was abnormally high—sometimes sky high. The doctors continued to worry about liver complications from the high-dose chemotherapy, in which blood vessels that carry blood through the organ become swollen and clogged. Should that happen, Sam would quickly become septic and probably die.

Other than the excitement of the high blood pressure, Sam remained stable and his care had the illusion of being routine. The intense days of the chemo, transplant, and GVHD were behind us, while a long draining recovery period awaited us. Steve's impressions of Sam's condition, the crowded IV trees, and the constant beep of med pumps helped break the illusion. Suzanne and I had become so accustomed to his appearance, treatments, the cacophony of alarms, and the constant nursing care that it had become normal. Steve helped remind us that it was not normal. He shared his impressions of his weekend with Sam in an e-mail to our network of family and friends.

Date: March 8, 1999
Subject: Visiting Sam

For those of you I don't know, I'm John's brother Steve from Chicago but in Cincinnati for the weekend. The snow in Chicago has made this a real adventure!

I've been reading the almost daily updates via e-mail for quite a while now, but it can't really compare to being here and seeing Sam in person. As far as I can tell he's got 10 fluids being pumped into him at the moment, including whole blood, Methadone, Ranitidine, Cyclosporin, Piracillin (sp?), Vancomycin, Ciprofloxacin, good old dextrose, and formula through a feeding tube. He also gets at least four other medications— and probably more—on a periodic basis. He's got a toe monitor which continuously measures the oxygen content in his blood. I think there are a total of six computerized monitors in his room, just to regulate the flow of fluids and to measure his heart and vital signs. These monitors beep almost hourly for one reason or another and they're also linked to pagers that the nurses carry around.

The hospital appears quite modern—I hear this wing is only 5 years old—and is decorated for children. They call the patient rooms "bedrooms" and some of the older kids are free to walk around. There are a lot of toys and places for kids to play. Sam has some kid videos to play in his room, with Teletubbies a personal favorite. The parents are well looked after, too. They pretty much have the run of the place and are free to get their own non-medical supplies as needed. The coffee is free and there's a place to do laundry and the like.

Because of the high dose of steroids, Sam's face and body are quite puffy. If you haven't seen him in a while, you might be caught off guard. His cheeks crowd his nose and chin, and stick further out than both. Especially after receiving blood, his cheeks get very red, almost raw looking. (Of course he's also taking medication to try to reduce water weight.) He doesn't have a lot of energy and sleeps intermittently throughout the day and night. He does produce a welcome smile on occasion and John said he laughed today for the first time in many days.

Sam's condition continues to move in a positive direction. I'm not sure how to interpret all the counts and measures, but John believes he's getting past the most dangerous stage. The doctors, in their way, will not be hurried into being overly optimistic. There's still a long road ahead. Vitals have to be taken on a regular basis and the worst is the blood pressure. Sammy hates it. With a puffy arm to start with, the pressure sleeve is just plain uncomfortable. To make it worse, they often have trouble getting a good reading, which means they have to repeat it more often. They finally looked all over the hospital to find an old-fashioned manual blood pressure cuff and are leaving that in the room for now.

The nurses are among the best I've seen. They're professional in practice and they all seem to really care about Sammy's welfare and comfort. Sarah is Sammy's primary care nurse and looks after him most days. She knows the most about his day-to-day condition, what to look for, and what makes him uncomfortable, etc. The before and after care is what counts in a place like this; good care really does save lives here. The night and weekend nurses are less well known and John and Suz have to break them in at times.

The good ones anticipate when the medications are ready to run out and arrive just before the dreaded beeping starts. They also recognize when another half hour of sleep is more important that getting the vital signs and the like.

Sam's a tough kid. He may be president some day.

Steve

I had a secret plan for Suzanne during Steve's visit. I wanted her to have a nice surprise, although numerous obstacles nearly prevented her from returning to Cincinnati in time to implement it. Despite a snowstorm at home, where she had visited for three days, Suzanne arrived back at the hospital with six hours of Steve's visit remaining—plenty of time to execute my plan. Steve was the key. I needed someone Suzanne was comfortable with to watch Sam for a few hours to enable us to get together, alone, in private. The surprise was that I had reserved a room at a nearby hotel. I had planned to enjoy a sumptuous brunch with Suzanne in the hotel restaurant, complete with champagne, and then entice her up to a room, where I planned to seduce her with all my charms. I figured ten minutes for the seduction and we would be curled up in the bed. After all, it had been six weeks since we'd last slept together.

Once Suzanne arrived, my plan instantly fell into jeopardy. Suzanne had the flu. She had the flu! It wasn't her fault. In fact, she had wanted some intimate times together herself. The plan wasn't a total loss, however. It was more of a good news, bad news situation. I did get to sleep with her. That is, sleep in the same bed with her, while she was sleeping. I never told her about my plan with the nice hotel, or the champagne brunch, or the ten-minute seduction. We simply went to the Ronald McDonald House for a nap. You gotta take what you can get sometimes. But damn, I was horny.

CHAPTER 17

A Typical Day in HEM/ONC/BMT

Midnight: *Beep, beep, beep.* The med. pump was signaling time for Sam's vancomycin, one of the many antibiotics he got daily. The pumps send a page to the nurse, in addition to the shrill beep in the room. Sam usually slumbered through the signal, though I never did.

I hoped to have gotten an hour of sleep in by this time. Often I went to bed not knowing who Sam's night nurse would be. The night nurse was the key to getting rest. Long, deep sleep was impossible. Always the night nurse would need to take Sam's vital signs around midnight; a very few skillful nurses could occasionally do this without waking Sam.

I was awake for at least a half hour while his blood pressure, temperature, heart rate, and respiration were measured. This night his nurse was Shelley, whom we had had several times before. The last time she was on duty, it turned out to be a bad night; Shelley and I had had a confrontation over vital signs. She had come into the room near the beginning of her shift, turned the lights on, made a racket, cuffed Sam, taken his blood pressure, and woken him up.

"Can't you be more careful?" I hissed in her face. I was angry and had moved into her space. "I just got him to sleep, and you storm in here like it's the middle of the day."

"I'm just doing my job," Shelley responded while backing away.

"Well, why don't you do it just a bit quieter? It took me forty-five minutes to get Sammy to sleep, and you walk right in and wake him up." I had calmed only slightly, but enough to know that I had frightened Shelley with my outburst. We eventually made our peace, but Shelley was wary around me. That was a good thing. She would pay close attention to the pumps—I hoped.

One a.m.: The vancomycin was done. The dosage, like most IV meds, was delivered over a set period of time. The med pump again signaled the nurse and woke me up, that is, if I had gotten back to sleep in the half-hour since the vitals were taken. I was so groggy, I wasn't sure if I slept.

Three a.m.: I had just completed my longest stretch of uninterrupted sleep when I was awakened by the incessant signal of the med pump. It was time for another antibiotic. This time it was Zosyn.

Four a.m.: There it went again. Shelley was quick; the alarm didn't fully awaken me. Soon, however, a second pump started its signal and finished the job. It was time for Sam to get his blood pressure medicine, nicardipine, along with his antiviral, acyclovir. Soon Sam was fully awake as the nurse again attempted to get his blood pressure and other vitals. Sam was starting to eat on his own again, so I went to the nurse's station and made a bottle of his special high-calorie formula. Sam settled down after consuming his bottle and getting some comforting cuddling. By 4:40 he was out. It took me longer.

Five a.m.: I had just fallen asleep when it was time for zantac, which Sam got by IV instead of orally due to his mucositis. Shelley anticipated the alarm, and I awakened for only a moment.

Six a.m.: Vancomycin started again. The pump beeped and signaled the nurse. The doctors have said they'll discontinue the vancomycin, commonly known as "vanc" (rhymes with bank), soon. I was grateful, since Sam got this med four times a day. While Shelley was in the room, she drew Sam's labs. He serenely slept through the blood draw. I did not. Labs were always drawn during the early morning hours so counts would be available for rounds.

Seven a.m.: Another beep signaled the end of the vanco-mycin. Sam slept through most of the interruptions. I was grateful he could rest at night. He went through so much during the day; at least the night was his.

Seven-thirty a.m: The night was over, and I survived it. The prize was down the hall in the parent living room: the vending machine dispensed free coffee and hot chocolate. The coffee was nasty, but I had grown to like it. The cups were tiny, so I always got two.

The resident always examined Sam between 7:30 and 8:00, so I tried to get dressed before she showed up. I failed, and she caught me in my shorts and T-shirt. This was no big deal; vanity among the parents on Hem/Onc was nonexistent. Dr. Jennifer examined Sam and questioned me about his night. I fed Sam. It was gratifying to see him enjoying his bottle; for too long he had been fed through his tube only. We had seen many residents in our hospital visits in Cleveland and Cincin-nati.; Jennifer was one of the best. She possessed fine communication skills and listened well. Moreover, she was available and was kind and gentle to Sam.

Eight a.m.: Two pumps let loose with the annoying beeps. Sam was due for his first dose of cyclosporine and his first of two doses of Actigall, which is a liver medicine. The day shift nurse, Sarah, arrived and checked his vitals. While she worked on his blood pressure, I got cleaned up and changed out of my sleeping attire in our private bathroom. We were not allowed to use the shower because Sam was bathed there and it must be kept sterile. We used the other facilities freely. Suzanne soon showed up with a newspaper, coffee, and a pastry from the cafeteria.

"How was your night?" we asked each other simultaneously.

"Sam slept okay and Shelley was on her best behavior," I answered. "What about you? Are you feeling any better?"

"A lot better, my stomach is a bit queasy yet, but I slept well," Suzanne answered.

Eight-thirty a.m.: Sam got his first dose of methylpredisone (22mg), the steroids. *Barney* was playing on the TV. *Teletubbies* was his favorite, but *Barney* was a close second. Suzanne and I enjoyed a respite and read *USA Today*. A staple of our morning routine was also a call home, where Zachary had learned to pick up the phone.

"Hi, Mommy." Zach always had many questions but never listened for the answer except for this one. "When is my daddy coming home?" Zach knew that since Mommy had just left the day before, Daddy would be coming home soon.

"Daddy will be home in two more days, Zach. Then he is going to bring you and Jacob back to Cincinnati, along with Grandma," Suzanne told him. I listened to her trying to carry on further conversations with Zach, but he soon gave the phone to Grandma; Suzanne got the morning report from home and delivered the update on Sam's condition. The hospital breakfast tray arrived, and we picked through it to see what might be edible.

Nine a.m.: Sarah popped back into the room and gave Sam his K-phos (potassium-phosphorus) through his NG (feeding) tube. The pumps let her know it was time for another dose of Zosyn. Then it was time for his thrice-daily mouth care. While I held Sam and forced his mouth open, Sarah swabbed his mouth with nystatin. Five minutes later, we repeated the procedure with Peridex, an antibacterial similar to Listerine. Sam never enjoyed the swabs, and he let us know it. The pain team visited. We all agreed it was time to reduce Sam's methadone dose, and he'll be slowly weaned off the narcotic.

Nine-fifteen a.m.: Playtime—and Sam was in his happiest mood of the day. The Hem/Onc physical therapist, Christy, young, attractive, and bubbly, arrived; she adored her job as well as Sammy. I thought of Zach's angel Chrissy while I watched Christy and wondered at the similarity of the names and the effect she had on Sam. Sammy liked Christy and always had a smile for her. He sat on the floor while Christy worked on his gross motor skills. She succeeded in getting Sam to reach for toys and exercise his arms. Keeping his balance while leaning over was a big goal of these sessions. Sam rarely used his legs anymore, so Christy worked on Sam's leg strength by encouraging him to put weight on them. Sam was so heavy and puffed up from the steroids, though, that he tolerated little of the leg exercises.

Ten-twenty a.m.: Suzanne offered Sam more bottle. He greedily sucked down three ounces. The play made him hungry—a good sign.

Ten-thirty a.m.: The docs finally visited on rounds. Dr. Jennifer explained that the liver function tests were abnormal; they were planning to do an ultrasound of his liver later in the afternoon. Because liver disease was a concern, the sonogram would give them the information needed to diagnose. I had a strong sense that his liver was fine, and this was a false alarm; Sam was looking healthier and more alert each day. My instincts told me he was getting better, not sicker. While we discussed the possibilities, Sam took a nap; he was worn out from the morning's play. The docs cut out his feedings until after the ultrasound. We hoped he would sleep until the ultrasound was completed.

Ten-fifty a.m.: A knock on our window. We looked up to see our friend Steve Carter. We had made friends with the Carters weeks ago when their nineteen-month-old son, Zachary, was diagnosed with HLH. We had been visiting the Carters weekly when they came in for clinic. But this wasn't clinic day. Quickly Steve explained that Zachary was back in the hospital in the next pod over. He had been vomiting, along with diarrhea. Suzanne and I walked over to Zach's room and offered our moral support to Steve and Tammy. They both looked shot. Steve told us they had been up all night, and they looked it. Their story was familiar: Sam was hospitalized at about the same time in his treatment protocol, at six weeks, with diarrhea and vomiting. Steve was too upset to nap, but I had a chance to go to Ronald McDonald House and catch some rest. On my way out, I stopped for a visit with Allison. She barely stirred from her couch as I waved to her through the glass front of her room. Allison was two days from her bone-marrow transplant, and she looked miserable. She'd undergone the same chemotherapy regimen that Sam had three weeks earlier. I visited Allison every day and had never found her feeling this low. I was happy to see that her mother was with her. She needed love now more than ever.

Eleven a.m.: More IV meds. Sam got a dose of an anti-fungal med called ciprofloxacin, which, like most meds, was delivered over sixty minutes. He woke up hungry at eleven-thirty but was not allowed to eat due to the upcoming sonogram; Suzanne could not console him despite herculean efforts at distraction. Then we learned the ultrasound tech had scheduled Sam for any time between noon and two o'clock. Suzanne was not pleased.

Noon: A busy time for meds. Sam got his third dose of vancomycin and his second dose of acyclovir and nicardipine. He calmed down slightly while *Teletubbies* was on the TV, enough so that Suzanne could sort through the hospital lunch tray and find enough to subsist on.

One p.m.: Only one medicine this hour—zantac, for Sam's stomach (ulcer protection). The ultrasound tech finally showed up in the room with a portable unit. After she checked Sam's gallbladder, she allowed Suzanne to feed Sam while she finished the ultrasound test. Sam was inconsolably angry; feeding him was the only way to calm him enough to complete the test. He chugged three ounces from his bottle and promptly vomited all over himself and the equipment. I was quite happy I missed that episode. Once the test was over, Sam ate again and fell into a deep slumber. Good news! The tech informed Suzanne that the liver looked great: all functions were normal. Quiet time arrives.

Two p.m.: Sarah came in hoping to do vitals and Sam's mouth care. Sam was sleeping, and she had plenty of other chores, so he snoozed on. Each day at this time, Sarah replaced his meds on the IV tree. It was a formidable task. There were many bags, bottles, and syringes to replace and reconnect to the pumps. From the pumps the lines connected into a manifold of valves, then into three lines, which extended from the pole to Sam's C-line. Two of the lines connect at a "Y" into one line, since Sam had only two C-line ports.

Two-thirty p.m.: Platelets arrived from Hoxworth Blood Center. Sarah crosschecked the bags with another nurse, a security measure to ensure that Sam got the right blood products. She then hung the platelets on Sam's pole and connected them to his C-line. The platelet transfusion took only twenty minutes.

Three p.m.: Another dose of Zosyn began to drip through Sam's IV lines. He woke up while Sarah was giving him his second dose of K-phos. While he is awake, more mouth care is given, nystatin, followed by Peridex. I arrived refreshed from a nap at Ronald McDonald House. Sam was ready to play again, and we put him into his playpen loaded with toys to work with his motor skills. Like the therapist had taught us, we set toys just out of his reach, forcing him to stretch and reach. We put funny hats on his head so he'd lean back to lose them. These simple exercises were the first steps to regain his mobility. Three months ago, Sam was far more advanced in his motor skills than today. It was difficult to watch him struggle with such simple tasks while his twin was soaring through stage after stage of development. Worn out from the exercise session, Sam took another snooze.

Four p.m.: Suzanne and I took the opportunity to check up on the Carters. A brief visit revealed a family in distress: Zach was pale and listless. He was dehydrated with a high heart rate and alarmingly low blood pressure. We offered a quick word of support and got out of the way. We heard a short time later that Zach was moved upstairs to the "unit"—hospitalspeak for Pediatric Intensive Care Unit (PICU).

Six p.m.: A three-hour break from the pumps and alarms ended: time for more vanc. While the vancomycin dripped, the second shift nurse, Melinda, came in to give Sam his daily dose of an antifungal medication, itraconozole. This is an oral med, so Melinda injected it through Sam's feeding tube. The hospital tray with dinner was delivered to our room. Upon inspection of the tray, Suzanne declared, "This is John food. You can eat this. I'll go downstairs and get dinner from the cafeteria." Suzanne was right, the meal was my hospital favorite: roast beef, gravy, and mashed potatoes. After our dinner, Sam dined on more delicious high-calorie formula. He was tired and cranky after his meal; Suzanne held him and read several children's books.

Eight p.m.: A busy night of medications began: IV meds this hour were nicardipine, cyclosporin, and acyclovir. In addition, Melinda brought a second dose of Actigall, which she delivered through his feeding tube.

Nine p.m.: Sam vomited up his formula, along with a load of mucous. Melinda came in and disconnected his feeding tube, allowing Suzanne to change his T-shirt. While she was in the room, we did his last mouth care of the day, more nystatin and Peridex. He also got his IV zantac, another dose of Zosyn, and a third shot of K-phos through his tube.

Nine-thirty p.m.: The first of Sam's soft snores drifted up from his crib as he settled in for what we hoped was a good night's rest. Suzanne, still weakened by a flu bug, had her bags packed and was ready to go to Ronald McDonald House for her rest. This would be my seventh straight hospital night. My sleep had become harder to come by, at least at night, however, I try not to complain, because Suzanne covered the hospital far more nights than I did. Once Sam was asleep, Suzanne and I walked over to Ronald McDonald House together. The walk wasn't long, since the house is next door to the hospital—but the neighborhood was not safe, and Suzanne needed her big strong man to protect her. I felt useful for at least a moment.

Eleven p.m.: Ciprofloxacin, Sam's thirty-fifth and last medication of the day, was delivered shortly after the pump beep. Still, the next day's meds would begin in one hour's time—a repeating cycle, but at least we had another day behind us, and eventually this nightmare would end and we'd all go home.

This was the time I made my first attempt at sleeping . . . but my eyes remained open as I waited for the incessant shrill sound of the pumps. I wondered anxiously if the night nurse would be capable of doing her duties without waking up my little world. Sam was sleeping peacefully.

CHAPTER 18

The Road to Recovery

Sam felt better as each day passed. The daily improvements were no longer minute, but apparent. He was more interactive in his play sessions, which now occurred several times each day. He smiled frequently and enjoyed short games of "peek-a-boo," and "how big are you?"

We talked more and more about Sam's release to outpatient status in several weeks. Even Dr. Filipovich voiced optimism about his leaving the hospital by the end of the month. Our concerns remained high about this phase, and the docs continued to warn us about the trials associated with the initial release period. Sam continued to get platelet transfusions almost daily. Nonetheless, the fear of losing him to HLH, chemotherapy, transplant, GVHD, or liver disease was fading with each day. Many hurdles remained, yet every day that passed brought a reduction in fears and an increase in hope that soon Sam would be home.

Tentatively dipping my toes into the pool of thought that Sam would be healthy, happy, growing, and developing normally brought me intense pangs of joy. Despite my faith, I had been hesitant to plan for good times, in fact had not dared to think of them until recently. Now that it appeared that Sam was going to defeat this disease and all its accompanying dangers, I could picture our three sons playing and laughing together. I could picture Sam learning to walk—and run.

There was more good news for Sam on this day: two antibiotics were discontinued, his feeding pump was removed, and his pain medicine, methadone, was reduced. The methadone reduction would proceed slowly to prevent withdrawal symptoms. Suzanne felt good for the first time in a week, and was ready for an intensive bonding weekend with Sam. I was ready for the same with our other boys. My lighthearted mood stayed with me for the four-hour drive. Feeling the optimism, I phoned work to share my hopes of returning to duty soon. I had taken a leave of absence since Sammy was admitted. Through my employer's incredible generosity, the paychecks never stopped flowing. Suzanne had been away from IBM for nine months by this time. Her job was waiting for her whenever she was ready to return. The continuing support from our employers at least kept the bill-collectors at bay during the siege of Sammy's illness.

Jacob and Zachary were in the middle of long naps when I arrived. Grandma had learned not to build up their excitement about Dad or Mom coming home. Naps would be impossible if they knew I was returning.

There was good news for the Carters also. Zachary was feeling better and had been released from PICU; he was back on the floor. Suzanne and Tammy spent what time they could enjoying conversation and supporting each other. Suzanne brought coffee in to Tammy during the quiet times of the morning, and their friendship strengthened.

While I was away, Suzanne called frequently with good news about Sam. Each day he seemed better. His personality was returning, and his counts continued to stabilize. Sam's beguiling smile was back, and he once again charmed whoever came across his path. He continued to need platelets, but the frequency of transfusions dropped from daily to every three days. Sam's hemoglobin also stabilized. Red cell transfusions had not been required for over a week. Suzanne seemed relaxed and enjoyed her time with Sam as much as I enjoyed my time with Sam's brothers.

Something was bothering Melinda on the day of my return.

"You seem upset, Min—what's happening?" I asked as she attempted a blood pressure on Sam. It took some coaxing, but she finally let it out.

"Some parents just drive me crazy. One of my primary kids was due in for chemo today, but his mother called and said she couldn't get a ride. This kid is a real sweetheart, and his cancer relapsed last month because his mother failed to bring him in for his treatments. He is supposed to be in every Thursday for chemo, and she misses it again. I just get so frustrated," she said.

"I can't imagine some of the things you must see in this place. It's got to drive you crazy."

Melinda wasn't finished yet. "One time this same boy was in for a transfusion. His blood was going to be done by late afternoon, and he was able to go home. I was in the room when he called his mom to pick him up. I could just see his face drop as he talked on the phone. His mom was going to a party that night and wouldn't be able to pick him up."

The pain, suffering, and heartbreak I witnessed in my short residence in Hem/Onc had to be minuscule compared to the experiences of the nurses here. As anyone would, I wanted to find a way to comfort those in distress, but had little to offer. A kind word, a hug, maybe an open ear was all I could come up with.

In the past week, I had finally become acquainted with the parents of Maria, the three-year-old with HLH next door. Only serious, drawn faces were ever visible in Maria's room. I could sense her condition was grave from the few glimpses in the room as I passed by. I wanted to offer my support, and finally got a chance when the family was gathered outside her room. Maria was being moved to the PICU when I introduced myself and shared news that Sam had the same disease as Maria. Her mom was in tears as she spoke to me in broken English. The family had moved to Chicago recently from Italy. She was obviously devastated by Maria's disease but seemed grateful to talk about it. They looked in on Sam, and he responded with a wave and a smile. For some strange reason, I wanted to tap into their pain. I wanted to know how they felt and feel it too. You see, Maria was going to die. Her brain consisted of almost all white matter, or infection. Her mom said they were just waiting for God to take her. *Why? Why is it so important to empathize with this family and feel their pain?* I tried to sleep that night with those thoughts in my head. Clarity came to me after hours of tossing and turning. *This could very easily be us. Sam could be in a bed with a machine breathing for him while we wait for him to die. In fact, he is yet at high risk. He might be there yet. How would I handle that?* Suzanne and I had reveled in Sam's remarkable recovery, but devastating complications could appear at any moment. I needed to feel the pain of Maria's family as a sample of what might have been. Fears that Sam might die had been on the perimeter of my consciousness since his diagnosis. I sensed them, but never allowed them to bloom. Visiting these fears through another family's experiences allowed me to sample the feeling from a distance, protected by the knowledge that I could walk away from them. In the end, I was not really providing as much comfort as I was receiving from this anguished family. The days ahead provided numerous opportunities to give back something to them. I would often run into Maria's mom in the elevator, the hallway, or at Ronald McDonald House. A pat on the back, or a word of encouragement, and a promise to pray for a miracle was again all I had to offer. My gestures were of little help, but were always returned with a smile and an inquiry about Sam.

A month had now passed since Sam's transplant, seemingly in a blur. Imprisoned not just by space, but also by his own body, Sammy had not left his room in over six weeks. Steroids had swollen his tissues such that he could barely move. A first-time visitor would be shocked by his appearance. Sam's jowls were so large that they hung well below his chin and much wider than his ears. I lovingly called him "Walrus Boy," but a dispassionate stranger would likely call him "the elephant kid."

Often disconnected from the pumps and monitors, Sam loved to sit by his window and look out around the floor. He would tilt his head and crane his neck to see as far down the hall as possible, looking to expand his tiny world. He attracted the attention of all passersby. Sammy began to lose a bit of his shyness as he healed. Despite his limited mobility, his signature wave became more aggressive as he now lifted his arm slightly before rotating his wrist Miss America–style. Although the puffiness masked his once radiant smile, Sam no longer hid his face as he grinned at visitors outside his room. He sought, and usually received, smiles in return to his waves. That afternoon, I watched as Sammy joyfully played with his physical therapist. Too big for his bungee chair, Sammy was content to sit in a playpen next to the window for his workout, where reaching for a toy was the extent of his regimen.

In the evening, Sammy rewarded me with a big surprise.

With the college basketball tournament in full swing, Sammy and I settled in to watch a few games. On my lap, he seemed disinterested in the riveting drama of a number fourteen seed beating a three. He occupied himself with observing the goings-on at the nurse's station. When he became bored, Sammy began playing with my ears and nose. He finally managed to get my undivided attention when he touched my cheek and spoke a real word.

"Da-da."

The biggest grin exploded across my face. Sammy put on a sheepish smile and said it again.

"Da-da." He giggled as he saw my excitement. I forgot about the basketball as Sam and I set about playing a round of "Da-da, Ma-ma." I would say Da-da and touch my cheek. Then I would touch his cheek and say Sammy. He only wanted to say Da-da and repeated it over and over. Even when I tried to get him to say Ma-ma, he would only say Da-da. It was the sweetest sound I had ever heard.

Sam's brain, according to the docs, hadn't grown in some time, but it didn't seem to slow him down. I often had to remind myself that the side effects, at least some of them, would be temporary. The others, whatever they might be, would be a part of Sam. As long as we brought him home, we could live with whatever legacy the HLH left with him.

CHAPTER 19

A Speck of Trouble

The smooth recovery Sam had been enjoying suddenly hit a rough spot. It started on a Friday, my weekend at home. Although the initial symptom was just a case of diarrhea, nothing is simple with transplant patients. The docs warned us that the diarrhea could mean several things—some of them routine, others very serious.

By the time the weekend ended, Sam was going through several diapers each hour. By Monday, Day +31, Sam had lost almost two pounds and began vomiting along with the continued diarrhea. The docs were concerned. Graft Versus Host Disease (GVHD) of the digestive tract was a strong possibility. Suzanne and I exchanged many phone calls that morning as information came available.

Meanwhile, the docs decided to do an intestinal biopsy—a minor surgical procedure—in order to diagnose GVHD of the gut. Sam left his room for the first time in weeks for a trip down to the surgical floor.

Suzanne's phone calls the next morning described Sammy's condition as worsening.

"I'm going to head back as soon as I can," I said. "Zach is going to be really upset, so I'm going to take him someplace special for lunch, then I'll get on the road."

"I think you'd better get here. I'm really worried about Zachary though. Maybe I can get one of my sisters to bring the boys down this weekend. I really miss them," she said.

"Okay, hon, hang in there. I'll see you in five or six hours." Of all the places Zachary could pick from to have lunch— Chuck E. Cheese's, Discovery Zone, and so on—he chose Burger King. Jacob was happy to stay home with Grandma and take a nap. Zach had a blast climbing through the tunnel and tumbling down the slide in the play area. Our time together was precious, though not nearly enough.

"Scotty, beam me to Cincinnati. I cannot handle this drive today," I said to myself later as I headed down the long highway. The never-ending series of good-byes were wearing me down, and Zachary had had enough.

"Daddy, please don't go! Please don't go away!" he cried, as I explained that I had to leave him once again.

"Can you stay with me, please?" he pleaded, as I walked out the door once again. Leaving Jacob and Zachary left me with a shattered heart. Jacob slept through my leaving, but the disappointment in Zachary's eyes sufficed for both boys.

They'll be fine, I thought as the miles ticked slowly away, *but what about Sam?* I wasn't so sure about him.

Within moments of my arrival back at the hospital, Dr. Jennifer entered Sam's room with news from his biopsy.

"I just finished consulting with the pathologist," she said. "The biopsy reveals a classic presentation of GVHD of the gut." She continued, "He also said it's very common for transplant patients with unrelated donors to present early with GVHD of the skin, which then clears, and then to see GVHD of the gut around Day +30. The GVHD often shows up about the time the patient is ready to go home, which is obviously the case with Sam."

"So this isn't really unexpected, is it?" I asked.

"It's not unusual," Dr. Jennifer answered. "But I understand that Dr. Filipovich has warned you about the seriousness of GVHD of the gut."

While holding Sammy moments later, the severity of his diarrhea became quickly apparent. By nightfall I was doing laundry because his overflowing diaper had soiled all my clean clothes. Sam was indeed a very sick boy. In addition to his constant diarrhea, he seemed listless and unusually fussy. The docs had cut off Sam's feeds that morning, yet he was still having bowel movements every fifteen minutes or so.

GVHD was like civil war inside Sam's body. His new bone marrow did not like being in his body and wanted to destroy it like a rebel army wants to destroy a country. The marrow or stem cells opened hostilities by attacking Sam's skin. The doctors used steroids in defense. The stem cells then opened this second offensive against Sam's digestive system. He would no longer be able to eat food. I couldn't imagine how awful that must feel.

The doctors would have to use smarter weapons to defeat this new attack. The treatment would be ATG, an immuno-suppressant given by IV for a period of seven days. Sam had received this medication during the destruction of his stem cells prior to transplant.

Sam would also start that evening on IV nutrition called TPN—total parenteral nutrition. The docs had been reluctant to put Sam on TPN in the past due to his compromised liver but now had no choice, as his digestive system was too diseased to handle food. Sam would not be allowed to eat again until his bowel healed. Even worse, as we were to soon learn, no drinking either; he would be allowed only tiny sips of liquid to soothe a raging thirst.

Suzanne and I had let our guard down with Sam's remarkable recovery from the HLH and transplant. Once again we had to deal with a life-threatening illness. The suddenness of his change—from recovering to critically ill—struck us like a hammer blow. Suzanne gave me a long, warm comforting hug after I laid Sam in his crib. The intimacy felt really nice. For a moment, I felt loved. I could tell Suzanne needed to cry in a big way, but she wouldn't let her tears out in front of Sam. Helplessly watching Sam suffer hurt me as well. This was a time for me to be the strong one again, but I didn't feel strong. Holding Sam while he searched my eyes looking for an answer to his hunger pained me to the core. His downcast eyes and soft moans told his story.

Daddy, why don't you feed me? Can't you see how very hungry I am? he seemed to say. The little comfort I could provide was pitifully less than he needed, and oceans less than I wanted to provide. Only a few days earlier, Sam's IV pole was nearly empty, supporting only one pump and one bag of fluid. Now the nurses paraded in pump after pump loaded with bags and syringes. Just days ago, we had been planning Sam's release. Now we again faced restless nights of constant beeps from med pumps along with numerous interruptions of nurses taking vital signs. The depth of Sam's setback remained unknown, but the depth of despair that Suzanne and I felt was easily measured by our drooped faces and the silence of our commiseration.

While Suzanne would not leave Sam's side, I needed a break. Short walks outside his room were a staple of survival for me, and this one was vital. Most often, I simply would walk the halls of Hem/Onc, but something led me upstairs on this night. I soon found myself in the intensive care unit, standing outside Maria's room. Although I would often visit Maria's parents, this was my first visit to her room in PICU. Anthony and Carla greeted me warmly and invited me in.

"I want you to see my little angel," she said.

The sight of Maria shocked me. This could not possibly be the same little girl so recently living next door to us on T5A. Maria's head and body had swollen up like an over-inflated balloon. Her hair, but for a few scraggly clumps, was gone. She was comatose, her breathing done by machine. Contrasted with Maria, Sam looked wonderful. Yet Anthony and Carla were seemingly euphoric. I didn't know if they had incredible faith in an impending miracle, or were simply unable to face the gravity of Maria's condition. There are probably few secrets in most hospitals, and this one was no different. I had kept track of Maria's condition through several grapevines. I knew her brain was gone and her chances for recovery nil. Sadness for Maria and her devoted parents gripped me as I moved along on my walk.

Soon I was back on T5A and at the door of our special friend, Allison. Suzanne and I could no longer visit Allison because she, like Sam, was in isolation. Allison, now two weeks beyond her bone-marrow transplant, looked miserable from the window. I tried hard to coax a smile from her, but at plus two weeks, few transplant patients find any reason to smile. With improved emotional balance and a new perspective from seeing the desolation, despair, and denial going on around us, I was back in Sam's room ready for the night shift. After seeing Maria, Sam's issues seemed like a minor inconvenience. I prayed quietly they would remain so.

After four straight nights covering the hospital, Suzanne was tired but reluctant to leave Sammy. It was late when she finally declared it was time to walk her to McDonald House for a night of sleep. Tears tumbled down her cheeks only moments after leaving T5A. Unable to hold it back, she cried throughout our short walk and while settling into our room. Like old times, I held her close and she cried on my shoulder.

"Just let it out, it's okay," I whispered softly to her.

"You can let it out too."

"I know. It will come," I said, enjoying the closeness.

"You better get back to Sammy. He was pretty upset when we left," she told me as our hug broke. The day had been pure hell. The news was devastating, and our spirits were deeply wounded, yet the warmth of our embrace left me with lightness and a feeling of hope as I made my way back to what was sure to be a long, tough night in Hem/Onc.

I tallied forty-seven diarrhea-filled diapers in twenty-four hours when I finished up Sam's chart at midnight. An intake of only six ounces of formula during the same span made for a major fluid imbalance. The night brought sporadic rest for Sam and only stolen moments for me. The nurse spent far more time in Sam's room than out. Once again, the hours filled with beeping pumps and the sound of a whimpering baby. Finding comfort for our treasured child was an impossible task. The night, a precursor to the interminable suffering of the next few weeks, mercifully ended when Suzanne arrived early, bearing the gift of coffee.

During this crisis, Sam had to fight back without the comfort of food and drink. He cried or whimpered with hunger, thirst, and pain nearly every hour that he was awake during that long week. And Sam was almost always awake. The most heart-wrenching part was watching him suffer from thirst. The docs allowed him very limited amounts of fluid as even water inflamed his bowel. Sam's only drink came from frozen Pedialyte Popsicles that he sucked through his bottle as they melted. The few times a day Sam was allowed this treat, he furiously attacked his bottle trying to quench his unbearable thirst. His only comfort came when he slept, which was rare and never lasted more than two hours. Only a cocktail of Benadryl and Ativan relaxed him enough to allow sleep. Even then, slumber came only for short periods while either Suzanne or I rocked him in our arms. Sam's twin IV ports were kept busy as he received meds twenty-four hours a day.

Sam, Suzanne, and I went through seven days and seven nights of hell together. But Sam did all the suffering.

Suzanne's normally upbeat attitude was rocked during this intense crisis. Never during Sam's treatments and hospitalization had Suzanne focused on herself. Despite encouragement from many friends and me, she refused to take a night off and/or enjoy herself. She never took breaks, relaxed, or allowed herself fun. Suzanne admitted that she reached rock bottom during this crisis. The stress and physical exhaustion finally took its toll on her. Something had to give. She was sleep-deprived, run-down, and emotionally spent. Her fears brought forth the tears that she had kept under control so many months. They streamed down her cheeks that seventh hellish afternoon while Sam mercifully snoozed. Her fears and frustrations could no longer be held within.

"I don't know if I can do this anymore," she wailed.

But then, when our despair was deepest, something wonderful happened. Suzanne and I began to draw closer. It happened slowly, almost like when we first met. We started talking to each other, really talking—and listening. And we touched. Quiet moments alone were rare, but we used them to hug or exchange back rubs. We admitted that we missed each other and longed for intimacy. We both had focused our love on Sam, Jacob, and Zachary—to the exclusion of each other, unfortunately. This crisis brought us back together.

"Where did you get this medallion?" I asked Suzanne one night after walking her to Ronald McDonald House. I studied it carefully after picking it up from the nightstand in our room. "It's beautiful."

The pewter medallion looked ancient. It was not

symmetrical and the edges were worn. On the medallion, carved out of the metal, was an angel.

"I've never seen that before," Suzanne said, leaning for a look. "It's lovely, where did you find it?"

"Right here on the nightstand. I wonder where it came from."

"That is really weird," she said as we looked at each other with wide eyes.

We both knew that angels were watching over Sammy. We had seen firsthand the peacefulness brought by the angel Chrissy months earlier. Krissy at this hospital certainly had some connection with angels.

"This is a reminder that angels are with us," Suzanne said.

"Why do I keep forgetting that?" A long pause followed while I formed a thought in my head. "It seems like God is sending these angels to remind us that we are not alone, that God has a plan. I just wish I knew what it is."

No one else ever came into our room. There was no maid service at Ronald McDonald House. It could not have been inadvertently left there. The mystery of the medallion led to only one possible conclusion: angels were among us. The medallion was a reminder. As soon as I arrived back at the hospital, the medallion found a new home above Sam's head in his crib.

But Sam's GVHD was not going away. The diarrhea continued, and he remained sick, weak, and tired. He was also hungry and thirsty. A second week without food or drink began with no relief expected in his near future. The transfusions continued, platelets every other day, red cells every five days or so. The docs seemed unconcerned, yet failed to explain why Sam's blood counts continued to drop.

Suzanne and I, looking back to nine months earlier, remembered how absolutely stunned and frightened we were by the
word *transfusion*. Now we viewed them as a routine segment of
Sam's care. We could tell by looking at Sam when he was due
for blood products. Tiny circular bruises appeared on Sam's
legs and arms when his platelets dropped below 30,000. He
became very pale and listless when he needed red blood.

During this time, Mom visited us for an emotional five
days; it was one year after my dad died. Tracking Sam's condition and progress from her distant home through phone calls
and occasional pictures had been excruciating for her. To actually see Sam and hold him touched and relieved her. Sam
nearly jumped out of my arms and into hers when she walked
into the room. They bonded instantly. Sam had not seen
Grandma Henkels for more than four months, yet was drawn
to her immediately. He soon fell asleep in her arms with a
contented smile on his face. Mom refused to let me move him
into his crib. He slept for nearly two hours while Mom,
Suzanne, and I visited quietly.

Her visit overlapped a night that Suzanne and I were both
in town, so Suzanne and I had a date night, together, both of
us, at the same time, at the same place. We couldn't believe our
good fortune. Dinner was wonderful. The stress melted off as
we enjoyed pleasant conversation, excellent, non–hospital food,
and a few cocktails. The best part: we didn't hurry back to the
hospital after dinner. We did hurry to Ronald McDonald
House and our private room. I had promised Suzanne a
complete massage that night and she got it, although I may
have enjoyed it more than she. After the massage we . . . well
suffice it to say I had a spring in my step the next morning and

slept deeply and contentedly that night. For one, brief, sparkling evening amongst a hundred dark ones, Suzanne and I shared intimacy and concentrated on each other. I hoped we would find more soon.

Although Sam's condition remained stable throughout Mom's visit, the GVHD stubbornly refused to fade. On Day +40 Sam needed yet another red-cell transfusion, along with three units of platelets. His blood pressure continued to be very high and his diarrhea continued. The days passed slowly with little change in his misery. Talk of leaving the hospital was nonexistent. We faced more time on T5A, and our spirits were low.

But a walk around the floor was all that was needed to remind us how much worse it could be. Some of our friends were in trouble. Sarah gave us regular reports on Allison's deteriorating condition: her liver function was decreasing daily and breathing was becoming difficult. Allison was desperately ill, and Sarah was frightened. In the next pod, Elijah had taken a turn for the worse and was now suffering from GVHD of the gut. He faced his first introduction to high-dose steroids. Isabelle, Elijah's mom, visited Sam to get an idea of the effects of steroids. Elijah and his family had been on T5A two months longer than us, and were much, much farther from home.

The holistic health specialist, Krissy, continued to visit and work with Sammy. She performed her healing touch once or twice a week, usually when Sam was asleep. As Sam's naptime was precious, Suzanne and I spent it reading the paper or dozing. When Krissy came around, I gave her the space she needed to do her thing with Sammy. I relaxed for those few moments. After our initial emotional conversation weeks earlier, I'd never again gotten into a discussion about her work or therapy with Sam. That is, until I walked into the room as she was leaving one afternoon during Sam's long recovery from Graft Versus Host Disease.

"Angels, little blue angels—they are just floating all around Sammy today. I could see them very clearly, and they are so pretty." Krissy was radiant as she described them to me.

Angels had become such a part of Sam's story that I believed Krissy's vision of the blue angels without a second thought. And I was excited to hear about them.

"Have you ever seen angels around him before?" I asked.

"Oh, they've been in Sam's room for a long time. I usually see them in the corners, but this is the first time I saw the blue angels around him. They were very pretty," she said.

Angels must be something to see. Krissy described these blue angels as "very pretty" several times. I really wanted to see them, too, but how? How could I get myself to a consciousness level to be able to see them? Was it possible, or was Krissy an angel herself?

CHAPTER 20

Meltdown

Suzanne lost it first, although my own emotional collapse wasn't far behind. I was asleep at Ronald McDonald House in the wee hours when the phone startled me awake. Suzanne was covering the hospital after completing a four-day visit home, her longest since Sam had been admitted. A solid night of sleep was the reward for my four long nights in the hospital. In fact, I had stayed up late enjoying a good book, knowing I could sleep in as late as I wanted. That plan failed! Initially frightened by the late-night phone call, I became angry once I found out Sam was fine, just restless. Suzanne was in tears, having not slept a wink during the night.

My anger softened once I arrived back at the hospital to take over. Suzanne had reached her emotional limit. The tears of frustration, anger, and helplessness flowed freely as I walked her to our temporary home.

"I just can't take it anymore," she cried. "I want to go home. I want to take Sammy home. I want everything to be normal," she sobbed.

"I want that, too, Suzanne. I'm so tired of this place." I

stopped her on the sidewalk long enough to embrace her in a bear hug. Suzanne had only started looking after herself a bit in the past week or so. She had given and given to the point she was emotionally spent.

Her eyes were still red when she returned late in the afternoon. Suzanne admitted to crying for over an hour before falling asleep. She then insisted I talk about how I was feeling. Alarms screeched in my head. *Oh no, anything but that. Why does she need to hear about my feelings? She's the one who cried herself to sleep, not me. I want her to need me but not at this extreme.*

I had a canned response ready just in case such an emergency arose. "I'm okay, just getting through this one day at a time," I said with a soft but serious inflection in my voice. I hoped it was enough. After all, I'd admitted it was hard, but I was tough enough to take it. Suzanne nodded her head slightly. I thought I was off the hook.

"Seriously, John, cut the bullshit. I want how you're *feeling*."

I was trapped and I knew it. The only thing to do now was actually try to figure out how I was feeling and then verbalize it. It took me awhile, but I came up with something.

"I'm scared Suzanne. I'm scared and I'm helpless. Sammy is suffering so much. I'm angry that this perfect and innocent child has to go through this nightmare. I'm supposed to be able to protect my family and I can't. I cannot take proper care of one single member of my family and that drives me crazy." It started flowing—real feelings put into words. It wasn't as hard as I thought. "I'm exhausted all the time. I miss Zach and Jake. I can't do this as well as you. I know I need more breaks, but I feel like I don't deserve time away if you don't take it," I said.

"What else are you feeling?" she asked softly. "I'm listening."

"I want to go home. I want Sam to get better, and I want us all home—soon. And I want to stop being afraid."

Somewhere inside myself, I found and then described the feeling I hated the most. I was afraid—afraid Sam was going to die. And I was frightened life would never be the same—we would not feel the top-of-the-world joy of days past. I also knew discussing my fears with Suzanne could not happen. Sam dying was an out-of-bounds discussion. So I turned it back on her.

"But I am still worried about you. I know you are exhausted and emotionally spent."

"I'll be okay. Why don't you drive home tonight and sleep in your own bed?" Suzanne offered. "Go home tonight and bring my mom and the boys back on Friday. We'll all be together for the weekend. We can celebrate Jake and Sam's birthday a few days early."

It was a good plan, and I agreed to it. There were only a few glitches in the arrangement. The first: it was after eight p.m. when I finally hit the highway. The second: my meltdown was not yet over. My fears had bubbled to the surface, and now I had to find an outlet.

Rev Ron, maybe the warmest human being alive, was at home doing his taxes when my cellular call reached him an hour later.

"John, I have been expecting this call for weeks now," he said gently after learning Sam was fine but I was hurting.

Ron called us religiously (pun intended) twice a week, always trying to understand how Suzanne and I were faring. He never accepted "I'm hanging in there," the stock answer of all parents on Hem/Onc. He always ended the call with a mild chastisement to call any hour, any day when, not if, I needed to talk, or needed a shoulder to cry on. I needed his shoulder this night.

"Talk to me, my friend. What is going on?"

And I spilled it out to him. On the phone driving north on I-71, I let my overloaded emotions pour forth.

"I just don't feel like I am taking proper care of one single member of my family right now. Jacob and Zachary need so much more than I can give them. Suzanne is completely exhausted. Sam is so sick. I just feel like I am giving none of them the love and attention they each need and deserve. Plus, I am worried about Marilyn. She has so much on her plate to care for Jake and Zach. She is doing an incredible job. Jacob is growing into a wonderfully happy, exuberant boy, but I'm worried that she may run down also. I am just so tired of it all. I want it to be over. I want my family home."

Ron allowed it all to come out, and boy, did it come out. "Sammy could die, Ron, and I don't know how we could survive that."

When I was done, his words of wisdom, understanding, and support were compassionate and sincere.

"John, you are being asked to do a herculean task right now that no human being could do perfectly. God doesn't ask you to be perfect, only to do what you can do. And, John, you are— listen to me, John—you are doing the best you can do. These are very trying times. You are in the worst of the worst places, and you are doing the best you can, and that is all that God asks."

Ron paused to allow his message to sink in before continuing.

"John, I told you I have been expecting this call, and, frankly, I expected it much earlier. You have been carrying an enormous burden. Jesus is there to carry it for you. Let him, John. Let Jesus carry your burden."

"I know," I sobbed. "I need to let it go. I need to let God handle the pressure for me. I just can't go on like this any longer."

Rev Ron's soothing words calmed me. I slowly began to feel peacefulness for the first time in days. We talked a while longer, and Ron gently probed my emotions, looking for ways to ease my tensions. He issued his final words of wisdom before giving me a warm telepathic bear hug.

"John, you cannot take care of anyone in your family, until

you take care of yourself first. Hear me, John. You must *first* care for yourself."

I heard him and promised to try. And I did try, but the situation required only more perseverance.

Living in a cancer unit changed my outlook on every aspect of life, especially the time spent with our children. Suzanne and I had both learned to cherish each moment with our little boys like it was the most precious treasure on earth. We had already learned how fast they grow and how they change every day. The time apart from Zach, Jake, and Sam could never be replaced. Thus, the times together were spent with an intensity of love and a level of appreciation for our wonderful children that we might never have reached had we not lived through this ordeal.

I believed the trials our family suffered would change Suzanne and me forever. And I prayed that we would be better persons for it. I hoped our appreciation for the blessings bestowed upon us would not diminish once the ordeal was over. I held that our marriage would be stronger, our spirituality greater, and our outlook on life brighter. Before all those good things happened, however, we had to get Sam healthy. And I knew not what would become of faith, marriage, optimism, or spirituality if Sammy died.

But Sam *had* started to improve. He was becoming more playful again. He even smiled occasionally. To a stranger, Sam might look almost monstrous, but to me, Suzanne, the docs, nurses, and therapists, he was getting better. Despite a long period without eating, Sam was still swollen and largely immobile. His cheeks and belly were huge; his legs, arms, and fingers were puffy and spotted with tiny round bruises from chronically low platelets. His back and bottom were speckled with a mysterious rash. And he was growing hair in strange places, such as his forehead, back, and cheeks, a side effect of the cyclosporine medication; his sideburns resembled the 1970s Elvis. Sammy now looked nothing like the Gerber baby. And the developmental disparity between him and Jacob was widening at an alarming rate. *Will Sam ever be normal and healthy like Jacob?* My demons came during "pretend to take a nap" time. *What will Sam be like when he is two years old, or four? Will he catch up to Jacob by the time they go to kindergarten? Will he be retarded? What an ugly word that is. No one uses the word* retarded *any more. John, what are you worrying about? Sam might not make it to two. Stop that! Don't even think about that.*

After my weekend at home, it was time to plan a party. Our twins were turning one year old. I brought Grandma and the boys with me to Cincinnati. But the celebration for Jacob and Samuel lacked the joyfulness of typical first birthday parties. The logistics of having half the family in Sam's room and the other half in the hallway separated by a glass wall robbed much of the celebration's charm. That Sammy and Jake were forced to be separated by isolation rules sucked (for lack of a more appropriate word). Worries over Sam's condition kept my spirits subdued. But we did our best to see that the kids had fun, and we enjoyed the attention they received from the staff and visitors. Jacob enjoyed eating his cake, and spreading it over his face and hair. Samuel was allowed only a Pedialyte Popsicle that he vigorously sucked through his bottle as it melted. The remainder of the week went better. Despite our worries, Suzanne and I left Sam in Marilyn's care and visited the Cincinnati Children's Museum, where the boys found stimulating games and delighted in the water activities. As we were leaving, Zachary led us into the gift shop for his obligatory toy. Only one thing in the entire store interested him, one thing he had to have: an inflatable jet plane—a Blue Angel jet plane. Hmmm, it seemed Zach was once again letting us know his angels were present, and like Krissy's angels, they were blue.

The doctors talked of allowing Sam outside for a brief walk during the weekend when few people were around; again we heard talk of Sam being released to Ronald McDonald House in a week or two. According to the docs, everything looked rosy. But Suzanne and I remained quietly concerned that all was not as it seemed.

Sammy's progress earned him the promised treat. He was allowed a one-hour furlough from the hospital on Sunday afternoon. Suzanne had taken the boys home, so Sammy and I were alone for the big event. The rules were many, and the time away brief. Sam would not be allowed near people, plants, animals, insects, sunshine, or cars. The nurses found one hour between IV medications to free Sam from his lines.

Despite the limitations, I was giddy with excitement. I dressed Sammy in a new pair of khaki coveralls with a navy-blue sweatshirt he had received on his birthday, then tucked him in his stroller. As I fantasized that Sam was cured, we walked out of the unit amidst applause from the skeleton Sunday staff. Sam, however, seemed disinterested, perhaps even frightened. Once outside, the event turned anticlimactic as we looked for a place to walk that fit the stringent rules. At home, Suzanne missed the excitement of Sam's stroller ride around an empty parking lot. The fantasy ended when Sammy's explosive diarrhea stained not only his new overalls, but covered his stroller seat as well.

The day after his outdoor excursion, the illusion of Sam's recovery also ended. Sam spiked a fever and began hourly vomiting. His hemoglobin and platelets, steady for nearly two weeks, nose-dived. He received transfusions of both. Sam entered into another crisis, this one of unknown origins.

Photographs from Chapter 20 can be viewed at:
SamuelsMission.com

CHAPTER 21

Death Comes Calling to HEM/ONC

The next morning brought sad news from another front: Reverend Sue gently informed me of Maria's death. Anthony and Carla's rock-solid faith would now be tested by the loss of their daughter. I hurt for them. They had been so certain their precious daughter would recover.

Maria and Sammy shared the same rare disease, but Maria went much too long undiagnosed. By the time she'd arrived at Cincinnati Children's Hospital, it was already too late: her brain was massively infected. She really had no chance. I was again reminded to thank God for the awesome work of Rainbow Babies and Children's Hospital and their prompt diagnosis of Sam. Although we switched hospitals for his transplant, the doctors at Rainbow had surely saved Sam's life.

Two kids died on the floor later in the week. Neither Suzanne nor I knew the families, but we knew of the kids. We had watched them suffer every day through their room windows. Darkness enveloped T5A that week. Other than Zachary Bowlin, all of the long-termers we had come to know were fighting for life. Elijah struggled with numerous issues and complications. Allison was critically ill and had been moved to the ICU with serious liver problems, and Sammy, of course, battled his mysterious symptoms.

A few days later, the hardest blow yet landed. Sarah Smiley brought the news. Her voice was barely audible, but I knew what she was going to say before she said it. A veil of despair masked her normally ebullient face. Her eyes were red; she had been crying.

"Allison died this morning. She suffered a brain seizure last night." Sarah whispered the words in a clinical way. It was the only way she could get the news out, I figured. Sarah had cared for Allison nearly every day for six months. Now she was gone.

Her death hit Suzanne and me hard also. We had come to know and love this beautiful child. Allison's family had been with her night and day during the past month or so. It would have been humorous if it hadn't been so sad. Her dad, her mom, and her mom's boyfriend all stayed in the same room at Ronald McDonald House. But at least they found a way to come together to care for her. She died with the love of her family around her. I was thankful for that much.

Allison had lost the fight, but would not be forgotten; we had taken a photo of Allison playing a board game with our Zachary months earlier. The photo captured a happy moment between two giggling children. She'd had few happy moments after that. Now sweet Allison was dead. It was hard to absorb. Suzanne and I talked that night about our need to get Sammy out of this place. Death was heavy in the air of T5A, and we needed to get away somehow.

But then something wonderful happened, good news that brightened the spirit of the entire unit. Zachary Bowlin, the little baby who had been abandoned at birth and undergone a bone marrow transplant for a rare immune disease, was being adopted. His new mom was the cousin of his primary nurse. This was a beautiful new chapter in what had been a very sad story. Suzanne and I eagerly sought out Zach's new parents and introduced ourselves. Jeff and Mary were grateful that we made the effort, especially when we told them that we were the parents of an adopted son named Zachary. They were very excited to bring this magnificent baby into their family. Zach's prognosis looked good. He was very tiny and under weight but recovering nicely. Much paperwork remained to be completed on the adoption, but Zach was getting a new start on life with wonderful new parents. As we got to know Jeff and Mary better over the next few days, we found we had much in common. They had been trying to conceive a child for nine years without success and now had the child they had been dreaming of. Although he appeared to be recovering, there were no guarantees that Zach would develop normally. To give this critically ill child a home and their total devotion was a tremendously loving commitment. Jeff and Mary inspired not only me, but also many others on the floor. Their presence made Hem/Onc a happier place.

As soon as one child close to our hearts was gone, another moved in. The day after Allison died, Zachary Carter was admitted to the room next door for his bone-marrow transplant. Steve, Tammy, and Zachary Carter had already become dear to us. Our bond strengthened as they began treatment to cure Zach's HLH. That Zach and Sammy's rooms were side by side was only a coincidence as far as we could know, but we were all grateful for having such close support.

Sam's condition did not reverse as my fervent prayers requested—not that week, and not in the next month. In that time, several devastating setbacks put Sam's recovery into a downward spiral. Sam's bowel shut down and began hemorrhaging. Suzanne and I thought a change might help and requested Sam be transferred to Rainbow Babies & Children's Hospital. The doctors could not pinpoint the exact cause of Sam's problems despite a month of tests and experimental drug therapies. They eventually concluded it was just that Sam had been dealing with so much for so long. Chemotherapy, steroids, and antibiotics before and after transplant had left his digestive tract severely inflamed and sore; his bowel had simply shut down to heal. Dr. Filipovich made it clear that Sam was much to sick to transfer.

I tried to imagine the pain Sammy must have felt. His guts were raw and bleeding. His bones were thin and fragile. X-rays showed hairline fractures in both his legs caused by the long-term medications. Sam winced in pain whenever he was moved. He could not sit up. He could not play. He could not eat. He could not even drink water. Sam lived with tubes stuffed down his throat and sticking out his chest. His suffering was unlike anything I had ever experienced, and he was barely a year old.

We knew we were not alone in praying for Sammy. Family, friends, church members, and strangers routinely prayed for his recovery. Evidence of such support came through our e-mail.

Date: May 15, 1999
Subject: Prayer for Sammy

Hi, everybody!

A quick update before I get to the important part of this message. Sammy's bowel now has completely shut down. This is a complete blockage in the intestine. Sammy now has a number of fractures in his bones due to the long-term high dose steroids. Although it didn't seem possible a month ago, Sammy's suffering has vastly increased yet again.

Some time ago, the suggestion was given that we all pray for Sammy on a specific day and time, and I think the time has come when we need to try it. Let's all stop what we are doing at 7 p.m. Ohio time on Tuesday and pray together for a swift recovery for Sammy, with a specific emphasis that his gastrointestinal problems are resolved. I'd suggest that wherever possible, we pray in small groups together, because God has told us that whenever two or more of you gather in His name, they will be heard. I spoke with John twice this week, and he is very discouraged at this time. I'm not sure how Suzanne is feeling, but I assume it is about the same. We need to remember to keep them in our prayers, to give them the strength to get through this horrible time.

Kathy Ott

Our hope to transfer Sammy back to Rainbow Babies & Children's Hospital was not forgotten. We entered into negotiations with Dr. Filipovich to make it happen. She agreed that Sam could safely be transferred once his condition stabilized in four areas: bowel, blood pressure, fevers, and nutrition. These were no small issues. Sam would have to learn to eat; a process she described as more difficult than one might imagine. Other secondary issues also remained. Destruction of Sam's red blood cells continued as his blood type changed from his O-positive to the donor's A-positive.

Obviously the transfer could not happen for some time. The big turnaround needed to begin soon to make a June transfer date happen. Once at Rainbow, Sam could remain hospitalized for two weeks or two months. We just didn't know. We did know the hospital time would last much longer than we'd anticipated at the beginning of the transplant process.

Over the next weeks, Sam's condition improved only slightly. The docs now referred to his condition as chronic GVHD, possibly a long-term or lifetime condition.

During Sammy's slow recovery period, he reached Day +100. This was the magical date we had circled on our calendars so long ago. This was the day Sammy was to go home. But Sammy was far from leaving the hospital. His misery multiplied as the GVHD worsened. Sam's donor bone marrow had launched further attacks on his own tissues in attempt to destroy them; Sam's new stem cells did not yet recognize his tissues as self. The bone marrow manufactured T-cells and other weapons to defeat the defensive medications, such as ATG and steroids. A war raged inside Sammy's body. And Sammy was losing.

CHAPTER 22

A Peck of Trouble

We thought that we had seen the worst. But the panic on Marilyn's face as she frantically waved for help through Sam's window proved us wrong again. Suzanne and I had been playing with Zach and Jacob outside the room when the catastrophe began. It was late in the afternoon, almost time to take the boys to the hotel. Reverend Sue, visiting at that moment, took charge of the boys as we flew into the room. Marilyn's white slacks were stained bright red from her hips to her knees where Sam sat on her lap. His diaper was overflowing with blood—lots of blood. Inside his ravaged little body Sam was hemorrhaging profusely.

Suzanne gently eased Sammy into his crib while I summoned help. Minutes after the bloody diaper was cleaned up, blood began pouring out of Sam's feeding tube. Sam was bleeding from both ends, his stomach and his bowel. Dr. Morris came in to assess the problem. He showed calmness by examining Sammy with deliberateness and speaking to us in a soft and controlled voice.

"I'm going to call for a GI consult. I'll be right back."

Moments later he was gone.

Niki, Sam's nurse at the moment, was not demonstrating calmness; her frantic actions were shot through with alarm. Her face was drawn and her eyes wide as she attached a collection bag to Sam's feeding tube to capture the blood flowing from his stomach. She then removed the blood-soaked sheets from his crib.

The next thirty minutes were a whirlwind. Suzanne reluctantly left to deposit Marilyn and the boys safely in the hotel as the crisis unfolded. I looked for Dr. Morris and spotted him on the phone at the nurse's station. Niki kept busy taking vital signs, drawing labs, and again changing Sam's blood-filled collection bag. I forced my fears down, but my insides were churning as I waited for word from Dr. Morris. Sammy moaned softly in his crib but seemed no different than earlier in the day.

Before long, one of the gastro-intestinal (GI) docs arrived in response to Dr. Morris's urgent summons. The doc examined Sam and explained that he needed to be scoped immediately to have a look at his digestive tract in order to locate the source of his bleeding. Sam had had a recent endoscopy so I understood the procedure. The doc explained that if they found a bleeding ulcer or a perforated intestine, they could possibly cauterize it with the scope.

Minutes later, a surgical transport team arrived. Niki shifted vital equipment and meds to one IV pole and disconnected others. The team whisked Sammy away. I found myself alone in the absolute stillness of Sam's room. The chaos of the last fifteen minutes echoed in my ears as butterflies swirled in my stomach. Moments later, I looked up to see that I was in the surgical waiting room—desperately frightened and shocked by the swiftness of the events. I wasn't even sure how I got there, but I was still alone. The room was deserted, as the day's busy surgical schedule had been completed. The quiet of the empty room unnerved me.

Her face ashen with fear, Suzanne arrived and hugged me tight. I told her everything I knew, which was precious little. Sam was bleeding heavily and in emergency surgery. With little to do but wait, we called our families. Prayers were needed. Phone calls and e-mails went quickly around the country. Suzanne arranged for her sister to drive to Cincinnati and take Marilyn, Jacob, and Zachary home.

Our wait on the surgical floor seemed like an eternity. I paced the floor of the huge, colorful waiting area many times while Suzanne wept quietly in her chair. The GI doctor I had spoken to earlier finally arrived with news. His face was grave as he described the procedure.

"We ran an endoscopy down Sam and found general bleeding throughout his small intestine. There were no ulcers or perforations that we could repair, only severely inflamed tissue pretty much all the way through from his stomach to his rectum.

"How much danger is Sam in? Could he die from this?" I asked.

"Dr. Morris will speak to you in a moment. He was in the OR for the procedure and said he would be out to see you."

"Can we see Sam?" Suzanne asked.

"Once he comes out of the anesthesia, someone will come and bring you into post-op."

All my expectations for Sam to survive left me. I didn't realize it at the time, but losing Sam suddenly seemed not a distant possibility, but a likely end. Suzanne and I wept silently in each other's arms while waiting for Dr. Morris to give his spin on Sam's condition.

"I've never thought Sam was going to die, Suzanne, but I'm

really scared right now," I sobbed. Her strength picked me up.

So much of the time I am the strong one, always positive when Suzanne is in despair. But in the unlikeliest of times, she comes through with unexpected strength. When I fail, when I expect her to be at her lowest point, when I have no emotional reserves to support her, Suzanne takes over. She carries me. And she carried me this day—a day with yet more trials awaiting us.

We waited a long time to see Sam, but no one came for us. In frustration, I searched the post-op area for either Sam or Dr. Morris. The place was nearly deserted, but I finally found a nurse with information.

"I'm sorry," she said. "Didn't anyone tell you? Sam's been moved to the intensive care unit."

Sam was supposed to be home by this date. It was June 4, 1999—104 days after his transplant. Our family had survived five months apart. Sam had lived through devastating chemotherapy, suffered through months without eating, and survived six months of debilitating steroid treatments. How much more suffering did God expect him to endure? Was God planning to take Sam from us after all he has been through? Having faith in God's plan for Sam was becoming difficult. I wondered what would become of my new faith if Sam died now. Would I still believe in God's plan and God's goodness? Would prayer remain in my life, or would I abandon it as easily as I'd picked it up?

"The unit," hospitalspeak for the intensive care unit, was not hard to find. It was located one floor above Hem/Onc on T6A. The floor plan of the unit was nearly identical to T5A. The surroundings looked familiar, but we soon realized we were in an alien world. We found Sam in one of the rooms surrounded by medical staff. Suzanne and I elbowed our way to his side where we hugged him and told him we loved him. It was a tear-filled moment. We did not know if Sam would survive this crisis, as the bleeding continued unabated. The

NG tube continually suctioned blood from his stomach. Sam filled diaper after diaper with bright red blood mixed with wormlike black blood clots. A unit of packed red blood cells dripped steadily through Sam's C-line, one of ten transfusions he would receive over the next forty-eight hours.

I phoned Kathy to get out an e-mail asking for prayers for Sammy. She had sent a note earlier with information that Sammy was in surgery.

> Date: June 4, 1999
> Subject: Sammy Update
>
> I just spoke with John, and Sammy is in very grave condition. They scoped his GI tract in surgery to find where the gastrointestinal bleeding is coming from, and they found that it is profusely bleeding from all over the small bowel. They are giving him blood, but there is not much else they can do for him. Sammy is now in ICU room T-628. John says that this complication is potentially fatal, so Sammy needs lots of prayers now.
>
> Kathy

Kathy's note was correct; there was little the docs could do for Sam at this point other than give him nearly continuous blood transfusions.

There were now two separate hierarchies of doctors treating Sam. The critical care doctors who ran the ICU were essentially in charge of Sam's care, but the BMT doctors advised them on his transplant issues.

The attitude of both nurses and doctors in the ICU was different than we'd encountered in Hem/Onc. We were accustomed to the never-give-up-hope attitude of the medical staff, families, and the kids on T5A. It took a day or two to absorb the atmosphere and to understand the vibe of T6A. Once we understood, we were stunned. Suzanne felt it first and became angry. She fought the nurses and doctors to change it, but the ICU was a strange land. The rules were different, and the expectations were not the same as on Hem/Onc. You see, the staff expected Sammy to die; the nurses and doctors assumed he was at the end. Hope was missing in the ICU. Emotional survival for parents in Hem/Onc depended on hope. Without hope, there was only despair. And despair enveloped the ICU.

The attitude of the staff was not imagined. We quickly found that much friction existed between the critical care and T5A doctors. Dr. Filipovich explained how frustrated she got working with the ICU physicians.

"They assume that all the kids who come up here from the fifth floor are in the final stages of leukemia. We've held meeting after meeting trying to create a better understanding of our patients. Apparently we haven't yet succeeded."

I asked Dr. Filipovich a direct and simple question about Sam's chances.

"Can he recover?" Her answer lifted my spirits immensely.

"I'm certainly planning on it," she said with a confident smile. I had lost hope when Sam came to the ICU. Now, with Dr. Filipovich's quiet proclamation, hope came back. I was so thankful.

One of the ICU residents demonstrated the attitude with an off-hand comment to Suzanne: "Dr. Filipovich tells me that she has seen kids recover from GVHD like Sam has."

She said it as if she was completely startled that Sam might recover. Suzanne shivered with anger as she related the story to me. We simply could not believe the negativity of the unit. We wanted Sammy out of ICU and back on T5A as quickly as possible.

As we entered the second day of Sammy's ICU stay, Suzanne and I felt alone and frightened. Sam continued to bleed from both ends, and the docs continued to transfuse him. Sam, on significant narcotics for pain, seemed reasonably comfortable. Further complications developed, however. His respiratory status had diminished over the past week. He now required low-pressure oxygen to keep his red blood cells saturated.

The treatment for the GVHD would be another round of ATG, or anti-thymocyte globulin. Dr. Filipovich explained that the ATG on this round would be made from rabbits instead of horses.

"Rabbit ATG is used extensively in Europe, although it has been used very little in the United States," she explained. "Our pharmacy doesn't have it, but we found some at the University of Cincinnati next door. We should have it in a few hours and will get Sammy started on a course yet today."

Dr. Filipovich further explained that horse ATG is made from antibodies of only a few horses, but rabbit ATG is made from antibodies from hundreds of rabbits and may provide better T-cell suppression. The T-cells were the type of white blood cells that were attacking Sam's digestive tract; they were being manufactured inside Sammy by the donor bone marrow. Although she quickly lost us in her explanation, we were willing to try anything that might help beat the devastating GVHD that was attacking Sam.

I found comfort that night from a favorite parable called

"Footprints." In the story, a Christ follower visualizes his life as a walk on the beach. Most of the time there are two sets of footprints, but at the most difficult times, he can see only one set of footprints. He asks the Lord why He would desert him, a faithful man, during trying times, and Christ replies, "When you see only one set of footprints, I was carrying you."

I thought about this for a long time and imagined myself and my family being carried in Christ's arms through this harrowing time. And then I slept.

Suzanne and I were learning to adjust to the rules of the ICU. The unit, unlike Hem/Onc, did not cater to family needs. Parents were not allowed to sleep in the patient's room, and the furniture was designed to prevent accidental dozing. A hard-bottom rocking chair was provided, along with a short, narrow bench along the wall. Eating in the room was forbidden, and food trays were not provided for parents.

Sammy had been in Children's Hospital for over five months by this time. Either Suzanne or I had been with him twenty-four hours a day, seven days a week, with only short exceptions when a family member visited. Suzanne and I had not slept together for one single night in that five-month period. Our personal relationship was largely nonexistent. Our marriage was stored away for a time in the distant future when the hurricane winds of our life eased. We were tired beyond description and stressed beyond comprehension. We needed help.

Some day, when we look back on this time in our lives, we will see that God carried us through these days. We will see one set of footprints. More and more each day I prayed to God to protect Sammy and to hold him and give him the strength and courage to carry on. I prayed that God make His plan known for Sammy, that He would ease his suffering.

Samuel taught me many things in his first fourteen months. His presence affected me more than any person had since my parents had nurtured me. Samuel taught me what faith in God really meant. I found it didn't mean that God would provide miracles or make everything perfect—or that God would fix Sammy. My understanding of faith began to emerge: that God is all-powerful, that God has wisdom that we cannot imagine, and that God has a plan for each of us. This understanding came from Samuel. He taught me things that priests and ministers, over many years and countless sermons, were never able to teach. Yes, my faith grew as time went by in the hospital. But I was like a kindergartner in my faith journey with so much yet to learn. I did not know if Samuel's stay on earth would last a long time, or even one more day. I was beginning to understand, however, that Samuel had already accomplished much in his life. The lessons I had learned while watching him fight for his life would stay with me. I wouldn't understand for some time the point of his lessons, but clarity would come.

As God carried us through the storm, we prayed for help to arrive. Suzanne and I had little emotional and physical reserves remaining to bring us through the crisis. We needed help.

"It's time to call in the cavalry," Dr. Filipovich gently encouraged. "You haven't left Sammy's side for even one night. It's going to be even rougher in the ICU. This is the time you really need family or close friends to help you."

The first weekend in the ICU, my brother Joe and his wife Donna drove twelve hours to spend a few days with us.

With no regrets, I openly admit that Joe is a favorite sibling.

This declaration likely doesn't ruffle too many feathers in my family, as my brothers and sisters claim him as a favorite also. Joe is quick with an impish grin and simply has an aura of warmth, sincerity, and friendliness about him. A chuckle is never far away in a conversation with Joe. He enjoys laughing at himself as much as anything.

The second youngest in my family, Joe's name was synonymous with the word *mischief* as a child. He was always into something that didn't please Mom but was never quite enough to label him a troublemaker. As a toddler, Joe entertained the household with a daily concert of banging pots and pans until they were moved to a higher shelf. But the cereal boxes transferred to the bottom shelf were equally fascinating when dumped on the floor of the kitchen. Joe loved the feel of *Wheaties* crunching under his bare feet. And later, when the optometrist recommended a newfangled "unbreakable" frame for Joe's glasses, he had unknowingly issued a challenge. The frames stood no chance when Joe repeatedly hurled them against the brick wall in the family room.

As a young adult, Joe eschewed the family goal of college and enlisted in the navy. As advertised, Joe saw the world from the deck of an aircraft carrier, the *USS Kitty Hawk*. While exploring distant lands, he learned a trade as an electrician. (Sometime during his years in the navy, something must have gone awry with his training, but Joe bore the nickname "Darkened Ship Henkels" with aplomb and a sense of humor.) His naval career led to a lifetime of employment in the electrical contracting field.

Like some of his siblings, his first marriage didn't survive, but Joe found incredible happiness with a beautiful, warm, friendly woman. Also from a large Catholic family—and a stereotypical Midwestern farmer's daughter as idolized by the Beach Boys—Donna fit Joe like a glove. Suzanne and Donna became instant friends when she married Joe. Over the years, we have spent many weekends together, playing golf, traveling, laughing, and hanging out. Joe and I spend many of those hours comparing notes on marriage and sharing what we have learned about women since our last visit. As the latter part actually took just a few seconds we went on to other important manly subjects, like football, golf, and any new favorite micro-brews we had discovered. It seemed like we could always hear Suzanne and Donna giggling in the next room. Joe and I assumed they were repeating some of the jokes we had taught them earlier.

Joe and Donna's visit came at a time of great fear for Samuel's life, a time of uncertainty, and a time of incredible stress. The four of us spent a weekend watching, holding, and comforting Sammy. Somehow in those dark hours, Joe brought laughter into the room. He found a way to ease the tension and lighten the mood.

Samuel sensed the change. Blood continued to pour out throughout the weekend while new blood steadily dripped back into him from a transfusion bag above. Yet he found a way to smile and spread his love. Sam's eyes would tell the story of his love and trust. He was too weak to play or even to laugh. He was too weak to hug or to babble. His eyes revealed his pain, but also revealed his love and trust as he gazed up at his caregiver of the moment. Joe and Donna learned of the power and spirit of this child during their short visit while Suzanne and I learned to lean on others for help. And we learned to let God help carry our load.

Photographs from Chapter 22 can be viewed at:
SamuelsMission.com

CHAPTER 23

The Slow Spiral

Despite the rules of the ICU and Dr. Filipovich's advice, Suzanne and I were determined to continue supporting Sam twenty-four hours a day. He remained very critical and neither of us felt comfortable leaving him. Continuing such a commitment meant Zachary and Jacob would do without a parent once again. Marilyn continued to be the rock our boys so desperately needed. Suzanne and I divided up the night shifts, shared the day shifts, and prayed for additional help to arrive.

Those prayers were answered. Like the cavalry suggested by Dr. Filipovich, waves of family came to the rescue. Steve's wife, Elise, drove in the weekend after Joe and Donna left. Judith visited and came to know Sammy. Paul and Terri spent a weekend in Cleveland watching our boys allowing Grandma a break and then made a quick Trek to Cincinnati to see Sam. Suzanne's sisters, Catherine and Lavonne made a number of visits. Kathy phoned from her home in California with news that she would be arriving soon. The trip came at no small sacrifice for Kathy's family. Her husband David would stay home with their teenage twins as Kathy cashed in the family vacation fund to purchase an airline ticket.

In many ways, Kathy was the perfect choice to help care for Sam. Her years of experience as a registered nurse, including critical care, would provide the comfort for Suzanne and me to get away. Her intimate knowledge of Sam's condition, medications, and monitors would be helpful. The love and support she had shown our family further encouraged us. In another way, however, I worried about her making the commitment to care for Sam for an entire week, as Kathy was moderately disabled with a degenerative muscle disease. She could walk only with the aid of a walker. She could not lift heavy weights. Lifting Sam in such a swollen and weakened condition with wires and lines sticking out from all over his body was as difficult as carrying a forty-pound water balloon with one hand and balancing a tray of hot coffee mugs in the other. Yet Kathy was determined to help out. She insisted on taking care of Sam through the nights, allowing Suzanne and I some rest. We gratefully accepted her offer and looked forward to her arrival the next day.

In the midst of our despair, wonderful news from T5A found its way upstairs. Baby Zachary—the child abandoned at birth by his crack mom; the child born without an immune system; the child who had survived a bone-marrow transplant and six months in the hospital—was going home with his newly adoptive parents. Zach had been one of the long-term BMT patients on the floor when we arrived at Children's Hospital. Of that group (which included Allison and Elijah), Zach was the first to go home. Allison had died two months earlier. Elijah was now in critical condition a few doors down from Sammy. Good news was hard find in our world, and we rejoiced for Zachary and his new parents.

Kathy arrived and immediately convinced us that she was ready, willing, and able to care for Sammy. Suzanne hadn't been home for weeks and was grateful for the help. She quickly developed a trust in Kathy and soon headed for home to a couple of lonesome little boys. And Sammy was showing signs of improvement. Although the bleeding continued, the bright red blood slowed considerably, leaving only the old black blood flowing from his NG tube as well as into his diaper.

Sam bonded with Kathy instantly. Her disability failed to deter her from holding him. The nurses were happy to assist Sam into Kathy's lap. They spent hours cuddling, singing songs, and talking. Kathy did all the singing and talking, but Sam's eyes lit up with trust and love. Kathy chased me from the room during the night with a promise that she and Sammy would be just fine. She came to care for Sam and give us a break, and insisted on some private time with him. Sammy responded to her love, as did I. I slept for eight hours at Ronald McDonald House while Sammy dozed quietly for much of the night. I chuckled as Kathy later described her night: Sammy, slumbering peacefully, would occasionally open one eye a tiny crack, search the room to confirm that Kathy was still with him, then drift back to restful oblivion.

Kathy stayed for a week. She took all the night shifts, and fell in love with her special nephew. The cheerfulness she brought clearly affected Sammy's spirits as well as mine. Kathy never complained about her own disability as she cared for Sammy. She made the walks to Ronald McDonald House by herself with the aid of her walker. She took complete notes of the nighttime events, gave her stamp of approval or disapproval to each nurse, and taught me much about the medications Sammy was taking. One afternoon, several days into her visit, Kathy shared her feelings about Sam and the way he had touched her from afar, and why she had to get to know him.

"John, I don't know if you recognize how many people's lives Sammy has touched through his battle. Do you realize the countless times the e-mails have been forwarded and reforwarded around the country? People who haven't prayed in years have turned to prayer for Sam. Just look at our family. Sammy has brought our family closer than we've been in years," she said. "Sammy is teaching lessons of courage, love, and determination to a group of people who probably will never meet him. I had to come and get to know Sammy. He is a *very* special child."

"Yes, he is," I whispered while drying a lone tear from my cheek.

Kathy's visit ended too soon. She promised to return in August.

Meanwhile, Sam continued to hold on, but only just. The hemorrhaging inside him would moderate one day, then increase the next. Blood and platelet transfusions continued daily, often two units of each. Sam completed the course of ATG, and we waited for the big turnaround while not really expecting it.

Day after day went by with little change. The first two weeks of Sam's ICU stay passed with little reason for optimism. During that span, Sam received fifty-one blood and platelet transfusions.

Although Suzanne and I had each visited home during Kathy's visit, we found ourselves running toward emotional and physical exhaustion once again. Life in the ICU was more stressful for the patients and families than in the Hem/Onc unit. Sam's biological clock ran askew in the ICU. Lights were rarely turned off as medical staff buzzed around Sam and other patients around the clock. The doctors referred to a syndrome called "ICU psychosis," in which patients and, as I discovered, the parents, cease to differentiate nighttime from daytime. Sleep cycles become nonexistent.

Sam's pain medications were frequently increased or changed altogether in attempts to bring him comfort. Little success was achieved. Sam's misery level was at an all-time high as we struggled to console him. His medical issues mounted as the weeks went by. The docs were forced to install an additional line into his foot to monitor increasing hypertension and provide additional access for his uncountable meds.

The downward spiral remained unchecked.

I missed the support that other parents provided in Hem/ Onc. For some reason, the families did not come together in the ICU. Sam's nurse explained the difference: the average stay in the ICU was five days—as opposed to the weeks or months in Hem/Onc.

Occasional walks down to T5A brought me to the Carters' room, where I found the fellowship I needed. Steve and Tammy were becoming ever-closer friends. We shared much, compared our children's progress through HLH and transplant, and leaned on each other for emotional support. On one of those visits I found three bright smiles in the room. Zachary Carter, only thirty-three days post-transplant, was going home. (Since the Carters lived nearby, Zach was allowed to go home instead of a Ronald McDonald House room.) He was the second of the two Zacharys on T5A to escape the hospital. His bone-marrow transplant came from an unrelated donor, as did Sam's, but Zachary seemed to be recovering well. I kept my thoughts to myself as I remembered how well Sammy was doing one month after transplant. I shared in their joy, yet couldn't help being angry that Sammy couldn't be going home. Sammy had passed his hundred-day milestone weeks ago, yet faced countless more hospital days.

Any hope of taking Sam home was such a distant fantasy that we no longer contemplated it. Our only dream at the time was to see him moved back to Hem/Onc, to see his bleeding stop, and to see him reverse the downward spiral. Secretly I had begun to lose hope that I would ever see Sammy learn to walk, talk, or play. I never verbalized my fears, nor did I even consciously accept them, but they were there.

Suzanne and I had seen enough death in our time at Children's Hospital, enough to last a lifetime. But death always hovered nearby in the ICU. Elijah's parents stopped by Sammy's room for a visit late one afternoon. In the hospital two months longer than Sammy, Elijah had been making a fabulous recovery from his bone-marrow transplant. His extended family had been a fixture in Hem/Onc. They were with him every moment of his seven-month stay. Elijah became our touchstone of hope for Sammy's recovery. One month ago, they had been packed up and ready to leave the hospital; Elijah had beaten his disease and was going home. But the very day he was to be discharged, Elijah suffered a devastating brain seizure. He never recovered. His parents had come to say good-bye to us. They told us that Elijah was to be taken off life support at nine o'clock the next morning. They're precious child would be going home, but in a casket.

Suzanne and I barely moved after they left. I just stared into space as if in a trance and concentrated on the shivers running up my arms. There was little to say. That we could soon be feeling similar grief remained unspoken. Sam's possible death was forbidden conversation.

That night was especially long. My heart ached for Elijah and his family. I thought how sad it must be to know when your son was to die.

In the morning, I joined the vigil outside his room. These events were not uncommon in Hem/Onc or the ICU. I had seen somber groups like this gathered before. Oddly, imminent death was sometimes quietly scheduled to allow for good-byes. Family members had arrived from New Mexico to say farewell to Elijah. In addition, several local Native Americans joined the vigil to show support for the family. I introduced myself and was greeted warmly by the group. They welcomed me to wait with them for the end. The curtains were drawn across Elijah's room. The floor was silent but for a few mumbled prayers in a strange language. At ten minutes past nine o'clock a nurse slipped out of the room and whispered that he was gone. Elijah was dead. Tears and fears welled within me. I couldn't stay any longer. I hurried to Sammy's room and held him for a long while.

Next-door to Sam lay a two-year-old child who had climbed over a fence and jumped into the family swimming pool. Jason was comatose. A ventilator machine breathed for him. Rushed to the hospital five days earlier, he showed no signs of life. His parent's eyes showed incredible sorrow. Tests over the next few days suggested that Jason's brain was dead. In the parent's lounge, his dad talked to me of the bargain he'd made with God.

"If Jason recovers, I promised God I would quit smoking." Hope was lost for him when an MRI revealed no brain activity. Death was again on the ICU schedule. A parade of aunts, uncles, and grandparents came in to hold him one last time. Suzanne and I became caught up in the drama as we prayed for Jason to be spared. His beautiful face eerily resembled our Zachary, and I couldn't help but think how awful such a trauma must be for the parents. Their pain and suffering was unbearable to watch; yet we forced ourselves to comfort them. But there was no comfort. Jason's dad lay in bed next to him all through his last night. In the morning, the machines were shut off and Jason quickly died. I made certain to be away this time. After Elijah's death, I could not face another.

"No more!" I said to Suzanne later that day. "I am not getting involved with other families in here. I really needed the support for awhile, but all I see any more is death." Until Jason, Suzanne had steered clear of other families in the ICU.

In her chair in Sammy's room Suzanne put her face into her hands. From her eyes, red with weariness, tears flowed.

"I don't know how you do it. I just can't look around anymore. This is a horrible place." Her sobs escaped in bunches before more words came out. "We have to get Sammy out of here!" she wailed.

Suzanne and I again faced exhaustion as well as an over-whelming longing to spend time with Jake and Zach. Sammy continued to get round-the-clock care from one of us. Our limits were fast approaching, however. Each day, unfortunately, was followed by nighttime, which passed slowly, like a Cleveland winter.

Still, our relationship with the ICU staff had improved somewhat as they learned of Sammy's spirit and thus developed a grudging respect for his determination and will to live. Our respect for the staff's skills grew as well. The intensive care fellows (fellows were doctors who had completed their residency and were specializing in intensive care medicine) knew Sammy best, and we relied on them for consistency. The attending physicians rotated every five to seven days. The residents switched each month. The fellows were on a three-year training program and seemed to be on duty every day—bad for them, good for us. Dr. Khalid, an Arab, was not a great communicator; therefore it took awhile for us to learn to respect his medical skills. After two weeks in the ICU, it became apparent that Dr. Khalid was very capable and nearly always around. When trouble with Sam arose, Dr. Khalid was there to handle the issues.

The nurses seemed more standoffish in the ICU than in Hem/Onc. Nurses usually had one patient, two at the most on any shift. If not in the room, they sat at a desk outside the room with a view of all the monitors. Snarls could occasionally be heard from the ICU nurses when Sam's T5A nurses stopped by. Melinda and Niki visited nearly every day, Sarah several times a week. Unable to control themselves, the T5A nurses would examine Sam's pumps and lines, check out his med

schedule, and generally piss off the ICU nurse. Since entertainment was rare in the ICU, I looked forward to the inevitable
hissing of the ICU nurse as she came into the room to defend
her turf. In general, we found the ICU nursing to be very
competent, yet significantly less personal than the Hem/Onc
nursing. Of course, the nurses had every reason to be standoffish. Many of their patients died. They would be grieving all
the time if they became personally involved with the kids. ICU
nurses have a tough job. Not many can do it. Those who can
are indeed special.

Photographs from Chapter 23 can be viewed at:
SamuelsMission.com

CHAPTER 24

Home Again

Twenty-five days after entering the ICU, Sam was transferred back to Hem/Onc, his longtime home on T5A. What a strange experience to be delighted to have your child in a cancer unit! But we had escaped the ICU and its attendant aura of death. The critical care staff never expected to see Sam leave the ICU alive.

He fooled them.

Sam's medical issues were many, and his condition complicated, but he was stable. He had received eighty-one blood transfusions in the ICU. Sam's bleeding continued, although at reduced levels. He hadn't eaten in months, yet his weight continued to climb. His steroid doses were at an all-time high, the maximum dosage he could safely receive. Fluid management became the next critical issue. The dozens of IV medications and blood products he received daily were delivered with substantial volume of fluid. Sam's body had a hard time regulating the fluid. The treatment was, of course, more drugs. Regular doses of diuretics were added to his busy medication schedule. In addition, Sam's blood pressure remained at dangerously high levels. Risk of fatal infection remained our biggest fear, however. Sam's immune system was totally suppressed by the steroids and the ATG. Those medications were used with great risk and could easily be lethal with no other issues present. Still, the GVHD would certainly have killed him if unchecked.

Once back on T5A, we again began working toward a transfer to Rainbow Babies & Children's Hospital in Cleveland. Dr. Filipovich backed our desires and promised to make it happen as long as Sammy cooperated.

Suzanne contacted our insurance company to ensure coverage would continue. To this point, they had paid everything. We had not received a single bill from Children's Hospital. Suzanne learned that transfer by air ambulance would be covered for one trip only. Should Sam need to return to Children's Hospital, we would have to cover the cost. She also learned that Sam's lifetime maximum was nearly used up on my policy, meaning his bills had totaled close to one million dollars. Fortunately, Suzanne's insurance would immediately take over and provide an additional million dollars in coverage. But since Sam was only fifteen months old, and he faced many weeks or months of further hospitalization, we became concerned that another million dollars would not be enough.

Dr. Filipovich, along with her staff, began meeting with us more formally in scheduled care conferences. The meetings were designed to facilitate Sam's transfer to Cleveland. Julia Griffin, the BMT nurse practitioner, had begun passing Sam's medical records to her counterpart at Rainbow. Dr. Filipovich had also opened a dialogue with Dr. Nieder, Sam's primary physician at Rainbow.

Dr. Sam Vogelbaum was beginning his month on BMT service when Sammy moved back to T5A. Doc Sam, as we came to know him, emerged as the best resident we had yet encountered. He came to know little Sammy intimately, and he spent a great deal of time with him. He was then dealt the responsibility of drafting the transfer summary for the docs at Rainbow. Doc Sam got to know not only Sammy's medical issues, but also Sammy's personality and spirit. In addition to sharing Sam's name, Dr. Vogelbaum had a son named Jacob and planned to name his next son Zachary. Yeah, Doc Sam was special, and he would prove it in the coming weeks.

Far off in the distance, we began to see hope shining once again. The light was dim, but growing in intensity. I had a dream one night in which Sammy was two years old and walking around our house laughing and playing with Jacob. For weeks, I had not been able to picture Sammy getting better. Now the dream seemed possible. Sam's condition remained tenuous, his issues complex, yet he showed signs of getting better.

Physical therapists worked with Sammy each day, often resulting in only tiny movements like reaching for a toy or leaning over to watch a ball. Any effort to play was greeted with applause and joy. Each day we would attempt to sit Sam up only to find that he couldn't. Sam would arch his back and fight to lie back down. The pain in his belly must have been incredible. He had been hemorrhaging for six weeks. Yet one day Sam sat up—and stayed that way. Suzanne excitedly phoned me at home after it happened. Her voice bubbled with elation as she related the story of Sammy's return to laughter and playfulness. Suzanne sat him in a chair by the window, and he began looking around, waving to the staff and laughing.

"Not little titters," Suzanne said, "big belly laughs. It was unbelievable how happy he was. Sam had the attention of the whole unit. Work simply stopped as people came to see him playing. He laughed and played for an hour." I was beaming as I pictured the scene. When he was done playing, Sammy slept the rest of the day.

Sammy continued to bleed from the gut off and on. He usually received one unit of red cells and one unit of platelets daily. The docs, generally happy with Sam's progress, treated him with yet another course of rabbit ATG as well as the steroids.

Proof that he was doing well came with the news that we had a transfer date. Sam was going back to Cleveland. We were going home. The Rainbow staff was ready to take him, and Dr. Filipovich was comfortable sending him. Suzanne and I wondered if we were making the right decision. We took our concerns to Reverend Sue and Reverend Ron. Were we doing what was best for Sammy? Or were we doing what was best for ourselves? The answer was, of course, in prayer and trust that God would guide us. Both gently chastised us and reminded us that our concerns were with our entire family. Neither could tell us what to do, and neither would accept that we were acting in selfishness. We made the plan a go.

Just as our excitement was building, Sam's condition suddenly worsened. I was working on my last solo weekend shift when his bleeding suddenly increased. He filled diaper after diaper with a mixture of black blood, bright red blood, and thick gooey blood clots. I was grateful Doc Sam was on duty at the time.

In addition to the bleeding, little Sammy had a rising fever as well as raging thirst unquenchable by the tiny amounts of fluid he was allowed. With the active intestinal bleeding, the last thing the docs wanted was to put fluid into his GI tract. He suffered through the day. Doc Sam stayed at his side nearly every moment.

"John, I have to warn you. We may need to move him to the unit soon," Doc Sam advised late in the afternoon. "I'm going to call upstairs for a consult." As soon as one unit of blood was infused into Sammy, Doc Sam would order another as the hemorrhaging continued. I phoned Suzanne with the bad news. Our conversation centered on Sam's condition, but we were both thinking of the lost dream of taking Sammy back to Cleveland. Dr. Khalid came down from the ICU to assess Sammy in preparation for transfer. He checked his vital signs, studied his chart, and met with Doc Sam alongside the nurse's station.

"We've decided to wait it out a bit longer," Doc Sam said as he reentered the isolation room. "We'll keep him here a few more hours and see what develops."

I was relieved. Day turned slowly to night as my vigil at Sammy's side continued. I prayed in the spare moments between my feeble attempts to comfort him. Of his issues, thirst seemed to be the most agitating. Sammy was, as usual, only allowed an occasional Pedialyte Popsicle through a bottle. The Popsicle contained just three ounces of fluid, which melted slowly in the bottle and metered tiny amounts of liquid. Sam sucked frantically from the bottle, vainly trying to soothe his parched throat. Despite my prayers and Doc Sam's attention, Sammy's condition worsened. His fever increased.

"We're getting close," Doc Sam said to me around midnight, meaning close to the time to send Sammy to the ICU. I could see our dreams of going home slowly fading into the darkness. Dr. Khalid reassessed Sammy in the middle of the night.

"As long as his blood pressure remains up, we can keep him here [on T5A]," Dr. Khalid said after examining Sammy again.

"Hang in there, Sammy. Keep fighting," I encouraged. "You can do it, my precious son." And Sammy did fight. My eyes rarely left the monitors, even though the machine only checked his blood pressure periodically.

"This is one tough kid," Doc Sam whispered, as we stood at Sammy's side in the quiet hours before dawn.

"He is amazing," I answered. "And he has been through so much."

"Yeah, I know. I wrote up Sammy's transfer summary when I came on rotation. I pretty much know everything he's been through. Not many kids would have survived."

Dawn arrived. Sammy continued fighting. His fever

dropped. The hemorrhaging slowed. His blood pressure remained stable. We didn't go to the ICU that day. Sammy's rally allowed him to remain on T5A, to my immense relief. Doc Sam came in about noon Sunday to let me know he was leaving. He gave Sammy a pat on the head and smiled at him.

My voice broke as I said good-bye. "Thanks so much Doc. You were awesome with him. I . . . I just really appreciate it."

"No problem, just doing my job. Sammy, keep up the good work. I'll see you tomorrow."

Just doing his job . . . about as good as anyone can do a job. I wonder what time he was really supposed to have gone home. Sammy started a long siesta about the time Doc Sam left. I realized I had been standing at his side for most of the past thirty hours. The sleep chair actually looked inviting.

The crisis abated over a few days. Sammy stabilized. Our transfer plans remained. Knowing that soon we could count on seeing each of our sons every day brought such relief. Sam's suffering was obvious; Jacob's and Zachary's were more subtle.

"Jacob doesn't even come to me any more when he needs comfort," Suzanne cried on her return. Sammy was mercifully asleep when she arrived back from home. "When his diaper is wet, or he's hungry, or tired, he goes right to Grandma. He doesn't want me! He wants Grandma."

We sat on the bench seat by Sammy's outside window. Suzanne buried her face in my chest. I put my arms around her and she cried. "Zachary's the exact opposite. He didn't let me out of his sight when I was home. I couldn't even go into the bathroom without him following me. He won't sleep in his bed anymore. He slept with me every night I was home, and he sleeps with Grandma when we're gone."

"Thank God we're going home this week. Our boys need us bad," I answered feebly.

"I feel like I don't even know Jacob any more," Suzanne sobbed. "He's changing so fast, and we're missing so much. We're missing things that we'll never get back."

"I know." I had nothing else to say. I knew of no words I could use to comfort Suzanne. Hell, I couldn't even comfort myself. This was one of those moments that I felt totally helpless. The feeling of powerlessness overwhelmed me.

"When I left the house, Zachary cried so hard and begged me to stay with him. He wouldn't let me go. He grabbed my neck, and I had to pry him off me to get out the door. My heart just broke and then he screamed at me, 'Mommy! Don't leave me! Mommy, Mommy! Don't go.' I called him three times on the drive down here to tell him I loved him."

"Was he okay when you called him?" I asked.

"He was better. Grandma got him outside on the swing set and promised him she would fill up the baby pool. Jacob was just as happy as he could be when I left. Grandma had *Barney* on the TV. He never shed a tear."

Suzanne and I feared the abandonment issues our boys must have felt. Each of our children needed us—and we them. The transfer was the right thing to do. Sam was ready. We hoped a change in scenery would enliven his spirits. Jake and Zach would delight in having at least one parent home every night. We could begin rebuilding the trust Jacob and Zachary had lost.

I thought, too, about rebuilding intimacy with my wife. In fact, I obsessed about it. Our family ordeal magnified the difference in the way men and women approach stress or in this case crisis. I, frankly, was craving sex. To me, sexual activity was completely unrelated to Sam's disease, and I saw no reason that I shouldn't get laid every once in awhile. To Suzanne, asking her for intimacy would be akin to asking her to sprout wings and fly. Sex was the furthest thing from her mind, and she me let know it when I hinted about sneaking off to Ronald McDonald House for a "nooner" during one of Sam's naps.

"How can you even think about that when Sammy is so sick?" she scolded again.

I didn't tell her I thought one issue was unrelated to the other. After being married for nearly seven years, I realized I had yet much to learn about women. But how could she not understand men? I mean, we're so simple to please. Just feed us, give a little lovin', a big-screen TV with a nearby refrigerator, and that's it, we're completely satisfied. But Suzanne still mystified me regularly. I once tried reading the *Men are from Mars, Women are from Venus* book. I didn't really get it. The writer made men way too complicated and totally oversimplified women.

Our final week at Children's Hospital neared the end. Only forty-eight hours remained before Sam's transfer back to Cleveland and Rainbow Babies & Children's Hospital. We finally believed it was really going to happen. Sam was doing well, the docs were satisfied that he was ready, and our excitement was building. A more normal life awaited our family. With the exception of Sam being released from the hospital altogether, this was the best news we could hope for.

We spent much of the day planning a good-bye celebration. So many people in this hospital had loved and cared not only for Sammy but also for Suzanne and me. Leaving our hospital family would be difficult, and we had many people to thank and bid farewell. Suzanne shopped for gifts for Sam's primary nurses, who had become so dear. She also purchased delicious pastries to share with all the staff on our final day. I loaded the video camera to record all the good-byes from well-wishers who were already arriving.

Sam's transfer was big news on Hem/Onc. He had beaten away death several times. His remarkable will to live and enormous spirit were becoming legendary. Although Sam faced yet more hospital time, this was a giant step forward, and a time for rejoicing. The transport team visited Sam and explained the procedure and the schedule for the big event. Sam would be moved by ambulance to a nearby airport where he would be loaded onto the air ambulance, a jet specifically used to transport critically ill patients.

"The air ambulance is a mini-ICU. We have nearly every piece of equipment aboard that the ICU has," the transport nurse explained. One of the BMT doctors would accompany Sam all the way to his hospital bed in Rainbow. Several of Sam's primary nurses were clamoring to go on the trip, but the transport team denied the requests. Suzanne, using the power of motherhood, won our discussion over who would fly with Sam. I would be content to make the final drive home from Cincinnati alone. The transport team expected the trip would take two hours from hospital bed to hospital bed.

That Sam was doing "well" was relative. His condition was improved compared to several weeks earlier in the ICU. No longer was his gut bleeding but, although there were positive signs of healing throughout his digestive tract, he remained on intravenous nutrition. Sam also continued to require red cells and platelets. To date, Sam had received 175 blood transfusions in Children's Hospital. Medicine had grossly disfigured his body. His back, arms, and forehead were covered with hair, an effect of his daily cyclosporine medicine. I still called him "little Elvis" occasionally due to his jet-black sideburns. Sam also remained massively obese from the continued steroids. His weight put a great deal of stress on his cardiopulmonary status. Sam could breathe but required oxygen support. His movement was extremely limited by his swollen body. He could not sit up. He reached out for toys only rarely and would no longer kick his legs or put any pressure on them. The occupational and physical therapists worked with Sam each day, but he had little energy for play or a workout. Sam was doing well in our minds, but had to be in constant misery. Smiles were hard to come by since the last time he sat by the window and laughed and played with his mommy.

I tried to imagine his pain, but had no experience to judge it. His guts were raw and his legs were fractured. Steroids had swelled his body and shrunk his brain. Sam's entire world was a tiny room where he was tortured daily with toxic medicines. He suffered the loss of his twin and the big brother who so adored him. As parents, Suzanne and I had precious few tools to use for comforting our child. Feeding him had been taken away long ago. A walk in the stroller was unthinkable. A drive in the car was only a distant dream. Holding, singing, and talking to Sam were the only comforts we could provide. Those and just being with him twenty-four hours a day were all we had left to give.

Excitement building, I settled in for my last evening on T5A. I knew that many hospital nights were yet in front of me, but never again four or five consecutively. The light mood didn't last long, though, as the night turned hellish.

Among the difficulties that parents of a critically ill child go through, nighttime on a Hem/Onc unit must be the worst. Sammy slept little. I was up numerous times to hold and comfort him. Only in my arms would he sleep. When I put him down, he fussed and moaned. When sleep finally came near morning, he moaned continuously. *How much pain must this child be in to moan in his sleep?* I wondered. I lay awake those early morning hours and prayed to God to reveal His plan for Sammy. "If he is to suffer so," I asked God, "then please make his life after recovery be so wonderful as to make it all worthwhile."

In the months that followed, I often wished I could relive

that one night. Given a second chance, I would have held Sam in my arms and comforted him all night long. Suzanne relieved me at five a.m., and I went to Ronald McDonald House to get a few hours of rest. A big day was ahead, our last at Children's Hospital!

CHAPTER 25

Shattered Dreams

The telephone awoke me hours later. The tone in Suzanne's voice as well as her frightening words alerted me that something was very wrong.

"John, get over here right away. Sammy's in trouble." As adrenaline rushed into my bloodstream, I listened for the frightening details to follow. "He's in renal failure, and the docs think he is septic. His blood pressure crashed, and they're sending him to the ICU." Suzanne spoke slowly but with a trembling voice.

Simply stated, Sam was going away. His kidneys had shut down, and he had the long-feared infection.

"Five minutes," was all I said as I slammed the phone down and raced to the hospital. I made it in three, quick enough to find Sam on his way upstairs to intensive care. Suzanne was calm, yet very frightened.

"They're going to have to intubate him," she told me immediately. I had been around hospitals enough to know what intubation meant—life support. Sam could no longer breathe and needed to be put on a ventilator machine.

"What happened?" I asked as we walked alongside Sammy's bed as it was wheeled into the elevator and sent up one floor to the ICU. The elevator was packed with staff assisting with the transfer.

"I tried to hold off calling you as long as possible, but he kept getting sicker and sicker," she explained. "He quit peeing earlier and just before I called you, his blood pressure crashed. It got down to 60/30. They gave him epinephrine and dopamine, which are adrenaline drugs. His pressure is more stable now."

I wasn't sure how scared to be until I realized this was the strong and powerful Suzanne speaking to me. This was "Suzanne with the Plan," taking care of business.

"What are they saying about his kidneys?" I asked.

"They just shut down," she said. "He has a catheter in his bladder now so they can see exactly how much he is peeing, but nothing has come out for a long time. The docs don't know for sure, but they think he has a blood infection," she said. "That's what sepsis is, right?" she asked.

"I think so."

"The ICU doc came down to assess him after Dr. Sam called. Since his kidneys shut down, they're going to have to put in more IV lines and start him on dialysis. I already signed the consent form to do all that and to intubate him," she said as we arrived in the ICU. Sam was wheeled right into a room. Doctors and staff swarmed around him.

"You'll have to leave while we do the procedures," one the ICU docs said while he led us out of the room. "Wait in the family lounge out by the elevator. I promise to come and get you the moment your son is stabilized. It should be about forty minutes."

The doc closed the door and curtains to Sammy's room. I counted five doctors and five nurses surrounding Sam as we were escorted to the waiting room. The forty minutes turned into ninety, but seemed like a thousand. Suzanne and I sat in vinyl-covered chairs, alone in the lounge with vending machines, a TV, and a laundry room. The jumbled mass of thoughts, emotions, questions, and fears during that wait is impossible to describe. Was this the end? Would we even see Sammy alive again? Suzanne and I held hands and prayed. Her tears came now. Without faith, I do not know how one could survive crisis after crisis, especially this one. The prayers were simple.

"God, please save Sammy, please watch over him."

Later I quietly added this prayer: *God, if Your plan is to take Sammy, please let him suffer no longer.* Neither Suzanne nor I had ever openly spoken those words before, and I didn't say them aloud this time. We each later admitted a fear of being the first to say them. Neither of us wanted to sound like we were giving up.

Between her tears, Suzanne explained the events of the morning.

"None of the staff seemed too concerned until Dr. Sam came in this morning after rounds. He looked at Sam's fluid ins and outs on the chart and promptly called the ICU. Doc Sam ordered a super-stat blood test to find out what was going on. Sammy was breathing really hard, you know, really grunting. The blood gases were back right away and showed he was oxygen deprived. That's when I called you. Dr. Khalid was down here by that time, and he ordered Sam transferred upstairs immediately. Before you got here, John, Dr. Khalid asked me if I wanted them to proceed with intubating him."

"I don't understand," I responded. "Was he asking you if we should let him die?"

"I guess," she answered. "He said he had to ask. Some parents decide that their child has suffered enough at this point." She looked at me. "Do you think I did I right thing?"

"Definitely," I said after a long pause while I absorbed the idea that maybe the staff had lost hope. "I think we owe it to Sammy to give him every chance. These doctors have given up on him before. I think Sammy will decide if it's time to go."

"That's what I thought too," Suzanne agreed.

I sat stoically through the interminable wait, praying some, worrying a lot. Suzanne wept as she prayed. I thought how cruel a blow it was to be within hours of leaving this place, only to maybe lose Sammy. Suzanne had a different outlook.

"I'm so glad this happened here. If this had happened on the airplane or in Cleveland, I would never forgive myself for transferring him," she said. "Maybe Sammy wasn't ready to leave this hospital and this was his way of telling us." Suzanne, as usual, had a different and more introspective spin on the crisis than mine.

Dr. Khalid finally arrived with news of Sammy's condition.

"Okay, we're done," he said. "Sam is on the ventilator. We put lines in his thigh for dialysis, and we put an arterial line in his foot," he said. Our questions came rapid-fire.

"Is he stable?"

"No, his condition is extremely critical," Dr. Khalid answered. "He crashed as soon as we got him in the room. His pressure dropped to nearly zero. He is on high doses of blood pressure support medicines, epinephrine, and dopamine. We also gave him fluids. His pressure is holding, but he is not stable."

"Is he on the dialysis machine now?" Suzanne asked.

"No, we're consulting with nephrology—the kidney doctors. They will be down to see him shortly."

"Is he going to make it?" I asked.

"I don't know. The next few hours will be critical."

"Can we see him now?" Suzanne asked.

"You can see him, but he is sedated. We gave him drugs to paralyze him while we put the tube in. He will be out for an hour or so."

My own breathing became ragged as I looked at Sammy moments later. He was alive, and for that we were grateful. But seeing him on the ventilator was the most difficult experience of my life. He was totally dependent on a machine to sustain his life.

The ventilator—with its numerous dials, lights, hoses, displays, monitors, and alarms—looked and sounded like a spacecraft control panel. Sam had a thick tube inserted down his nose into his airway. This tube was in addition to the tube in his other nostril that continued to pump his stomach contents. The intubation tube was connected to two larger hoses. One hose supplied oxygen under pressure that expanded his lungs at a breathing rate determined by the docs. The other hose removed his exhaled carbon dioxide. The ventilator also had a suction line attached that would periodically be inserted into Sam's airway to suction mucous from his lungs. The whole contraption was attached to his face with wide strips of medical tape.

The suffering Sam had endured to this point in his battle for life was tremendous. It was about to get worse. Of greater concern at that moment, however, was his renal failure, which had not yet been addressed by the docs. Suzanne and I had understood that he would be put on the dialysis machine immediately. We were confused by the delay and asked the ICU docs for information.

"The nephrologist is reviewing his chart now. He will be in to examine Sam in a moment and then we will talk," Dr. Khalid explained.

"What is this machine?" I asked pointing to another machine with hoses and dials that was making a steady humming noise.

"That's a warming blanket," Dr. Khalid responded. "Sam's temperature dropped to 95 degrees when his pressure crashed. We're still trying to get it back up."

Dr. Khalid and the other docs left us alone with Sam's nurse and respiratory therapist. Out the window we could see a group of six or eight of Sam's doctors deep in conference.

The nephrologist seemed in no hurry to begin dialysis on Sam when he did arrive. Suzanne and I continued to question both him and the ICU docs about getting the dialysis started. Finally, the nephrologist came out and asked us directly if we really wanted them to do the dialysis.

"What do you mean?" I asked. "He needs it, doesn't he?" One of the ICU doctors explained it in words we never wanted to hear.

"When kids get this sick—when they have what we call multi organ failure—it is nearly impossible to bring them back. Sam's kidneys have shut down, and he is in respiratory failure. We may be at the end of what we can do for him."

He paused while we tried to absorb what he was saying.

"We can start him on dialysis if that is your desire."

Suzanne and I looked at each other and assimilated an agreement. She was holding the catheter tube, almost willing Sam to start peeing on his own as I responded with our wishes.

"We both think we owe it to Sam to give him every chance. Start the dialysis. Sam is tough. He might surprise you guys again."

As I finished speaking, Suzanne quietly made an announcement.

"He is starting to pee. Look!"

And there was—not much—but definitely urine in the catheter tube. Sam's kidneys had restarted. The docs decided to wait before starting dialysis.

"Perhaps Sam is coming back on his own," Dr. Khalid said.

Within in hour, Sam was peeing steadily. His temperature returned to normal. Sam was indeed coming back—again. The docs had given up on him—again. But Sam was not ready to leave us.

We sat at Sam's side for many hours that evening, watching him, holding his hand, and talking quietly. The nurse and respiratory therapist bustled around Sam constantly, but we found space to be close to him. Sam opened his eyes for only seconds at a time that night, long enough to be certain we were with him before he lapsed into sleep or sedated restfulness.

"He is so quiet. Can he cry with the tube in?" I asked the nurse.

"No. The intubation tube is passed through his vocal cords. He won't be able to make any sound except little gagging noises."

Earlier, we had asked if we could hold Sam.

"It's impossible while he's on the ventilator," she explained. The pain of watching Sam lay so helplessly was excruciating. There was little we could do to comfort our precious little boy. The familiar feeling of powerlessness again overwhelmed me. Sam's suffering had to be incredible, yet we could do nothing to help him. The docs promised to keep him as comfortable as possible.

Even though Sam's kidneys were again functioning, the staff gave us little hope for recovery. The evening shift nurse made an offhand comment that further eroded our hopes. "Sam is about as sick as a kid can get," she said.

Her comment was the last thing Suzanne needed to hear that night. "The ICU is already driving me crazy. They all just assume Sammy is going to die."

But Sam did not die that night. In fact, he rallied—another legendary Sammy comeback. The docs shook their heads in wonder that night as Sam fooled them again. We later learned from a nurse that in private conference, the docs discussed Sam's amazing resilience.

Sammy awoke on his second day in the ICU to find himself in a nightmarish predicament. He fought with his bonds as he attempted to claw the ventilator tube from his face. His arms, restrained to the bed, would not move. Sammy attempted to cry out only to choke on the tube in his throat. Sam could not move; he could not tell of his pain; he could not talk; and he could not cry.

But his eyes told all. His eyes were his only means of communication. They told a story of immense misery. He looked at me as if to say, "Daddy, why are you doing this to me? Why can't you help me?" My heart broke as I gazed into those frightened eyes.

Sammy grasped my finger with his swollen hand for only a second before he returned to his frantic fight to remove the equipment from his face. *Is it time to let him go?* I asked myself. The question had no easy answer. I did not feel comfortable even discussing the subject with Suzanne. *Besides,* I reminded myself, *hadn't Sammy showed us before that he can come back from the bleakest of situations?*

By the third day in PICU, the docs seemed to be giving Sammy a chance. Dr. Filipovich led the charge, as she ordered multiple tests to clarify Sam's cardiac, as well as GVHD, status. A CT scan of Sam's belly showed he was healing. An echocardiogram showed Sam's heart was strong and normal. His bleeding was reduced as well. He required no red cells this day, only one transfusion of platelets. Suzanne and I grasped the straws of good news and began to rebuild hope. With the arrival of each lab report, Suzanne and I scanned the data, searching for good news hiding in the numbers. The details became more important than the obvious. One look at Sam would tell far more than any lab report could, but then we were looking for hope, not despair.

Sam's first week on the ventilator was the darkest period yet, full of suffering. His condition changed day by day, often hour by hour, while on the vent.

Complications continued to mount. Sam's blood sugar skyrocketed, and his white count plummeted. The docs were forced to start Sammy on an insulin drip to control his sugar and gave him drugs to support white cell production. Sam battled all weekend just to stay alive. Fluid management, such a critical issue only a day before, became out of control as each new medication delivered more and more fluids into Sam's bloodstream. He swelled up even greater than before; his belly expanded bigger and bigger, stretching his skin ever tighter.

While Sammy received adrenaline from doctors, mine was produced naturally. I lived each moment of that period on pure adrenaline—not knowing if Sammy would survive another day, afraid to sleep for fear of missing his last breath. I remember staring trancelike at the monitors—and jumping out of my skin when the alarms sounded. Time slowly marched on. Sammy clung to life by the tiniest of threads. And fear enveloped my heart.

Photographs from Chapter 25 can be viewed at:
SamuelsMission.com

CHAPTER 26

Heart of a Lion

Ravaged by disease, weak and frail, Samuel fought back. Unbelievable courage, determination, toughness, and grit—I don't know where he found these qualities, but Sammy was not ready to let go. He rallied once again. Each comeback left Sam in worse shape than before, yet he hung in there.

"Sam could be like this a long time," Dr. Filipovich warned. Her unspoken intent was to encourage us to back off on our twenty-four-hour bedside watch. She knew how badly we wanted to be closer to home, how greatly we missed Zachary and Jacob, how much they missed us.

Dr. Filipovich's words came through clearly. Along with Sam's crisis and the cancellation of his transfer came the huge disappointment of not being with our other boys. Zachary and Jacob needed us nearly as much as Sam did. They had lived six months without consistent parenting. Suzanne and I reached a difficult decision. One of us had to try to be home with our other sons despite Sammy's tenuous condition. This decision was not reached without some heartache, for it meant that Sam's caregiver would have to leave his bedside at night to get sleep. To this point, we had not left him alone for a single night of his hospital stay. With tears on her cheeks, Suzanne hugged Sam good-bye and left me alone with him as she went to our sons at home. Late that night, Suzanne sat down and updated the Sam network and implored all to pray hard for Sammy's recovery.

Sam's condition bounced from one critical issue to the next over the next few days. X-rays showed his lungs were diseased and fluid-filled. Internal bleeding started anew as Sam once again filled diaper after diaper with blood. His pressure continued to fluctuate from high to very low, as did his blood sugar. The BMT docs treated him with more ATG to fight the GVHD. The ICU docs were kept busy with numerous episodes of sudden blood pressure crashes, which by this time were being treated like a routine procedure. Suzanne and I became immune to the dangers of Sam's crashes. Often mesmerized by his monitor, we watched as each episode unfolded by the data flashing on the screen. The blood pressure alarm sounded so often that it no longer made us jump up to look. Usually the nurse would come in and adjust his epinephrine and dopamine levels, watch him respond, and then return to her paperwork.

Just when it seemed like Suzanne and I had reached our emotional limit, rescue came. My sister, as promised, returned for a second stint of Sam duty at the time that we most needed her. Kathy, known to be a willful person, expressed her desire to have Sammy to herself for a few days. She encouraged Suzanne and me to go home together, to be a family for a short while, to sleep in our own bed—together. We did just that. Our trust in Kathy was complete. Sam loved her as much as she loved him. Jacob and Zachary screamed with delight when they saw us together at home for the first time in half a year.

The boys never let us out of their sight as we embarked on a mini vacation. We swam, took a day trip to Sea World, and then another to a kiddie amusement park. Every minute of the day was spent with our boys. The never-ending smiles on their faces attested to their joy in being with Mom and Dad at the same time.

At night, Suzanne and I slept together in our own bed. Intimacy was difficult, however. Every time I thought I had a chance to score, I found a grinning little three-year-old on the bed between Suzanne and me. Zachary had faced plenty of abandonment issues in his short life, and neither of us had the heart to chase him out of our bed those few nights.

Back at the hospital, Sammy struggled. He made no improvement. Kathy settled into a routine in which she would sit with him until one or two o'clock in the morning, then catch forty winks at Ronald McDonald house.

The glow of happiness never left the faces of Jacob and Zachary until the time came for me to make my exit and once again head south. The pleas for me to stay just a little longer cut like a knife into my heart. I wanted to stay—yet I wanted to go.

"I'm going to stay with you both for a few more days, then Daddy will come home again," Suzanne told the boys. Although the family time together was a great break in the constant tension of the hospital, I was anxious to return. I needed to be with Sammy.

I arrived an hour before Kathy's departure. It was the most emotional time I've ever spent with my sister. Kathy had come to Cincinnati with a mission in mind. She encouraged me to ask direct questions to Dr. Filipovich regarding Sam's prognosis. Kathy understood our tendency to become so involved in the micromanagement of Sam's care that we lost sight of, or perhaps refused to see, the big picture.

Dr. Filipovich happened by Sam's room immediately after Kathy delivered her advice. Dr. Filipovich gave me the update on Sam's condition, reviewed his latest lab results with me, and informed me of his care plan for the next twenty-four hours. I then asked the direct question Suzanne and I had avoided.

"Have you seen other kids recover who have been this sick? Can Sam get better?"

Dr. Filipovich paused a long moment before answering.

"John, it's a real long shot right now," she finally said. "He is very, very sick. It's not impossible, but the odds are not in his favor."

I will never forget those words.

Dr. Filipovich had always expressed optimism for Sam's recovery, even in the worst moments. Her bleak outlook on this day affected me greatly. In times of crisis, Suzanne and I had feared losing Sam. However, he had always fought back from the brink of death. He had shown he wasn't ready to die so many times that somehow we made ourselves believe he was going to make it. The emotional ups and downs of Sam's physical ups and downs had been draining; keeping a positive outlook was absolutely necessary for our emotional stability. So this declaration by Dr. Filipovich was a devastating blow to my optimism.

It was also the reality check I needed at the time to begin preparing for the worst.

Kathy then took my hand and softly explained her mission. "John, it has been obvious to me from your e-mails and phone calls that Sammy is on a steady downward spiral. I came to visit this time not only to take care of Sammy and give you and Suzanne a break, but I came to encourage Dr. Filipovich and the ICU doctors to be very frank with you. I felt it hadn't been made clear to you the graveness of Sammy's condition. Once I arrived, I quickly realized how far Sammy has gone down. I think both you and Suzanne need to begin to prepare yourselves for the fact that Sammy could die."

Kathy delivered her comments in a most loving and gentle way, but the words were difficult to swallow.

"Wow," was all I could say for a moment. "I guess you accomplished your mission about five minutes after I arrived. I knew Sam was in a tough spot, but Dr. Filipovich really laid it on the line."

"When I was here in June," Kathy said, "Sammy was very alert, loved to be rocked and cuddled, and he had a light in his eyes. When I look at him now, he is not there. He doesn't focus on activity. He doesn't react to stimulation. The Sammy I knew in June is gone. I'm afraid he has quit fighting."

I nodded slowly as Kathy spoke, not wanting to hear those words, yet knowing they were true.

"Sammy won my heart the first day I spent with him two months ago," she said. "He is a very precious child, and it is so difficult for me to talk to you like this. I just want you and Suzanne to be prepared for some difficult decisions that may lie ahead."

For the first time in my life, I told Kathy I loved her. The words she spoke to me that morning were not pleasant; however, I needed to hear them. The old cliché about not seeing the forest for the trees certainly applied. When I finally sat down with Sam, he gave little response to my presence.

"Sammy, Daddy's here. I love you, Sam. I missed you so much, Sammy. Sammy, can you hear me?" I cooed. No response. Sam's face was so swollen I wondered if he could even open his eye if he wanted.

I held back from phoning Suzanne with the news until Kathy was gone.

Suzanne dropped what she was doing and hurried back to Cincinnati after I phoned. As much as I wanted her to stay home with the other boys for another day, she was determined to be with Sam. Later that evening, we openly discussed the probability that Sam was going to die. We had feared his death at several points in the past, but never talked frankly about it. We tried to imagine life without Sam—life as parents of a dead child. The pain was heavy. The hope that carried us for so long was nearly gone. I admitted to Suzanne that I had made a mental note of the name of a nearby funeral home in the past week. She admitted to doing the same.

Somehow, from somewhere, Sammy found the strength to keep fighting. Life came back into his eyes. He became alert to his surroundings and again responded to Suzanne's voice and touch. Sam's fighting spirit came back. Three days later, the docs talked of removing the ventilator. We were again upbeat and feeling like Sam was ready to pull another miracle recovery.

The docs took away the life support machine to give Sam a chance to recover. He still had a tube suctioning his stomach contents and now had a third tube, inserted through a nostril into his duodenum. Sam was being fed tiny amounts of formula once again, and the tube was used to deliver the formula directly into his intestinal tract, bypassing his stomach.

The positive signs, such as Sam getting feeds and breathing on his own, made it easy to believe that he was getting better. Maybe Kathy and the doctors were wrong. Suzanne and I prayed that Sammy would find the strength to continue breathing on his own. We anxiously awaited each blood gas and lab report. The gases, tested every four hours from a simple blood draw, would determine Sam's status. If he were appropriately removing the carbon dioxide from his system while maintaining adequate oxygen levels in his red cells, he could continue. And Sam was breathing just fine. Although he was working hard, he maintained his blood gases in the normal range. The doctors were encouraged by Sam's progress and quietly amazed at his resilience. Suzanne took the opportunity to race home to see Zach and Jake for a few hours.

Unfortunately for Sam, he faced another imminent battle, his addiction to narcotics. The docs did not want him sedated while learning to breathe on his own again. This meant narcotic withdrawal pains were again added to Sam's already monumental suffering. I spent that night and all the next day begging the docs to give him something to help him rest, or make him comfortable. Sam hadn't slept a wink in forty-eight hours. He twitched constantly, writhed back and forth, and made feeble gurgling attempts to cry. I could finally hold Sam again since the ventilator equipment was gone, but this gave him little comfort. Sam constantly reached for his face to try to remove his oxygen cannula and tubes. Watching his agony was nearly unbearable. I prayed to God throughout that long night to bring some peace to Sammy. I told myself that it would all be worth it if he just got through the next few days. I prayed for Sam to make the big turnaround.

Sam successfully passed the twenty-four-hour mark. Lab reports showed appropriate amounts of oxygen and carbon dioxide. My hopes soared when he reached forty-eight hours. Sam's respiratory status remained stable. He was doing fine, except for the excruciating hell of drug withdrawal.

Both Suzanne and I continued to pray for him, she at home, me, at his bedside. "Why, oh Lord, does this precious child need to suffer like this?" I prayed. "Please, God, make Your plan for Sammy clear to us now. If it is Your plan to take Sam, please let him suffer no more." I held Sammy's hand for long hours while telling him over and over that God had a plan for him. I felt that God's answer to our prayers was coming. I felt we would soon know if Sammy was to recover, if this were truly the big turnaround, or if God was going to take Sam.

I left Sam at midnight on Thursday, August 12, to get some sleep. Sharon, one of the ICU's best, was Sam's night nurse. He was her only patient. I made her promise to hound the docs to find a way to get Sammy comfortable. The docs had given him Ativan and Benadryl for comfort, but those drugs provided little relief. He had now gone over seventy-two hours without sleep. He had also gone sixty hours breathing on his own. I walked away that night humbled by the sheer toughness of this incredible child. He had gone two and one-half days breathing on his own while fighting through the unimaginable agony of narcotic withdrawal.

I thought of another old cliché, one of my favorites, that night. It goes something like, "It's not the size of the dog in the fight, it's the size of fight in the dog." Well, the size of the fight in Sammy was unlike any I had ever seen. Sam, nearly sixteen months old, never learned to talk. He never learned to walk. He never even learned to crawl. Yet he had taught me life lessons that I hadn't learned in forty-two years. He showed me courage I had only read about. He demonstrated the power of determination.

I would understand more of Sam's life lessons in the future, but for this night, I was overcome by the power of his will to live and by his courage. I cried softly to myself that night as I thought of Sam and tried to remember the words to Psalm 143, a psalm that had given me comfort in the past months. The only verse I could remember, verse 8, brought the comforting words I sought. "Let me hear in the morning of your steadfast love, for in you I trust. Make me know the way I should go, for to you I lift up my soul" (esv).

CHAPTER 27

Letting Go

Good news did not come in the morning. Sam crashed at two a.m. It was Friday, the thirteenth of August, nine months to the day that Sam had been diagnosed. I had just fallen asleep when the ringing telephone awoke me. Reverend Sue was on the line.

"John, I'm not sure what is going on, but there is a roomful of doctors with Sammy."

Upon my arrival, Dr. Bruce Grossman, the ICU fellow on duty, took me aside and advised me that Sam would need to be intubated once again. Sam had simply become worn out from his exertions trying to breathe. Without hesitating, I gave my consent to proceed. Giving up was not a decision I could make without Suzanne's input.

Knowing that Suzanne would need all the sleep she could get, I waited until seven a.m. to call her. Dr. Filipovich visited later in the morning. In her eyes, I saw empathy and compassion. I saw in her eyes that Sam was near the end. She left the room with a light pat on my back, her way of giving a hug.

Sam slept all day in sedated bliss. He suffered no longer,

and for that I was grateful. He awoke that day once, the moment Suzanne arrived from home. Sam opened his eyes a tiny crack, looked at his mommy, and closed them again.

At lunch, we discussed Sam's condition. Were we pushing too hard? By intubating again were we asking too much of him?

Finally I said, "I think God will send us a clear signal when Sam has had enough. I've been praying hard that God will make clear His plan for Sammy. I think we will know if it is time to let him go." Suzanne nodded and said that she had prayed that if God was going to take him, to not let him suffer like this.

Exhausted, and in emotional disarray, I left for home in mid-afternoon. But God's clear signal came before I'd passed the Cincinnati city limits. Suzanne sounded calm as she reported that Sam was having a brain seizure.

I turned around. People in the other cars were heading out of town for the weekend or going home from work. I was on my way to watch my son die.

I arrived in time for the CT scan, which showed nothing significant. Sam continued to seize. His toes and fingers twitched rhythmically. High fever, over 104 degrees, came with the seizures.

Dr. Filipovich was forthright is her assessment of Sam's chances. Seizures could be very damaging to the brain. It was important to stop them. To do that, they would need to give him enough sedation drugs to put his brain to sleep. When I asked if he could recover from this, she replied softly.

"It doesn't look good, John."

A technician arrived and attached thirty wires to Sammy's head, then covered his scalp with a cloth to hold them in place. The wires were connected to a computer, which showed the seizure activity on the screen.

Sam's twitching finally stopped around eleven p.m. The EEG monitor no longer showed activity; Sam's brain was asleep. The seizure was over. It had lasted seven hours. Sam's fever worsened, however, to 106 degrees, a lethal level. As the evening progressed, Sam required more and more blood pressure medicines. The ventilator was set on maximum support settings.

Prayers were being said around the country for Sammy. Kathy e-mailed friends and family with the grave news. Rev Ron started our church's prayer chain. The gloom that surrounded Suzanne and me that evening could only be described by Psalm 23. We were walking in the valley of the shadow of death. And we feared. And we prayed. We prayed for the Lord to comfort us, and to be with Sammy.

Dr. Filipovich returned at eleven-thirty that night. Her voice was choked with emotion, her eyes full of compassion.

"Suzanne, John, we are getting very close to the end. I don't know if Sammy can survive the night. We are maxxed out on blood pressure support medicines. I think you should call now if you want Grandma, or any one else to get here. We will do everything we can to keep Sam alive for the hours it will take to her to get here."

Suzanne wept. I sat stonily silent—shivering. More phone calls were made. We arranged a midnight ride for Marilyn. We found a neighbor to sit with Jacob and Zachary. I worried about them waking to find Grandma gone.

Our all-night vigil was on. This was a deathwatch. The desire to hold Sam was overpowering, but not possible without disconnecting critical life-support equipment. Doctors no longer came into the room, as they had nothing left to give Sam. The nurse and respiratory therapist kept busy keeping Sam alive with medicine and breathing support. Suzanne and I sat at Sam's side alternately weeping and praying. I visited the chapel to read the psalms that had given me comfort in the past, but could not find the Bible.

Word spread through the hospital that Sam was dying. Visitors began showing up. Several of Sam's doctors, residents who had taken care of him for one month, came by to say good-bye to Sam and to give hugs to Suzanne and me. Each told how Sam had inspired them throughout his long fight. Melinda came by after her shift on T5A. The room became a sea of tears as she hugged Suzanne and me, then said good-bye to her "Lovebug." Grandma, Grandpa, and Suzanne's sister, Lavonne, arrived at four a.m. to join our vigil. Suzanne and I took turns trying to sleep, but with little success.

Dawn arrived to find that Sam was still with us. The morning dragged slowly on. Marilyn sat in a corner crying. I had never seen Curt cry, but he openly wept for his grandson that day. Steve and Tammy Carter visited in turn to say their good-byes to Sam. Their child was again in the hospital with complications, after cruising through the first ninety days after his bone marrow transplant. We hugged, cried, and prayed together. Sometime during the morning Reverend Sue joined our vigil.

Suzanne and I knew it was time to let Sam go. God's plan was clear. He was calling Sammy home. But we desperately needed to hold Sam one more time. In consultation with Dr. Filipovich, we found a way. We decided to disconnect Sam from all his meds, wires, and IV lines, except for the blood pressure support and ventilator.

Dr. Filipovich wanted us to be sure, and to know what to expect, before she agreed to proceed. "When Sam is ready, I encourage you to let him go. I want you to avoid putting him and yourselves through the trauma of the crash cart and CPR."

Suzanne and I mumbled our assent. The decision allowed us to hold our Sammy one last time. No more labs were to be drawn, no more transfusions given. Sammy would receive no more steroids. We agreed to cut off his cyclosporine, IVIG, ATG, insulin, and acyclovir, along with the countless other scheduled meds. I personally removed the EEG wires from Sammy's head. Suzanne and I then shampooed and combed his hair.

It took a great effort to position Sam's equipment so that we could hold him. Each of us in the room held him for a few minutes. Suzanne was first, then me. Marilyn, Lavonne, and Curt each took a turn. The room filled with sounds of weeping as we each told Sam good-bye. We told him how much we loved him and that we would never forget him.

We positioned Sam in Suzanne's arms. I put my arms around them. We both knew it was time. We also sensed that Sam needed our permission to go. With tears streaming down our cheeks, Suzanne and I said the same words to Sammy.

"You can go now, Sammy. It's okay, Sam. You can go to God now, precious Sammy."

Sammy died seconds later.

My eyes swung from Sammy to the monitors as a cacophony of alarms sounded. Dr. Filipovich, at my shoulder, silenced the alarms.

"Just let him go. Let him go," she said softly. Sam slipped away quickly. Suzanne and I exploded in loud sobs.

"It hurts so much! It hurts so much!" I wailed.

Photographs from Chapter 27 can be viewed at:
SamuelsMission.com

CHAPTER 28

Coming Home

AUGUST 1999

Sam was gone. Medicine was no longer needed. Reverend Sue gathered us in a cocoon of warmth and led us in prayer. When she finished, I began ripping lines and wires from Sam's body. I desperately wanted him free of the medicine and equipment that controlled him. Tears flowing, we held Sam's body for an hour.

I had a hole in my heart. But I hadn't carried Sam in my body for nine months as he grew from a single cell. Suzanne was shattered.

Outside the room, friends had gathered to say their good-byes. Reverend Sue escorted in Melinda and Niki, Sam's favorite nurses, along with Steve and Tammy Carter, and led another round of prayers. A nurse came in quietly to make foot- and handprint impressions of Sam for our memory box. The handprints she affixed to a beautiful parchment with a sentimental poem.

Arrangements for Sam's body had to be made. It was Sue,

of course, who took charge and assisted with contacting the funeral home. We had to pack our belongings and leave the hospital. Our long stay was over. It was time to go home.

Sammy's body would stay a few more days. We agreed with Dr. Filipovich's request for an autopsy. Sammy had given his life to HLH; maybe the doctors could learn something from his body to help the next child survive.

After packing and loading the car, we returned to Sam's room. Medicine had grossly disfigured our precious son, but he looked beautiful to me. That he no longer suffered provided a tiny amount of comfort. Our faith that he was with our heavenly Father provided the strength we needed to function and move forward. Two boys who urgently needed our love awaited our homecoming. We dreaded the task of explaining Sammy's death to them.

Before we left him in God's hands, Marilyn, Curtis, Lavonne, Steve, Tammy, Nikki, Melinda, Sue, Suzanne, and I held hands and encircled Sammy as Reverend Sue led us in a final prayer.

"Dear God, we ask You to take Sammy into Your care now. For although we don't begin to understand Your mysterious ways, we put our faith in You to show us the way through the darkness we find ourselves in. Dear God, please be with John and Suzanne and Zachary and Jacob as they learn to live without their precious son and brother, Sammy. This we ask of You, who know what it is like to walk in our shoes and lie in our beds."

Leaving the hospital for the last time was the most difficult of walks. I had fantasized many times of wheeling a giggly Sam out of the hospital in his stroller to take him home. Never in our long stay did we expect to leave this place without our son.

Silence filled the car as we made the long, lonely drive home. Marilyn was filled with the need to hug Zachary and Jacob as much as Suzanne and I. The miles ticked slowly away, each of us lost in our own sadness. None of us had anything to give to the others. We carried our loads alone and in silence. When I look back on those days, this was the lowest point in my life.

The house was quiet upon our arrival, eerily quiet. Our eyes were dry as we endured the wait until our sons arrived home with their aunt and uncle who had picked them up earlier in the day. I remember sitting on the edge of the couch, staring into space, just waiting, enveloped in emptiness. The void began to fill when Jacob and Zachary walked in. Unaware of the tragedy, they flew into our arms with wide, happy smiles. Suzanne and I wailed openly as we hugged them tightly. Tears flowed freely down our cheeks. How would we ever explain to them that Sammy was never coming home? Startled by the emotion, Zachary squeezed me in a bear hug.

"Daddy, please show me a happy face. Please show me a happy face." Somehow . . . somehow I found a way to show him a happy face.

CHAPTER 29

Samuel's Mission

Throughout Samuel's short life and long illness, I often felt he was sent to us with a mission. Now that he was gone I was left with only questions. What of all the life lessons learned from Sammy? And what of the visits from angels and the connections made with God? What of all the prayers said for Sammy? Why were those thousands of prayers ignored? Does prayer have real value? What was the point to Sammy's immense suffering, anguish, and cruel stay on earth?

Sam was dead and I was at the lowest point in my life. I looked inside myself for the faith I had acquired during Sam's ordeal. I had to look deep. And then I had to search. Somewhere in that process I forgot how to listen to God. It had taken more than forty years of my life to learn to hear God speak to me, and now I'd lost the ability to hear Him.

I was like a teenager with an iPod blaring through the earphones: I knew God was speaking to me, but I couldn't hear Him through the hurt and sorrow. I had to *once again* learn how to listen. And before that, I had to be willing to listen. My stubbornness made this process a very long one.

Meanwhile I tried to figure out for myself the meaning of Sammy's short life. He was clearly special from the moment he peacefully exited his mommy's womb. But his mission had always seemed vague, clouded by the maelstrom of events that was his life.

In the days leading up to and during his funeral service, some of the clouds moved away as we learned of Samuel's accomplishments. Two days after his death, a letter arrived for Samuel in our e-mail. The letter was from my sister Judith. She had met Sammy only once several months earlier during a weekend visit to the hospital, but she aptly described his spirit, and defined his mission.

Dear Sammy,

While your visit to our world was a brief one, you have certainly impacted many lives. I have to believe that you were here as a messenger of God to teach us all certain lessons. I'm sure I can't begin to know even the half of it, but these are the ones I have witnessed:

The lesson of courage: You bore the unending pain and discomfort, the needles, tubes and drugs with a courage that is not easily forgotten. You showed each of us just how much a person can suffer for months on end without giving up.

The lesson of love, particularly the special love between a parent and a child: The bible tells us that there is no greater love than to lay down one's life for another, and that is truly what your parents have done for you in many ways. Despite all adversity, discomfort, complete lack of sleep, and even boredom sometimes, not to mention the giving up of any normal personal life and ambitions, John and Suzie have been there with you every moment of every day since this ordeal began. They truly laid their own lives aside in an attempt to save yours.

The lesson of determination, even when it is against all odds: We've learned this lesson time and again from watching you overcome almost insurmountable odds, and in seeing Suzie and John's determination to make sure that no stone was left unturned to help you in that effort.

The lesson of trust: I remember holding you in my arms and seeing the trust in your eyes. Having no children of my own, I felt somewhat incompetent while taking care of you, but you trusted me, and your parents trusted me, and it's something I won't easily forget. You stole my heart in a matter of minutes.

The lesson of family: Family is always there for you, no matter what. Whether you need a shoulder to cry on, or someone to take over the running of your household for six or seven months, or someone to fly across the country to give you a few days break; family to laugh with, to grieve with, to find comfort with.

And finally, the lesson of God's will: No one can put it aside, no matter how hard we try. What God wills, He will have, and we are here to do His bidding. God has called you back to be one of His angels, and we can only take comfort in that fact. You will be hurt by this world no more.

Sammy, you've left behind two beautiful brothers who have missed their parents desperately over the past several months. Watch over them and help them through the years.

We lost a brother, too, when we were young, and while we miss him dearly, it's always been a comfort to know that he's in heaven helping us through the difficult times.

And while you're at it, please pray to our Heavenly Father to help John and Suzie to put their lives back together after this difficult and shattering loss. Help them draw together and find that the strength in their love for each other has not been diminished, but rather increased significantly by the trials of the past year. They have only survived this time by drawing on their every inner reserve of strength and determination. Help them now find peace and comfort in God's will.

You will be missed, Sammy. Go in peace and love, as we all wait to meet you again in joy. And by the way, give a hug to Billy and Dad for us.

Love,
Aunt Judy

Kathy asked to speak during the service. With her box of tissues on the lectern, she tearfully described her time with Sammy to the congregation.

I had the privilege of meeting Sammy this past June, while he was in the ICU for the first time. While in constant pain, with continuous bleeding, Sammy played and waved and talked with his eyes. We spent many, many hours during those nights in the ICU rocking and talking and singing. I lost my heart to Sammy. He showed a courage and forbearance which I had never seen before in a baby. He was truly a special child.

Sammy touched so many people's lives in his few short months on this earth. The prayer chain for Sammy crossed the entire country, with hundreds of people praying for him separately and together. The e-mail updates on his condition were forwarded again and again.

We could look at this and say that God did not listen to our prayers, that He did not heal Sammy. But God worked in so many ways in Sammy's life, and in the lives of those who loved him.

God worked in their lives to provide Marilyn to be a constant source of care and love for Sammy's brothers Zachary and Jacob, allowing John and Suzanne to stay with Sammy in the hospital. Thank God for Marilyn.

God provided John and Suzanne with employers who allowed them to take the time off work to be with Sammy, and they provided financial security for them.

God provided family and friends to be with them during the worst times, always sending someone during the scariest, hardest times, or when they were at the ends of their rope and needed a break.

God gave John and Suzanne the strength to make the decisions they needed to stop treatment, and tell Sammy that it was okay for him to go at the end.

God allowed Sammy to die peacefully, in his mother's arms and his father's love.

God did answer our prayers, in His own way, and was with Sammy every step of the way. Sammy's personal legacy to me was a better understanding of how God answers our prayers, and how He acts in our lives. My faith in God has grown because of Sammy.

I truly believe that Sammy was able to accomplish God's plan for him in his few short months on this earth. He touched many lives and hearts of more people than many of us will in seventy or eighty years. We are all blessed by having known him, and having been touched by him.

Reverend Sue spoke also. Among her words were these:

The way in which God's spirit dwelled in Sam was like a magnet. Sam's room during his months with us was a room of activity—a room of activity beyond the medical necessities and tests. Staff would come by before or after work and even on their days off! Other families whose children were also on the unit would stop in. Sam had a way of teaching us about what it meant to reach out beyond ourselves—to care enough about another person, to make an extra effort.

Sam was not his disease. His HLH was a part of who he was, a significant part, but it was not all of him. Sam reminded us that no matter how we try and talk about God or experience God, God is always more than that.

Perhaps most importantly, when Sam was the weakest and sickest—when he couldn't have held his bottle if he wanted to—it was then that he showed us that as God carried Sam in his frailness, God will also carry us in our frailness, even as we grieve the loss of this precious one.

These words of Kathy and Sue touched all who heard them. "Sammy's funeral was one of the most profound events of my life," one friend told me. "The things that were said about him touched me so deeply. He was truly a remarkable little boy."

Sam's mission was different to each one he touched. Doctor's talked of underestimating his will to live and the lessons learned in treating hypercritical patients. Nurses talked of Sam's will but mostly his love. Sammy taught me to value each breath of life, to live life to the fullest, to find joy in the simplest of pleasures. I learned the meaning of true courage. I learned the meaning of adversity and the power of the human spirit to overcome it.

Samuel also taught a lesson in trust. Sam trusted Suzanne and me, as well as his doctors, to make the difficult and often painful decisions for him, seemingly without his consent. The consent, however, was given through the look of trust in Sam's eyes. Those eyes also radiated love. Sam's short life was lived in an atmosphere of extraordinary love. Nothing in the world compares to the pure, sweet love of a child. Sam, as well as Jacob and Zachary, like children do, taught me the meaning of unconditional love. No matter how much pain he was in, or the pleading in his eyes for relief, Sam loved. Without conditions— Sam loved. Others learned different lessons from Sammy. His life was short in years, but long in accomplishments.

The days and weeks that followed Sammy's funeral were filled with an odd assortment of anguish and sorrow mixed with relief, all stirred together by the love of two confused little boys. I looked back to the night in the hospital when Sammy cried out for me to hold him, when his only comfort was snuggling in my lap. I cursed myself over and over for not giving him more.

Nights would find me awake thinking of the enormous suffering Sammy endured and wondering why. Why? Why did God make Samuel suffer so? What did this perfect little boy, this tiny little child, do to deserve such punishment? The answers didn't come when I demanded them. Or they came and I refused to listen. It wasn't until I began looking back to that period of intense grief that I realized how angry I was. Didn't God remember how long and hard we tried to have children? How could He have snatched Sammy away from us? But God was patient. And I had much to learn.

During that period, Suzanne and I returned to Sunday worship service and our church. I'm not sure what brought us back, as I was so confused about my belief that God loved us. But we had received such support from the congregation during Sammy's ordeal that we felt a longing to be with them.

The high point of my anger came during one of these Sunday church services. It was late in the summer, and Rev Ron was on vacation. A guest minister was preaching. The title of the sermon listed in the bulletin was "The Power of Prayer in Times of Turmoil." I sat up straight in my pew ready to hear the wisdom of this out-of-town speaker. Maybe her words could soothe my pain and bring me back to prayer. She told a story about how a friend had approached her about starting a prayer chain for a critically ill loved one. She had my attention, but a bad feeling formed in my gut. The prayer chain was started, and the loved one made a miraculous recovery. Of course, the "power of prayer" made the difference. When she finished the story by telling the congregation that the loved one was the family cat, I shuddered with anger. The minister explained that God listens to all of our supplications, even to prayers for a pet. I left church that day livid. I spoke silently the last prayer I would say for some time: *God, I need to understand why you took Sam and why he suffered so much. I need you to help me with this soon, for I am so confused.*

During this darkest hour of grief, I deeply questioned my faith in God. But He was patient.

Samuel's mission, to our surprise, continued even after his death. Months after Sammy's funeral, during one of our lowest periods of grief, we received a note from Reverend Sue. Her heartfelt letter described the impact Sammy had made on her ministry.

> The time I was privileged to share with you and Sammy here was holy time for me personally. I'm finding that I have a growing passion for trying to help people understand what it's like to be in this place. There are really difficult and sad things that happen here, but real joys and holy moments as well. I know that Sam is not only one of the reasons I can do this, but that he's with me when I speak. What better guide to have?

Sue's words brought comfort as well as a sliver of light into our darkness. Suzanne and I often prayed for Sam to come to us, to let us know his spirit was near. Sue's letter brought the message that Sam's mission continued in the place that needed him greatly. To give of oneself so completely in a place as terrible as a children's cancer unit, one needs special guides. That Sammy's spirit could provide strength for Sue brought comfort and peace to my heart.

CHAPTER 30

Days of Gloom

Grief would disappear one day, then like a cloudy winter day envelop us in darkness. There were few days when Suzanne and I both felt upbeat. She would talk of her powerful desire to dig up Sammy's grave and hold his body. I would look for diversions to keep from thinking about him. Some weeks would find us at the cemetery every day, only to be followed by a month of no visits to the gravesite. For a period after Sammy's death, Jacob clung to Suzanne with ferocity he had never shown before. And despite our mighty efforts to get Zach to sleep in his room, morning would always find him snuggled safely in our bed.

We couldn't let Cincinnati and Children's Hospital completely out of our lives. Suzanne and I made several pilgrimages back to the site of Sam's death in an effort to touch his spirit, as well as to thank those who knew him best—his nurses and therapists. Our one visit to the ICU was most painful. A walk past the room where Sammy died brought back fierce pangs of grief. The staff nodded brief hellos but never approached. There were no pleasant memories from the

ICU. We never returned. Visiting Hem/Onc was easier. So many familiar families remained.

Bright spots in our Cincinnati trips were the time spent with the Carters. Zachary Carter was the one child able to fend off this devastating disease. All the HLH kids we had come to know had died except Zachary. Zach spent many months at home mixed in with periods of hospital time. Steve and Tammy always found a way to spend several hours with us during these visits. The Carters continued to provide much emotional support. Back home, few friends understood the ordeal we had been through; few friends knew the Sammy the Carters knew. Steve and Tammy were very much a touchstone to our ordeal.

Several months after Sammy died we received a visitor: Dr. Filipovich drove to our home to personally deliver the autopsy report. The event made me realize what dissimilar places Suzanne and I were in our grief. Quietly over coffee, after a few pleasantries, Dr. Filipovich explained what took Sammy's life.

"The HLH came back. Sam's brain was full of infection," she said softly. I remember little else of the meeting. I took it simply as information. I didn't really care what Dr. Filipovich said; nothing was going to bring him back. But Suzanne went into an emotional nosedive, angered by what might have been. Once Dr. Filipovich left, Suzanne and I discussed the "what-ifs?" To me, it didn't really matter. Sam was gone. He had so many other issues to deal with at the time that maybe the HLH didn't matter.

As summer turned to fall, Zachary Carter, too, began to struggle with recovery. Issues with graft versus host disease, along with digestive problems, kept Zach ricocheting between the hospital and home. The steroids kept him swollen beyond recognition. The medicine failed to prevent his light from shining, however. He always found a way to smile when we visited. Zach always told us about his guardian angel Sammy in the special language of a two-year-old. Zach's ability to fend off his medical issues while maintaining his sparkling personality repeatedly surprised visitors and uplifted hospital staff. The staff of T5A referred to Zach's spirit as the "Z-factor." Zach knew how to love. He spread it around freely to anyone and everyone he encountered. I later realized Zach ministered the chaplains as much as they ministered to the Carter family. Reverend Sue, Father Mike, Pastor Andy—Protestant, Catholic, Jewish—Zach loved them all.

But even the Z-factor was not enough to defeat this vicious disease. The world was busy celebrating the arrival of the new millennium when Zachary Carter died in the arms of Steve and Tammy.

As it was for Sammy, Zach's funeral was a celebration of his short life and the enormous impact he'd made on hundreds of people. For Suzanne and me, the funeral brought back knifing memories. The progress we had made through the grieving process seemed lost as we relived the first few days after losing a child.

Reverend Sue again addressed a funeral congregation. "Sammy and Zach are together now in heaven."

We heard that phrase enough that it began to sound trite. It turned out to be not so trite. Others at Zach's service brought news of Sammy's presence and his continuing mission. Reverend Sue grabbed us shortly after our arrival at the funeral home. She quickly related the story of Zach's death, and her overpowering feeling of Sammy's presence as an angel of God.

Moments later Krissy, the Children's Hospital holistic health therapist, hugged Suzanne and me tightly, then with a bright smile excitedly related the ever-present guidance that

Sammy brings to her. Krissy said she could see Sam and his blue angels at her side as she tended to the children and families in her special practice. "Sammy keeps me focused. I'm so much better at my job when he is with me." Krissy's enthusiasm bubbled over, brightening the despair of the day.

Signs from God, I came to realize, are rarely as obvious as graffiti painted on a bridge. God does speak to us, but only when the heart is open. The answer to my questions would come, but I was not yet ready to listen.

CHAPTER 31

Marriage

Now that the war was over, it was time to pick up the pieces. The trauma of Samuel's illness and death rocked our marriage. Divorce rates of couples who have lost a child are staggering—something like 80 percent.

Suzanne and I did not immediately speak of the state of our marriage. We had to figure out what we had left for each other. But neither of us was ready to face the prospect of rebuilding intimacy while grieving our loss.

We moved into our post-Samuel life well aware of the devastating statistics. We sought counseling, joined a group of parents who had lost children, took a grief recovery class. I wrote this book for therapy. (The first version ended with Sammy's death but no clues to what it all meant.) We both tried being workaholics. Over the years, we've turned to food, sports, travel, and sometimes too much wine to try to forget. But we've learned that we don't want to forget. Sammy's life and death will always be with us. It's a part of who we are.

My parents lived with similar grief through my entire life with them. It wasn't until I was grown that I came to understand the emotions of their loss. Looking back, I see the grief in the joylessness that made up Mom's personality. She never got over losing Billy, her firstborn son. The undeserved mom-guilt must have been an enormous load to carry all those years. I knew so little of the shadow that grief cast over my childhood. Only now, eleven years after Sammy died, have I discovered the proper perspective to look back on my childhood. I wish I had more time with Mom and Dad, now that I understand them. But Mom is gone now too.

Grief affected me in three areas of my life—marriage, spirituality, and emotionally. I craved one of the kitchen table discussions that I enjoyed so many times with Mom and Dad. Their experiences handling the grief and the effects on marriage and faith would have been enlightening and perhaps helped pull me out of increasing depression.

Suzanne and I each had long periods of despair and anger. And we had short periods of happiness and light. We fought and made up, drifted apart and came together. Some days we couldn't agree if it was sunny or gloomy (it was sunny). Other times it felt like Suzanne and I were together against the world.

I don't know if I would have survived our ordeals without Suzanne's strength, integrity, and character. She has been tempered and tested by life. Infertility, Sammy's death, and other private traumas have wounded her deeply. My life before Suzanne seems so trivial, like I was just treading water waiting to be rescued. Her strength brought us through the storm. Now we had to find a common ground to rebuild our relationship.

Raising our sons together kept us moving in the right direction. But I could see that Suzanne was not the same person she had been before Sam's illness. I remember when her thousand-watt smile disappeared about the time of Sam's diagnosis. Now I wondered if I would ever see it again. We had happy times and did fun things with our boys, but it was not the same. The smile was never powerful enough for her dimples to appear nor

bright enough to illuminate our darkness. She had a seriousness about her that was now a part of her personality, kind of
like my mom.

I wondered about myself and how I had changed through
the experience. It was easy to look out and compare the differences in Suzanne but much more difficult to look within. It
was also difficult to admit to my not-so-pretty personality
changes. I found myself irritable, close-mouthed, and temper-
amental. My mood swings were like those advertised for
women on fertility drugs. I could be happy like a child having
a birthday and then an hour later throw things at the TV
because my show was preempted. It couldn't have been much
fun being my spouse in those days.

Suzanne and I had many gifts for which to be thankful. For
one thing, we lived in a beautiful home in a great neighborhood with plenty of room and amenities for our lifestyle. We
had abundant close friends nearby. Playmates for our kids were
plentiful on our street, as were teenage babysitters. We had
bought the house before we had children and fixed it just the
way we wanted. We were completely satisfied in our home. But
a Sunday drive through a new development somehow made us
yearn for change. Neither of us can really remember why we
decided to buy a lot and build a new home across town, but it
seemed like a great distraction. And looking back, it was indeed
a diversion from our pain and also a way to reconnect on a
project that would require us to communicate and spend time
together. And that worked for us . . . at least some of the time.
I remember sitting in the office of the builder trying to agree
with Suzanne on cabinets, tile, or some other selection and not
caring a whit about what we chose—and then later being angry

when I thought she was making all the decisions.

Eventually the construction was completed and we moved into our new house. Somehow we had made mostly good decisions. We loved our home and new neighborhood. Suzanne claimed to be delighted, but I had yet to find real joy in her personality. After a few months at our new address, I was visiting with the woman next door, a fiftyish wife of a well-to-do entrepreneur. I related our story of Samuel and his fight for life.

"Oh, I could see in Suzanne's face there's been some recent tragedy," she commented gently. That a new friend could see Suzanne's pain caught me off guard and again made me realize how different my grief was from my wife's.

That was how I spent the first several years after Sammy's death—riding the emotional roller coaster and looking for a way to get centered. I had by this time contemplated the concept that I wanted to be happy and enjoy life, although I hadn't yet found the path.

My relationship with Suzanne continued to evolve during this time . . . and not always for the good. Over time, anger stealthily seeped into my personality and took up residence like a tiny but hungry parasite. The resentment was, of course, about losing our son, but I let myself believe it was caused by the little things in my relationship with Suzanne.

The intimacy we lost during Sam's fight did not return easily. As a man, I could separate my physical needs from any emotional wounds. But as a woman, Suzanne's affectionate side was still affected by her scarred heart. I wish I could tell husbands something different, but it was several years before real intimacy returned. My frustrations boiled over now and again, and resentment moved in next door to anger in my heart. The anger was growing and eating away at me, slowly and clandestinely tearing down my spirit and making me bitter.

Suzanne and I had our tiffs but more often kept our emotions in check thinking we were being kind. But our marriage started to falter as I let anger build and smolder within.. Bitterness crept into our daily conversation. When the words themselves were not acerbic, our tone of voice did the damage.

Although Suzanne and I did not blame each other for Sammy's ordeal and death, anger is so much easier to express than heartache. One only needs a target—and guess who was nearby to absorb it? I allowed my resentment and anger to fester for years.

Finally came the day the anger could no longer be contained. The trigger is unremembered and unimportant, but the eruption happened just after we'd ordered dinner at a favorite bistro on my birthday six years after Sammy's death. The menus were on the table, and we had just sipped our first taste of the wine when the dam burst with a fury. Neither of us remembers the words that set it off. One certainty is that my tone was less than loving. Suzanne had enough. She stormed out of the restaurant while I flung a few dollars on the table to pay for the wine. Anger bubbled and frothed within us as we drove home without speaking. Fortunately the boys were at Grandma's house for the night.

The fight was epic. Anger spewed from each of us like dueling volcanoes. Words hot as molten lava flung through the air. Suzanne and I cursed each other with shocking insults never spoken before. We both absorbed the fiery blows yet stood our ground as the eruptions continued. We both fired salvos that were to be regretted. It was the nastiest battle ever between us. The next day, when the kids were around, we switched to e-mail to maim and mutilate. We both used the D-word and meant it. When the magma was expended, glaciers moved in. Our only contact became evil looks and snide body language. The iciness lasted for five long days.

Those nights sleeping in the basement were cold and frightening. Lying awake, scenes of lonely apartment life drifted through my head. Divorce was certainly one of the possible outcomes of this fight, and thoughts of living apart from my family left me desolate.

When the firestorm ended, pain remained. Suzanne and I had absorbed enough wounds in our time together. The last thing we needed was the raw battle damage we had inflicted on each other. Our marriage teetered on a precipice. It was time to mend it or time to end it.

Many have walked away at this point. It wouldn't be unexpected by society. But we had so much invested. Two boys, fate hung in the balance as we battled. The olive branches were extended tentatively.

Suzanne's peace offering came with the words men dread more than any: "We need to talk."

I needed terms. I wanted the rules of engagement clearly dictated before agreeing to meet at the peace table. I wanted my say.

Suzanne's tears came as soon as we started. The tension between us had simply become intolerable, she explained. My condescending tone made her dread being with me. A revelation dawned on me as she spoke. I learned at that moment something about how women function, something important. I already knew the part about listening and not trying to fix, but this was different and so simple.

Read carefully, men. Anger is caused by hurt and heartache. Suzanne was hurting—deeply hurting. She had absorbed the growing resentment from me and truly missed the old John, the one not infected with anger and bitterness. Her tears softened me. She then heard me out and listened to my complaints.

This day became a defining moment in our quest for a joyful life.

I know what the men reading this account are thinking: *Yeah! And they had some bodacious makeup sex.* Maybe we did and maybe we didn't; I don't remember that part. What I do remember is going off by myself and willfully and intentionally letting go of my anger toward Suzanne.

Until that day, I hadn't realized the control anger had over me. It was like an infection of my spirit, and it controlled me and consumed me. The anger was gross, like the pus of a leaking boil. I needed to lose the anger and drain the foul infection.

After the first peace talk, I lanced that boil. Like an overinflated balloon, I let the pressure off and released anger's massive negative energy. Like you see in some self-help books, I exhaled the anger and inhaled fresh clean untainted air. I pictured the poison air leaving and could feel new positive energy flowing as I inhaled oxygen. I continued the exercise until I felt better.

What an unbelievable feeling it was to release all that anger! It didn't require any action from anyone to let it go. There was no need for amends or apologies from anyone. It was totally up to me and completely under my control. It just took my willingness to liberate myself from the stranglehold of anger. I felt like a new man. It was so easy. My heart thawed and the chains came off my emotions. The best part was that the anger I released wasn't only that toward my wife, but all the anger and resentment I felt toward God and the world for taking Sammy. Almost unknowingly, I let it all go. The release was truly life changing.

The next day I spoke to Suzanne of the change and my feeling of a new beginning. She fell into my arms and nestled her tearful face in my chest.

The thaw in our marriage was instant.

Suzanne must have released her anger in much the same way. A dark cloud lifted from our lives, and for the first time in years, lightness entered our relationship.

Together, we hauled our marriage off the edge of the cliff.

Photographs from Chapter 31 can be viewed at:
SamuelsMission.com

CHAPTER 32

The Path to Joy

Returning to a joyful life was a process of, as yet, indeterminate steps. Losing my anger was step one, and it opened the door to others.

Step two occurred a few months later. The moment, like so many others, is frozen in my memory. It was a nonevent, really. I was sitting in my backyard with my brother Joe when the revelation . . . just happened.

We were in the hot tub drinking a beer and having one of our deep conversations, the kind I don't have with my other brothers. I may have been explaining women to him. Like it often does with Joe and me, the conversation took a philosophical turn. Maybe Joe believed the words he spoke or maybe he phrased his question purposely to make me think.

"Do you ever wonder when you're going to catch a break in life, John?" he asked. "I mean, with all the infertility, fighting through the adoption hassles, and then going through what you and Suzanne did with Sammy, when is it your turn for good fortune?"

I didn't answer quickly. Instead I looked slowly around and

then engaged my other senses. I saw a beautiful home . . . nicer than I ever thought I would live in. I listened. Inside the house I could hear Zach singing to himself. From another room I heard Suzanne and Donna giggling, probably poking fun at dumb stuff wives do. Just then Jacob bounded out of the house in his swimsuit, sporting a huge smile and ready to join the men in the hot tub. I felt a strange emotion, one that had eluded me for some time.

I felt blessed.

I absorbed this new thought before speaking.

"I think life is starting to turn my way, Joe. I can feel a change in the wind, as Captain Jack Sparrow might say." I embraced the emotion and let it settle.

Over the next days and weeks, I explored the feeling of being blessed and of reawakened thankfulness. I discovered that I was no longer depressed and actually felt optimistic and happy. Feeling grateful is a huge component of living joyfully. Reflecting back on this time, an attitude of gratitude was step two on my road to bliss.

Not long thereafter, on a sun-splashed Sunday morning, magic reentered our lives: Suzanne found the long lost switch to her radiant smile. Her thousand-watt beam returned.

The effect was stunning. Like the Julia Roberts smile at the end of *Pretty Woman* when Richard Gere comes back for her. The room warmed from her radiance. Somehow Suzanne's heart had healed enough to allow genuine joy to fill her again. And that special Sunday morning her infectious giggles drew me into the room where she and Jacob were clowning around. I nearly sprained my neck when I first spotted it. The event was nothing special, but her long-gone dimples were suddenly there. Light spilled from her huge brown eyes and contagious joy completely illuminated our home. It occurred to me that Suzanne had embarked on her own separate path to a joyful life. Just as we dealt with Sam's illness in often divergent ways and handled the grief process differently, it makes sense that we also have individual paths to finding—refinding—joy. It had been nearly seven years since the day Sam was diagnosed and the day her smile disappeared. I had almost forgotten the effect her smile had on me . . . almost.

A few days later, Suzanne declared that she was going to be more social in the neighborhood and make new friends. She consciously decided to be happy, no doubt one of her steps on our parallel paths to fullfillment. And it worked. The old Suzanne was on a comeback, and from what I could envision, maybe better than ever. I was not blind to the results of her intentional decision to be happy, and perhaps a bit envious. I wanted some of what she had. So I emulated her decision to choose a life of delight and bliss. Whatever step Suzanne had achieved, this became my step three to a life of joy and contentment.

Our emotional paths that had diverged during Sammy's initial hospitalization so long ago were coming together. Suzanne and I were, separately but in parallel, each finding our way to a joyful life. As with my steps one and two, step three is a conscious decision one makes—to choose to smile, to laugh, to feel happy—because this is where a joyful life is to be found.

To my great delight, I once again found myself blinded by Suzanne's light. Marriage, now at eighteen years and counting, has become richly fulfilling. Suzanne and I truly partner in our relationship and share all the joys and day-to-day sorrows that come with it. And after the trials we've been through, few of life's ups and downs bother us. Suzanne and I are a couple. We are committed to our marriage and to our sons. We've been through the rocky times and came out stronger for it. I really can't remember much of my life before I met her.

So now that I had completed my three-step process to a life of joy, I rewrote this book to include the life-lessons absorbed in the years after Samuel's death.

In the end, the really important things were our family and

our faith, even though the *real* lesson of faith was to become yet another step and is discussed in the next chapter. Nonetheless, Suzanne and I will share whatever God put in front of us, whether it is joy or suffering. We've had both.

I like the joy better.

CHAPTER 33

So What Is the Value of Prayer?

As Sammy's ordeal progressed, God came to me several times and in dramatic ways. I learned to listen as well as speak to Him. I found the listening to be much harder. I claimed during this trial to have developed great faith and trust in God. But when Sammy died, I easily let go of that faith and trust, and forgot how to listen.

For several years, I remained subconsciously angry with God while simultaneously claiming to understand His plan. The way I lived my faith best is described by the old Platters tune, "The Great Pretender." I talked a good game, but deep down, I wasn't ready to embrace the concept that God loved Sammy and loved me as well. But God was patient and He doesn't hold grudges.

After all those prayers said for him, why didn't Sammy live? I suspect questions like this are the toughest asked of ministers, priests, and rabbis. I've certainly asked that question many times. We're preached to throughout our lives to pray and *God will listen*. So how could God let such an innocent child suffer and die? Does God not care?

Not long ago, I read a story written by a California woman named Esther whose two-year-old daughter nearly died from an infection. Arieanna was hospitalized for a month and hovered near death for two weeks in the ICU. Her family and friends prayed hard for God to save Arieanna, and somehow she pulled through. Esther's story tells of her gratitude for answered prayers and blessings from God. She wonders what made her family deserve God's mercy and why they were so special that God would bless them and save their child's life.

She goes on to explain how God spoke to her: "He impressed on me [that] He had done so because I was His child and we had called upon His name. That and that alone qualified us for His rich blessings."

The writer further explains her faith lesson. "His strength really is sufficient and His peace really will transcend all understanding; when we need it most."

My initial reaction to reading her words was my familiar anger, followed by disdain—as if I had more insight than the author on how God answers our prayers. I took Esther's explanation of prayer as meaning that perhaps my family didn't qualify for God's blessing; otherwise, Sammy would have been saved. I then let the arrogance take over and thought in my mind that Esther didn't understand prayer any more than I did when Sammy died.

Prior to reading Esther's story I thought I had a good understanding about how prayer works and how God answers prayers. Once I let humility wash over me, I read her words again and found appreciation for her explanation. The insight was that the way God answered Esther's prayers is *completely unrelated to the way he answered ours*. There is no parallel or comparison.

Through my conversations and e-mails with many parents of children with critical illnesses, I found prayer experiences to be almost polarizing. When you speak with parents of survivors, they feel blessed by God and are grateful. But while there are great stories out there of suffering Christians who never waver in their faith, many parents of dead children often feel anger and abandonment at first.

Nonetheless, the opportunity for growth in relationship with God is available to both groups. Some choose to proceed down the path of enlightenment. I did not choose that road for a long time. I'm not proud of my foolish and selfish anger that I carried for God. In truth, I'm ashamed that I could be so weak as to question faith after adversity. The shallowness of my commitment startles me when I reflect on this.

So how did I find my way back? I wish I could tell you that an angel appeared in my bedroom and took me by the hand and showed me Sammy, ecstatic in the kingdom of heaven. In truth, I had a feeling of emptiness in my heart that was more than just the loss of Samuel. I had strayed from God and found that I was missing my relationship with Him as much as I was missing Samuel. My heart softened, and I started praying again. My prayers were short and tentative and even a little shy. I was embarrassed and almost afraid to ask God to let me back into His fold. Soon I began listening to Him, paying attention to the signals he was sending.

The process continued on my way to finding and reclaiming a joyful life. Step four was rebuilding my faith. Without faith and trust in God, there will always be emptiness. I know; I lived without my faith for some time. I lost trust. But I was forgiven and welcomed back into God's fold.

When I learned to listen, I was struck by a sensation of love. An image kept recurring in my head of the way Sammy loved without any conditions. No matter the suffering, he was enduring. He radiated love to me. And then I tapped into the powerful feelings of the love I felt for Sam, the feeling that I would have given anything to trade places with him. In those moments, I realized that our feelings of unconditional love for our children are just a tiny fraction of the feeling God has for us, and for me.

It was love—powerful love—that brought me back to God. He provided the path I needed to find my way home. And God welcomed me with open arms—and immersed me in His unconditional love. I don't quote the Bible often, certainly not as often as I should, but the passage below strikes me as the purest and most eloquent description ever written of love. I believe this is Sammy's ultimate lesson and the way God wants me to live my life.

If I speak in the tongues of men and of angels,
but have not love,
I am only a resounding gong or a clanging cymbal.
If I have the gift of prophecy and can fathom all mysteries
and all knowledge, and if I have a faith that can move
mountains, but have not love, I am nothing.
If I give all I possess to the poor and surrender my body to the
flames, but have not love, I gain nothing.
Love is patient, love is kind.
It does not envy, it does not boast, it is not proud.
It is not rude, it is not self-seeking, it is not easily angered,
it keeps no record of wrongs.
Love does not delight in evil but rejoices with the truth.
It always protects, always trusts, always hopes,
always perseveres. Love never fails . . . .
And now these three remain: faith, hope and love.
But the greatest of these is love.
—1 CORINTHIANS 13:1–13 (NIV1984)

We hear these words often at weddings referring to romantic love, but I believe the words are meant in the context of loving your fellow man.

The word *extravagant* is used to describe richness, luxuriousness, or excessiveness. I remember the feeling of love that enveloped T5A, the way people of every walk of life shared and transmitted love in that beautiful/ghastly environment. The way love was expended and received on Hem/Onc was the ultimate in extravagance. The way Sammy loved without any conditions and despite his nightmarish tortured life. The way Suzanne and I loved Sammy and the way we love his brothers.

Extravagance.

I'll never forget Elijah and his poverty-stricken family—but on T5A, Elijah was among the richest in the currency of love.

I remember adorable Allison, and the crafts she made to cheer Sammy even as she fought for her own life.

Love.

I remember Alexandra and the joy she projected even as her last days approached.

Pure, sweet, unconditional love.

I remember Zach Carter and the way he spread joy, the way he attracted visitors like bees to honey. His magnetism was electric.

This was love.

And I recall the feeling that if the world could absorb the attitudes of Hem/Onc, we would live in a peaceful, tolerant society. That is the love as described in First Corinthians.

Call this lesson of love the fifth step. Giving love unconditionally is not easy. I am only beginning to understand its power and how to use it. My efforts are imperfect and far too selective when compared to the power of love I witnessed in Sammy and the kids of T5A. But I'm learning. And I want to develop this potent skill. Steps four and five were no small movements, but giant leaps that went hand-in-hand on my road to a joyful, fulfilled life. Of course, these insights called for yet another rewrite.

As I began to grasp the meaning of Esther's words, I also remembered that God never promised us a life free of suffering. In fact, He sent His Son to be with us and allowed Him to suffer and die violently. It's worth repeating. God allowed men on earth to brutalize and then kill His Son. Jesus lived as man. The pain and suffering He endured was real.

Another Bible verse was sent to me while I was writing this chapter. Esther quoted it in her story, and it came again the next day in a daily devotional e-mail. This was no coincidence as I had never read this passage in my life and it came to me twice while I was trying to find the wisdom to describe why Christians suffer. God sent me the words and I listened.

Blessed is the man who perseveres under trial,
because when he has stood the test,
he will receive the crown of life that God has promised
to those who love Him.
—JAMES 1:12 (NIV1984)

Between my moments of arrogance and close-mindedness, I have relearned to listen when God speaks to me. It's like I'm in second grade now when it comes to building my relationship with Him. Yet I've never heard the question of why prayers go unheard answered in any acceptable way. But God has impressed upon me the simple explanation to that most difficult question. Now I, a man with no training and with credibility based only on experience, will provide the answer in a way that makes sense.

Our prayers are indeed answered but in a way that is not always comprehensible to our limited, simplistic, human, rational, black-and-white way of thinking. God sees our role in a picture so much more immense and eternal than we can possibly envision. Sure, God has a plan for us. But our insistence that we think we can or should *understand* His plan is arrogant and a massive roadblock to our relationship with Him.

We Christians love to speculate on God's plan. We are quick to be angry with God and quick to believe that maybe God doesn't care because of the suffering we see and feel. But we must understand that His plan encompasses so much more than we can see—so much more than we can imagine. God's plan does not include just our time on this planet or the microscopic time that we live as men and women. We exist here as part of our eternity, and this is like comparing a tiny grain of sand on a beach to the entire planet. For us to understand God's plan is ludicrous . . . yet we try. We try to justify our anger and our suffering as if God does not care. We try to categorize God's actions in human terms and put Him in a box.

So back to the question; Did God answer our prayers? We prayed for God to save Sammy's life and cure him of his disease. The answer . . . God did indeed answer our prayers but in His way, not our way. And some time in the next thirty years or so, I will understand the way in which God worked in Sammy's life. For now, I embrace my dreams of Sammy in heaven and rejoice in his ecstasy in the presence of our heavenly Father.

CHAPTER 34

Zachary and Jacob Update

Like any parent, I get frustrated when our sons don't listen, misbehave, or throw a tantrum. Yet I treasure them immensely. My appreciation for life—its preciousness and its fragility—has increased exponentially since our family trauma. That we have Zachary and Jacob simply makes life infinitely fulfilling.

Since the time of Sammy's illness, our sons have grown into adolescents. Each has developed gifts and talents that will bring them through childhood into adulthood. For example, they each have a gift of music and have played the piano for years.

Zach is blessed with an ear for music and can play a piano riff from a tune in his head. When band was offered in fifth grade, Zach quickly gravitated to the saxophone and found he enjoyed blowing the horn even more than playing the piano.

When he went to high school, we all discovered his real talent was in vocal music: Zach auditioned for an elite competitive choir and made the cut as a freshman. In our huge suburban high school, that was a great accomplishment. When he started with a voice coach, she was stunned by his natural ability. When she asked Zach which of his parents is a singer, he explained about being adopted from Russia. "Well, there is music in Russia!" she exclaimed loudly.

Jacob's abilities are a result of hard work, plenty of practice, and sheer determination. It wasn't long before Jake surpassed Zach on the piano, and he never looked back. He began playing hymns at church periodically and received many accolades from our congregation. "Jacob plays with such great expression," we heard from many. From this experience, I learned that Jacob loves an audience. His performances always outshine his practices. Jacob brings his "A" game when a crowd is listening. At a recent Christmas piano recital, twelve-year-old Jacob finished his piece and we awaited the next pianist, a very talented eighteen-year-old friend of our family.

"I'm not following that, someone else go next!" the young man pleaded. It was one of those proud-dad moments.

Childhood sports are extremely competitive in our community, and like many dads, I want my kids to enjoy them. Jacob played on the offensive and defensive line in fourth grade peewee football. At the high school homecoming football game that year, I took a moment in the second half to remind Jake that in a few years he might be out on the playing field. Despite my dreams of having athletic kids, my heart soared when he answered.

"I'd like to be out there, Dad. But I think I'll be out there at halftime playing in the band."

He is still a year away from high school as I write this chapter but well on his way to playing the trombone in marching band. Jake is first chair in the middle school band, as well as the lead trombonist in the elite jazz band. And he still has his sports—fencing and diving. When I share that with others, many comment about how expensive diving is, what with all the air tanks and having to go to the Caribbean and such. But no, Jake just has to go to one of the local pools with a diving board and a coach who can teach him the twists, pikes, tucks, and flips required to put together five dives for a high school diving competition. Jake has his whole life planned out. He knows where he wants to go to college and what he has to do to make it happen. He is already planning a life as an entrepreneur and lacks only the financing to get there. I'm not betting against him.

Zach's athletic talent is swimming. He'll never make the Olympics or win any state championships, but he earned a spot on the high school varsity team as a freshman and loves the entire experience—especially the team camaraderie. The highlight of Zach's first year on the team? Singing the national anthem on Senior Night. It was breathtaking.

Jacob and Zach, too, live with a hole in their hearts. Jake, after all, lost a twin. But Sammy's life and death probably affected Zach more. After being abandoned at birth, he was separated from his parents for long periods of time at age two. And Zach adored his baby brother. The losses Zach endured at such a young age have largely shaped his personality. He is a homebody like no other. Zach would prefer to stay home and endure a Cleveland winter than go on vacation to the beach.

I refer to the days when our kids do something special as a "Great Dad Day." One of the best dad days occurred just as this book went into final editing in the summer of 2011. Zach, age fifteen, performed his first solo at church with Jacob, thirteen, accompanying him on the piano. The boys performed a traditional hymn and then the Josh Groban hit "You Raise Me Up." I nearly burst with pride.

So often during my workday, I find myself smiling at something Zach or Jake said or did recently. It's like they're with me all the time. And I still love the end of the day when I look in on my sons, sleeping blissfully and securely. I am, indeed, a blessed man.

Photographs from Chapter 34 can be viewed at:
SamuelsMission.com

CHAPTER 35

What About Me?

More than a decade has slipped by since Sammy's death. For the first few years, every cough, cold, or bug the boys caught brought out my worst fears. *What if Zach or Jake gets sick like Sammy?*

I've grown beyond those fears now. But the experience of Sammy's birth, disease, and death altered my outlook on nearly every aspect of my life. Marriage, family, faith, and career all mean different things to me now.

Throughout this book, I wondered how I was changing and evolving. I've discussed the changes in Suzanne and my relationship with her. I've talked of my growth and developing relationship with God. I've written of our sons and how Sammy's life and death affected them. So what life-changing effect did Sammy's life provide for me?

People I run across, especially those with older or grown children, often remind me to enjoy time with our young children because they grow so fast. "Yeah, I think I got that part down," I always say with a grin.

You see, the ultimate gift Sammy left me is the transformation of my heart. Although part of it is empty, it feels bigger—and more powerful. Where I used to try to survive each day, I now soar through them, embracing the parts I once passed by. I exist on a plane above where I did before Sammy entered my life. Even though it sounds like a country music cliché, I live better, love deeper, and experience emotions that I've never felt. The sun is brighter, the flowers prettier, and the grass greener. An even better change is that I don't live on the roller coaster anymore. I dismounted the wild up-and-down thrill ride and embarked on a pleasure cruise through peaceful calm waters.

Another lesson I learned through Sam's ordeal is that while bad things happen in an instant, wonderful life changes happen very slowly. Just as we always waited for a big turnaround in Sammy's condition, we also waited for joy to reenter our lives after his death. But such bliss never comes like lottery winning—in one giant swoop of fortune. It comes in tiny increments. Suzanne and I accepted the bits of joy as we moved along in our post-Sammy life and used them as building blocks to utter contentment. We consciously chose to live joyously. It was a five-step process for me.

1. Expulsion of the anger: Controlled by no one but oneself. Easy to do and life-changing.

2. Gratitude: I am grateful for the gifts that have been given to me.

3. Select happiness: A lesson I learned from Suzanne. Intentionally choose to live life with joy.

4. Love: Unconditional, extravagant love is a powerful life skill. The rewards from expressing love are infinite.

5. Faith: God is so patient and forgiving and loving. We are not promised a life free of suffering. God has a plan for us, but we may not understand it in this lifetime.

Today I feel like I have a secret—a secret to happiness, love, joy, and fulfillment. It came from learning how fragile life is and, to that end, how to treasure each day, hour, and moment. It came from learning to love unconditionally and extravagantly like the children and inhabitants of T5A. People around me stress about the tiniest of issues in life, and it affects their dispositions. Few things bother me like they used to. Our family has seen some of the worst life has to offer. But now we embrace the best of life and squeeze simple joys from the most mundane everyday living. And it is most comforting to know that our experience has brought us to a level of feeling joy, contentment, and happiness that was not there before our lessons from Samuel.

A recent experience provided an indication of my ability to embrace joy. It was Baptism Day in our church in December 2010. As the official lay leader of our congregation, it was Suzanne's job to assist with the service. Rev Ron had phoned earlier in the week to give her warning that twin baby boys were receiving the sacrament; he gave Suzanne the option to step aside if it would bring back too many painful memories. But no, Suzanne was up for it.

When the time came at the end of the service and the parents brought the babies forth to stand in front of the church, the memories did indeed come flooding back. The twins looked eerily like Jake and Sammy. In fact one of them was named Jacob. Suzanne was unfazed. She held one of the babies and recited her portion of the service. I observed the look of pure joy on the faces of the parents and remembered my top-of-the-world elation on this event twelve and a half years earlier. At the conclusion of the rite, Rev Ron took a baby in each arm and paraded them around the church, as is still our custom, to introduce them to the congregation. We sang the same hymn as on our own sons' baptism.

The memories were too much. Suzanne hurried off the altar and quickly dug in her purse for a tissue. I was grateful she found one as my tears were flowing and I had a lump in my throat the size of an ice cube. I could barely breathe. Suzanne put her arm around me. The twins, Rev Ron, the music . . . it was too much, right?

At my side, Jacob looked alarmed. "Dad, what's wrong?" he whispered.

The *déjà vu* was powerful. Yes, I experienced the excruciating feeling of loss—but at the same time I revisited a moment I now realize was the single happiest moment of my life. I felt again the pure joy of one perfect day spent with my wife and three healthy sons. My tears on this day were not so much from our loss but from delight of reliving a glorious moment in time.

It's a bit trite to say Sammy died but I lived. Trite . . . but true. What meaning does it give your loved one's life if you give up and live the rest of your life depressed and angry? Embrace the lessons learned, and look for the good that came of your journey. Embrace God's plan knowing that we have no ability to understand while we're here.

In the end, what is it we truly desire for our life? It's not riches. It's not power. What truly satisfies is happiness—a joyful life.

Guess what? I'm there. I can look at the rich and famous and smile. I have something they may not have. It's not exclusive. Anyone can have it. It is joy, it is happiness, it is satisfaction, and it is being loved. Life is not perfect and doesn't need to be.

Remember, our time on earth is minuscule compared to eternity in heaven. Live with what you are given. Radiate joy and love like a beacon. And then revel as it is reflected back to you.

I have a friend, a man of significant wealth, who is always trying to win the lottery, as if a few more millions will make him happy. There is always someone richer or with a nicer home that he covets. I tell him, "You're looking the wrong way. Turn around." And sometimes we *are* looking in the wrong direction. Look the other way. Look at what you have, not what you don't have. Consider the line of people who covet your lifestyle. Be grateful for the gifts you've been given.

As we move forward, our family will embrace the joys of life. I will continue to love and cherish Suzanne. I will celebrate the joys of fatherhood, and I will wake up every day with a smile of gratitude and treasure the hours ahead. I will live in the glow of a thousand watts of joy.

Sam taught me these lessons. He brought to me many gifts: joy, peace, and contentment. But his greatest legacy . . . is love.

EPILOGUE:
The Dream

Over the years, I've collected bits and scraps of a wonderful recurring dream about Sammy going to heaven. The dream comes in tiny fragments often scattered by months or years. In it, I get a glimpse, often just seconds, of what I believe is Sammy telling about traveling to heaven and meeting God.

This stuff of these dreams is farfetched and way beyond my typical spiritual awareness level. I've never told anyone, not even my wife, about them. They come in such short intense bursts that I often lose the feeling and emotions before I can describe them, even if I wanted to. A few years ago, I started an attempt to portray the dreams on paper. The writing also came in bits and pieces. Unfortunately, I found words of little use in expressing the emotions, color, sounds, senses, and power of these dream bursts. Nonetheless, this is my attempt at describing what I've seen in scattered dreams—Samuel's trip to heaven as described by him.

My trip to heaven began with a cacophony of noise. I later learned the clamor was the alarms on the monitors connected to my body. The doctor silenced the alarms and put her hand on my dad's shoulder. "Just let him go. Let him go," she whispered. I watched the scene from a strange perspective. I was in the room but not in my body. And I was suddenly intelligent and worldly . . . just in time to leave the world. I could see and hear but I was missing . . . something.

"It hurts so much!" Dad screamed. Mom cried out too—wails of despair. I tried to go to them, but I was being drawn away. I caught a last glimpse of Mom and Dad and . . . and my body before I was overtaken by an intense desire to go . . . somewhere. I didn't want to leave them, but I was being pulled toward a peacefulness that I had never known. For the first time since I was a tiny baby, I felt wonderful—no pain. I was free from the extreme agony that was my life as a child. I realized I was being drawn by an intense but wonderful force—like the gravitational pull of a celestial planet.

Then I was flying—soaring, really—through a vast passage and toward a radiant golden glow far in the distance. There was no fear, only intense desire to get to the source—to find what magnificent power was drawing me close. The trip seemed to be endless, and my destination a mystery. A sense of warmth and incredible peace came over me. I was enveloped in serenity and comfort like I had not known.

Then I found I was not alone. Soaring along with me were two little blue angels. They were smiling at me—welcoming me with tenderness and love. The angels were not unfamiliar. They had been with me for much of my life, one of them since I was born. We began moving toward a light—a warm, wonderful, indescribable light—a welcoming, lustrous, golden light—soft, yet luminous, rich and vibrant, yet comforting and peaceful. I felt incredible bliss.

My troubles slipped away as we came closer to the light. I knew I was dead but had no fear of death. Truly I felt more alive than I had ever been. Joy filled me up. I hoped my incredible journey would never end, while at the same time I yearned to arrive at the iridescent glow. Then the concept of time seemed to disappear. Speeding along we entered what seemed like a tunnel, a beautiful, celestial, infinite tunnel. Dots of light in the distance encircled me. I felt not confined, but freer than any time in life. Unencumbered by my ravaged body, I floated, sailed, soared, tumbled, spun, flipped, and flew.

My two angels were in front of me, while six and then eight appeared alongside. The angels were ebullient. They were grinning and bubbling with excitement. In turn, they approached and gently caressed me. Their warmth and affection touched my heart. Love radiated from them. I could feel the love in different way, as if I had a new sense.

The trip took weeks—or maybe it was only seconds. Speed, like time, became blurred as a concept. It seemed we were flying at a rate far beyond light speed, yet there was a sensation of floating. Nonetheless, I sensed we were nearing the end of the voyage. I was now surrounded by countless luminescent floating loving apparitions—angels, saints, heavenly bodies, all massed around my little blue friends. The speed was exhilarating while the silence was wondrous.

I had already learned several things about

life after death. I had a spirit and I had a heart—
not the muscle that pumps blood to a body, but
the heart that feels emotion and love, a heart
that seemed ready to burst with passion and
adoration.

The light grew in size or what seemed like
size. The end of the tunnel was apparent by the
lustrous, bright radiance now illuminating my
surroundings. Then beautiful music filled me,
like it was coming from inside me. I was the
instrument. The music filled the tunnel with
glorious sounds unlike I've ever heard—singing
and wondrous instrumentals. The music was
not just for the ears. I could feel it and see it. The
colors of the sound were vibrant and brighter
than anything I'd ever seen. The colors were
different than seen on earth, indescribable really,
except for the incredible intensity and . . . it's
like the colors and the music were one and the
same, awe-inspiring, yet serene and soothing. I
wanted the trip to last forever, while at the same
time I yearned to reach the end.

Then just like that, I arrived at my destination.
I found myself alone in a place of remarkable
tranquility and peace. I was bathed in the light
I had seen from the tunnel. The light was unlike
any on earth. I could feel it. It was warm and
gentle and luxuriously soft. It was not just around
me but inside me as well. My spirit swelled with
an intense feeling of pure, sweet, astonishing
love. It was inside this glorious light that I met
my heavenly Father. His words resonated with
gentleness and compassion.

"My precious, precious child, you are home
now."

God embraced me into His tender care and enveloped me in His heavenly love. There is simply no description to match His awesome gentleness, love, and kindness. I felt secure and comfortable in God's presence. I was at peace. I was not afraid or intimidated to be in attendance of such a power. I only felt His love and compassion and His acceptance. My devotion and adoration for God poured forth from me like the greatest waterfall ever imagined. The feeling of loving and being loved was of a magnitude of awesomeness that could fill a universe. If one could describe heaven in a word it would be *LOVE.*

God knew all about me. He knew of my life of suffering. He knew how much I already missed my mom, dad, and Zachary. He knew of my bond with my twin brother, Jacob, and how I longed to be with him.

"Do not worry my son. You will be with the ones you love," God promised. "You are home now. All the heavens are your home." God's great light was within me. I could feel my soul vibrating with it. "You have found eternal life Sammy. I am so happy to have you with Me. A great celebration awaits your arrival." And then God brought forth my heavenly guides to lead me to the gala.

RESOURCES
for Families Affected by Catastrophic Illness

www.carepages.com: Free patient blog site that connects family and friends during a health challenge.

www.caringbridge.org: Free websites that connect people during a significant health challenge.

www.jamiechavez.com: Developmental (substantive) editor of fiction and nonfiction for authors and publishers nationwide.

www.histiocytesociety.org: A nonprofit organization of over 200 physicians worldwide committed to improving the lives of patients with histiocytic disorders.

www.histio.org: Histiocytosis Association of America, a global nonprofit organization dedicated to raising awareness of histiocytic disorders, providing education and emotional support and funding research leading to better treatments and cures.

www.uhhospital.org/rainbowchildren: Rainbow Babies & Children's Hospital.

www.cincinnatichildrens.org: Cincinnati Children's Hospital Medical Center.

www.rmhc.org: Ronald McDonald House.

www.strongsvilleumc.org: Strongsville United Methodist Church.

www.eaci.com: European Adoption Consultants.

www.lebonheur.org: LeBonheur Children's Medical Center.

GLOSSARY OF
MEDICAL TERMS *and*
MEDICATIONS

Absolute Neutrophil Count: A measure of the number of neutrophils within the number of white blood cells. Neutrophils are one of the infections-fighting white cells in the blood.

Acyclovir: An antivirus medication.

ANC: Absolute neutrophil count.

Ativan: A drug used for treating anxiety.

Benadryl: A drug used to treat allergy symptoms and in Sammy's case to help with sleeplessness.

BMT: Bone marrow transplant.

Bone Marrow: The soft blood-forming tissue that fills the cavities of bones and produces blood cells.

Busulfan: Chemotherapy drug used to destroy Sammy's stem cells prior to bone marrow transplant.

Ciprofloxacin: An antibiotic used to treat various infections.

C-Line: Same as Central Line.

Central Line: Semipermanent IV port installed in the patient's chest used to receive medications, draw blood, and transfuse blood products.

CBC: Abbreviation for Complete Blood Count or a measure of the types of cells in a sample of blood.

Chem 7: A blood test that measures seven characteristics of the blood.

Chem 23: A blood test that measures twenty-three components and characteristics of blood.

CT Scan: Pictures of structures within the body created by a computer that takes the data from multiple X-ray images and turns them into pictures.

Cytoxan: Chemotherapy drug used to destroy Sammy's stem cells prior to transplant.

Echocardiogram: Noninvasive procedure to check the electrical activity of the heart.

EKG or ECG: Abbreviation for echocardiogram.

Endoscopy: Procedure to examine the digestive tract using a lighted flexible instrument.

Gamma Globulin: Blood proteins with antibodies to fight infections. Given to Sammy when his immune system was depressed by chemotherapy and also prior to diagnosis.

Hematology: Field of medicine devoted to the diagnosis, treatment, and prevention of diseases of the blood and bone marrow.

HLH: Hemaphagocytic lymphohistiocytosis.

Hemaphagocytic Lymphohistiocytosis: A genetic disease that affects the immune system. It can be set off by viruses, as it appears to have done in Sammy's case, or just on its own. It usually appears before age two, but sometimes not until age six. In HLH, the histiocytes (one type of white blood cell, which is an immune cell and should attack invaders to the body) become too populous and start invading other tissues and destroying normal cells, especially in the bone marrow, lymph nodes, liver, spleen, skin, spinal cord, and more rarely, the brain itself. This is generally described as a fatal disease.

Intrathecal Chemotherapy: Treatment with drugs that are injected into the fluid surrounding the brain and spinal cord.

Itraconozole: A drug used to fight serious fungal infections.

IVIG: Intravenous Gamma Globulin; blood proteins with antibodies to fight infections. Given to Sammy when his immune system was depressed by chemotherapy.

Laminar Air-Flow Room: Isolation room in which the air is constantly vented and replaced with clean filtered air.

Lasix: Diuretic or drug used to reduce fluid retention.

Methadone: Narcotic medication used for treating moderate to severe pain.

Methotrexate: Chemotherapy drug injected into the spinal fluid used to treat certain types of cancer. This medication works by interfering with cell growth and by suppressing the immune system.

Methylprednisolone: Steroid used to suppress the immune system. The drug has various effects on the body. It reduces swelling and inflammation. It is used in a variety of disorders such as skin diseases, allergic conditions, asthma, respiratory conditions, cancer, and blood disorders.

Nephrologist: Physician trained in diagnosis and treatment of kidney diseases.

Neutropenia: A condition in which the patient has a lack of neutrophils, a type of white blood cell. May be seen with viral infections and after radiotherapy and chemotherapy. Neutropenia lowers the immunologic barrier to bacterial and fungal infection.

NG Tube: A nasogastric (or feeding) tube is one that is passed through the nose via the esophagus into the stomach. Sammy's NG tube was used to pump baby formula into his stomach when his mouth sores were prevalent following his bone marrow transplant.

Nicardipine: Drug that relaxes and widens the blood vessels. It is used to treat high blood pressure.

Neutrophils: Type of white blood cells that fight infections.

Nystatin: Oral medication used to treat fungal infections in Sammy's mouth following bone marrow transplant.

Oncology: The field of medicine devoted to cancer.

Peridex: A mouth rinse that kills bacteria. It is used to treat redness, swelling, and bleeding of inflamed gums.

PICU: Pediatric Intensive Care Unit.

Ranitidine: Anti-inflammatory drug used to reduce stomach acids, such as Zantac.

Sinusoidal Obstruction Syndrome: Preferred name for Veno Occlusive disease.

Stem Cells: The human body's master cells—found in the bone marrow—with the ability to grow into any one of the body's more than two hundred cell types.

T-Cells: White blood cells known as lymphocytes of key importance to the immune system.

Vancomycin: Antibiotic used to treat serious bacterial infections.

Veno Occlusive Disease: A possibly fatal disease of the liver in which some of the small veins in the liver are blocked. It is a complication of high-dose chemotherapy prior to bone marrow transplant. The name "Sinusoidal Obstruction Syndrome" is now preferred when as a result of chemo or BMT.

VOD: Veno Occlusive Disease.

VP-16: Anti-cancer chemotherapy drug also used as high-dose therapy in bone marrow transplants.

Zosyn: Antibiotic used to treat various infections.

ACKNOWLEDGMENTS

Samuel's Mission evolved over a period of nearly thirteen years. In that time, there were many rewrites as life lessons were learned and Sam's legacy became clearer. I was inspired to write immediately after Sammy was diagnosed with a life-threatening illness that few had ever heard of. When finally ready to launch, I found my editor, Jamie Chavez, through a friend. I was forced to wait a few months to fit her schedule but then after more than a dozen years what are a few extra months. Jamie was way worth it. She patted me on the back when it was deserved. She read my mind and shaped my sometimes random thoughts into a beautiful story arc. Jamie has the ability to make my spirit soar with a little comment and she inspired me to find the perfect words to describe an emotion.

Thanks to James (Jay) Monroe and his stunning cover design. I was speechless the first time I viewed it.

I had a few trusted readers over the years who provided encouragement, advice, and reviews. Carolina Fernandez, author of *Rocket Mom! 7 Strategies to Blast You into Brilliance* and *Country French Kitchens,* has been there from the beginning when she volunteered to spend a day with Sammy in Cincinnati Children's Hospital. Carolina not only inspired me to write better but provided numerous insights into the murky publishing world. Denise Dean, a neighbor and friend, volunteered countless hours reading and encouraging. Denise then created and helped implement a marketing plan for *Samuel's Mission*. Her website is: 4simplemarketing.com

Steve and Tammy Carter not only shared our experiences with Sammy but allowed me to tell the story of their precious Zach and the "Z" factor. The Carters, too, have found great joy in their life. In a recent letter, Tammy talked of our time together in Cincinnati and their life since. "Not sure that I can even believe it all happened at times. We are so happy to have Nicholas and Katelyn. They have helped us to find the happiness that we deserve and are so happy that the two of you have found happiness again."

Their children, Nicholas, age nine, and Katelyn, seven, keep them busy and fulfilled.

Liseta Antunes befriended me the day I met Dr. Filipovich at the HLH seminar just days after Sammy was diagnosed. Liseta had lost her first child, John, to HLH and was awaiting bone marrow transplant for her second son, Charles, also afflicted with HLH. Liseta seemed to know everything about the disease, and she freely educated me in the early days. Charles was admitted to Cincinnati Children's not long before Sammy died, and passed away five years to the day that Liseta lost her precious John. I grieve with her to this day.

Thanks to Dan Mahoney. His poem "HEM/ONC/BMT" provides such a vivid description of life in a children's cancer unit from a nurse's perspective.

I am so grateful for the spiritual guidance of Reverend Sue during our time in Cincinnati and Rev Ron before, during, and after our family crisis. Rev Ron remains the warmest human I have ever met and has been such a spiritual mentor for our entire family.

There were so many medical staff that made an impression in our lives. The first and one of the best is Dr. Brian Berman from Rainbow Babies and Children's Hospital, who made the difficult diagnosis of HLH. Of course, the angel nurse, Chrissy, at Rainbow made a lifetime impact on me and I only wish I knew her last name. At Cincinnati Children's Hospital we encountered truly remarkable professionals. We have not spoken to her since she visited our home with news from the autopsy, but we are so grateful for Dr. Filipovich and her bone marrow transplant staff. Her dedication to finding a cure for this dreaded disease is inspiring, and I remain hopeful to see the day it is eradicated. We became so close to the nurses on T5A. Sarah, Niki, Min, and Mark were our favorites and so dedicated and loving with their care for Sammy. Suzanne and I will never forget them. Krissy and her blue angels also left their mark in our memories.

We could not have supported Sam 24/7 without Suzanne's mom, Marilyn. Now in her seventies, she still spends two to three days a week with us running the boys around, doing laundry, working in the yard, and fulfilling her role as the iconic grandma. We recently purchased an iPad for Grandpa Curt, who is now retired: he belongs to many clubs and organizations that communicate with e-mail. Jacob and Zach work patiently with him on every visit to teach him how to read his messages, but he still gets stuck. They have it down to two keystrokes, but somehow the digital world remains a mystery to him. We are blessed to have him with us.

I barely knew my sister Kathy until Sammy's illness. She made great sacrifices to travel to Cincinnati from her California home, fell in love with her nephew Sammy, and truly brought our family together. With our parents gone, Kathy has stepped into a family leadership role. Around the time of Sammy's funeral, Kathy began closing phone conversations to siblings with the words "I love you." It was uncomfortable for most of us at first. Since then, we have realized that we do love each other and don't mind expressing the emotions. My brother Joe and his wife Donna supported us at one of the most scary times in Sammy's long fight. I still remember the laughter and lightness they imparted in those frightening days. Zach and Jake look up to them like no other relative. Joe has reembraced Catholicism in a big way and has become a guide and mentor for our sons and their personal spiritual journeys. Joe recently experienced one of those mountaintop encounters with God like we read about in the Bible. His story is astonishing, and he has allowed me to write about it in my next book.

My sister Judith visited from Texas and inspired the name for this book in her eye opening letter to Samuel. Brothers Steve and Paul along with their wives, Elise and Teri, were all there for us, as were Suzanne's sisters, Catherine and Lavonne. Suzanne and I are thankful for their care and compassion. Suzanne's lifetime friends, Peggy Kennelly, Linda Hickle, and Andréa Rossiter visited as did Linda's mother Mary Kay. Peggy, Linda were present "the Night of Two Moons," when my life started over. As this book neared completion, my oldest brother, Tom, was battling leukemia and had achieved remission, the latest Henkels family crisis. Like with Sammy, our family showed up with financial and emotional support for Tom and his wife Kristina.

I remain deeply grateful that I have Suzanne in my life. As stated so often in the book, my life started over on the night we met. She is my soul mate, partner, best friend, and wife. I love her deeply, like the love described in Corinthians. We no longer are aboard the roller coaster yet I know that we could be forced to ride at any moment. But we have a strong foundation to help us survive the next plunge.

I thank God every day for our three sons. We became a family in a most special way when we were led to Russia and to our firstborn son, Zachary. Jacob and Sammy completed our family, and we lived in complete bliss until Sam became sick and our world turned upside down. The intense eight months that followed changed me forever. We only had Sammy for a short time. But he lived large in those few months. Zach and Jake raise me up. I am such a better man for having them in my life.

ABOUT THE AUTHOR

John Henkels grew up in Iowa amidst a family of nine kids to a road-warrior traveling-salesman father and a stay-at-home mother. John is a civil engineer by day and a family man all the time. This is his first book. He and his wife, Suzanne, are the parents of three boys. They live in a suburb of Cleveland, Ohio.